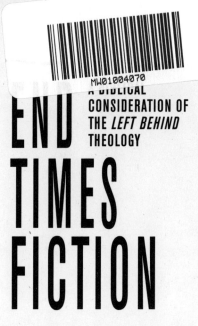

END

A BIBLICAL
CONSIDERATION OF
THE *LEFT BEHIND*
THEOLOGY

TIMES

FICTION

GARY DeMar

THOMAS NELSON PUBLISHERS®
Nashville

A Division of Thomas Nelson, Inc.
www.ThomasNelson.com

Published in Nashville, Tennessee, by Thomas Nelson, Inc.

Unless otherwise noted, Scripture quotations are taken from the NEW AMERICAN STANDARD BIBLE®, © Copyright The Lockman Foundation 1960, 1962, 1963, 1968, 1971, 1972, 1973, 1975, 1977, 1995. Used by permission. <www.Lockman.org>

Scripture quotations noted KJV are from the KING JAMES VERSION.

ISBN 0-7852-6642-9

Printed in the United States of America

01 02 03 04 05 PHX 5 4 3 2 1

CONTENTS

OTHER BOOKS BY GARY DEMAR

FOREWORD

From the time I learned to read as a child I was hooked on books. Reading opened my mind to a world that far transcended my limited local experience. There was adventure, mystery, fantasy—all the ingredients that captured the essence of both fact and fiction.

I rapidly read through the entire Hardy Boys series, vicariously enjoying the thrills and chills of Frank, Joe, and their buddy Chet, the creations of Franklin W. Dixon. Then I turned to the offerings of Clair Bee with the Chip Hilton series. When this series was exhausted, I joined the small library in our local community. My library card became an "open sesame" to another realm of literature. I read every single book in the library's sports section.

When the sports category was exhausted, I turned to sea stories to fuel my love of adventure. From there I went to the standard American novel.

In a word, from my youth I have been a voracious reader. I cannot stand to be away from the printed page. If necessary I will read the nutritional information printed on the cereal box.

I rehearse my personal love affair with reading to introduce a radical shift in my reading habits that took place in 1957, the year that marked my first year of college, but more importantly, my conversion to the Christian faith. In my first semester, as a new Christian, I made the dean's list. However, it was not the list of high achievement; it was the list of probation. My record card displayed an A in gym, an A in Bible, and all the rest were Ds. I was so gripped by a desire to know the Bible that all I wanted to read was the Bible and books about the Bible.

In the first few weeks of my Christian life I found a bookstore like none other I'd ever visited. It was a small bookstore in New Castle, Pennsylvania, that was billed as a "Christian" bookstore. Its stock was comprised strictly of Christian literature. A sweet lady owned and operated the store. On my first visit to the store I asked her for advice in choosing what to read. She immediately directed me to a trilogy of books written by a man named Watson (I cannot recall his first name). These books were fictional accounts of the return of Christ based upon the doctrine of the pretribulation Rapture. They antedated but presaged the blockbuster bestselling Left Behind series.

My memory of the content of these books is dim, inasmuch as I read them some forty-four years ago. But what remains vivid in my recollection is what happened when I finished them and returned to the store looking for more books. This time the proprietor handed me a copy of a commentary on 2 Thessalonians, written by Harry Ironsides. (I must note at this point that this was the very first commentary on Scripture I ever read.) Also I had no knowledge of any system of theology. I had never heard of labels such as Dispensationalism, Arminianism, Calvinism, *et al.* I was a baby Christian putting my toe in the theological ocean, and to mix my metaphors, experiencing my maiden voyage on the doctrinal sea.

I was initially thrilled to now have a teaching book to help me as I read through the New Testament. Things progressed nicely until I got to a puzzling passage in 2 Thessalonians 2:5–10.

Do you not remember that when I was still with you I told you these things? And now you know what is restraining, that he may be revealed in his own time. For the mystery of lawlessness is already at work; only He who now restrains will do so until He is taken out of the way. And then the lawless one will be revealed, whom the Lord will consume with the breath of His mouth and destroy with the brightness of His coming. The coming of the lawless one is according to the working of Satan, with all power, signs, and lying wonders, and with all unrighteous deception among those who perish, because they did not receive the love of the truth, that they might be saved. (NKJV)

Ironsides reasoned as follows. *Premise A:* The Holy Spirit is the restrainer mentioned by Paul. *Premise B:* The Restrainer must be removed before the man of lawlessness is revealed. *Premise C:* Since the Holy Spirit indwells every Christian, the only way for the Restrainer to be removed from this world is for Christians to all be removed. *Premise D:* Since the Bible teaches that Christians will be raptured, this text must refer to the Rapture. *Conclusion:* The rapture will occur before the unleashing of the man of lawlessness and the great tribulation.

When I read this argument, I was befuddled. I was already disposed toward believing in a pretribulation Rapture from my reading of Watson. I had taken no courses in theology nor in logic. Yet, even as a rank novice the argument didn't set well with me. The nagging question was: "How does Ironsides know that the one who restrains is the Holy Spirit? I know in some Bibles the word "He" when used for the restrainer is capitalized. (Yet a marginal note indicates that it can also be lower case since nothing in the text indicates a divine person.)

I went to the library and checked out other commentaries and saw quickly there was no consensus as to the identity of the restrainer. What may have been self-evident to the Thessalonian recipients of the epistle was not self-evident to subsequent generations of biblical scholars. Various candidates included the Roman government or one of its emperors, the Jewish state, or even the ministry of Paul himself. The restrainer is introduced first as an "it" and then as a "He," fueling speculation that the one who restrains is a person who embodies an institution such as a king or emperor. The Scripture teaches that government has the task from God of restraining evil.

Ironsides's argument rests first on pure speculation regarding the identity of the restrainer, then upon the bizarre and gratuitous leap of the need to remove all Christians from the world to remove the restraint. This is imaginative exegesis at its worst. Not one word of the text explicitly teaches a pretribulation Rapture.

Fast forward to the decade of the seventies. I had finished college, seminary, and my graduate work and was now teaching theology. I was invited by a friend in Pittsburgh to meet privately with Kathryn Kuhlman, the faith healer. During my visit with her in her offices, she showed me a large vault that contained hundreds of audio tapes carefully preserved with proper air conditioning and the like. She explained that the purpose of these vaulted tapes was to have witnessing materials for the benefit of those left behind after the Rapture and during the tribulation.

Fast forward to the present. In my years of study and ministry I have yet to discover a single text of sacred Scripture that teaches a pretribulation Rapture. In my opinion the notion, which is quite recent in church history, is pure fiction.

The Left Behind series is clearly fiction. But it involves the literary genre of fiction to teach a theological viewpoint that the authors do not believe is fiction. I do not think one can account for the phenomenal sales (over 40 million copies) of this series by the strength of the fictional story line. I believe these books are devoured by people who regard the theological premises upon which they are based as true and valid. I find that a sad and tragic matter, for if I am correct, millions of earnest Christians are being taught manifestly flawed doctrine.

I am delighted that Gary DeMar has taken the time and made the effort to do a painstaking analysis of the theological premises of the Left Behind series. I think he clearly demonstrates that the theological premises upon which the series is built is a house of cards. DeMar, with surgical and exegetical precision, dismantles the house of cards.

He shows the inconsistencies of LaHaye's hermeneutics in which literal interpretation is ignored when the plain meaning of the text does not support his thesis. DeMar also reveals the ignoring of the time-frame references of Scripture, which would destroy LaHaye's thesis altogether if compared to his principle of literal interpretation.

I wish that every person who has read the Left Behind series would read *End Times Fiction*. I, for one, am deeply grateful for this volume and pray that it will bring a sobering approach to biblical interpretation that is so needed in our times.

R. C. SPROUL
Orlando

INTRODUCTION

In 1973 I was introduced to the gospel by a friend who was caught up in the frenzy generated by the belief of many at that time that Jesus was coming soon. Scared to death, I heeded his call to read everything I could get my hands on related to the topic of Bible prophecy. Soon after becoming familiar with the fascinating world of "eschatology," the study of the "last things," I became acutely aware of all things prophetic. Finally the bumper sticker that I had seen plastered on cars on campus made sense. You know the one: "Warning: In case of rapture, this car will be left unmanned." Of course, the warning was referring to the pretribulational Rapture of Christians who would be taken to heaven—"in the twinkling of an eye"—at the invisible return of Christ just before the start of the seven-year tribulation period. Before reading my stack of newly purchased prophecy books, I didn't have the slightest idea what these "rapture" bumper stickers were getting at. Now tens of millions of avid readers of Christian fiction are keenly aware of the "rapture" and what it means for cars without drivers causing wrecks on our nation's highways and planes without pilots falling from the sky. Tim LaHaye and Jerry Jenkins have turned a slogan on a fifty-cent bumper sticker into a multimillion-dollar publishing industry that shows no signs of losing momentum or enthusiastic readers.

Left Behind was conceived by Tim LaHaye while he was sitting on an airplane flying to a prophecy conference. "I saw the pilot flirting with a flight attendant," he recounts. "He had on a wedding ring and she didn't. I thought what if the rapture were to occur now and the pilot was left behind but his wife wasn't."[1] From this germ of inspiration, a publishing phenomenon was born. Originally, *Left Behind* was planned for only three volumes. The series is now projected to include a total of twelve volumes. That's not counting the forty volumes projected for children, the audio- and videotapes, CDs, radio drama, movie, wallpaper, postcards, and page-per-day Left Behind calendars. Don't be surprised when *Left Behind* action figures hit the stores. As of this writing, the series has sold more than forty million copies and has been translated into more than twenty languages. Of course, these figures will climb only steadily upward as each new volume is published and another spin-off hits the market.

In terms of sales, *Left Behind* is following in the publishing footsteps of Hal Lindsey's *Late Great Planet Earth* which has sold more than thirty million copies since it was published in 1970. It was named the "No. 1 Nonfiction Best-Seller of the Decade" by the *New York Times Book Review.*[2] It sold "seven million copies through the bookstores in the 1970s."[3] The book spawned a movie with the same title in 1976. Considering that *Late Great Planet Earth* is a single volume and not a multivolume series such as *Left Behind,* thirty million copies sold is a staggering number, especially when the means of distribution in the 1970s and 1980s were not what they are today. There were no megastores like Borders, Barnes & Noble, and Amazon.com. Sales were helped along when *Late Great Planet Earth* was picked up by secular publisher Bantam Books, whose address, in an ironic twist, is *666* Fifth Avenue, New York, New York.

The *Left Behind* books are easy to read. It took me a few hours on a quiet Saturday afternoon to get through the first book. *Left Behind* is not great literature, and it was never meant to be. Cranking out two 450-page books a year doesn't lend itself to too much literary introspection. Jerry Jenkins, the writing member of the dynamic prophetic duo, is cutting back to one book per year. There is even talk about a prequel, made popular by the comic book industry. The prequel will tell us what these characters were doing before the Rapture. In an interview, the authors mentioned that they are considering writing a book that will recount what takes place after the Tribulation and during the Millennium. So far, *Left Behind* deals only with events just before the Rapture and seven years of tribulation that follow immediately after.

I began reading the books in the *Left Behind* series when radio talk-show hosts, newspaper columnists, and magazine editors who were familiar with my book on Bible prophecy, *Last Days Madness*, began calling me to ask my opinion of these runaway bestsellers and the newly released *Left Behind* movie. Most people I encountered in the press had little knowledge of the theology behind the left behind premise. I often spent thirty minutes just outlining the basic assumptions of Bible prophecy so they had some grasp of the subject. Even though they admitted their lack of knowledge, they noted that *Left Behind* was impossible to ignore as a news story. The books can be found everywhere. All the big chain bookstores are cashing in on the craze. Supermarkets and the ever-present Wal-Mart stores are joining in on the excitement and the money generated by the series. When secular bookstores take notice and create huge promotional displays to promote a Christian book series, you can be assured that there is a remarkable publishing event in our midst.

THE PLACE OF FICTION IN CHRISTIAN LITERATURE

Since you are reading *End Times Fiction*, you already suspect that this book is critical of *Left Behind*. Let me assure you that my disagreement with *Left Behind* is not based on its fictional format. Christian fiction has found a large niche in today's publishing world. Check any catalog or Christian bookstore. The niche was started years ago with John Bunyan's *Pilgrim's Progress*. *Pilgrim's Progress* was first published in 1678, went through eleven editions during Bunyan's lifetime, ninety-two editions within a century, and had been translated into Dutch, French, and Welsh before he died in 1688. The book has been translated into more than seventy languages and remains a perennial best-seller.[4] The *London Times* called *Pilgrim's Progress* "the world's best supplement to the Bible."[5] Bunyan's vivid characters and unforgettable imagery are part of our vocabulary. What would our language be without phrases such as "vanity fair," "worldly-wiseman," "slough of despond," "city of destruction," "celestial city," and "house beautiful"? Written for the masses and criticized by the masters, "critics now vigorously agree that it is one of the world's masterpieces; and the common people [diligently] leave it unread."[6]

General Lew Wallace's bestselling novel of the nineteenth century, *Ben-Hur: A Tale of the Christ*, has sold in the millions. It has never been out of print since it was published in 1880. A silent film version opened to audiences in late 1925.[7] Before its screen debut, stage productions had been running for twenty-five years. *Ben-Hur* came to the screen again in 1959 and picked up eleven Academy Awards, with Charlton Heston receiving his first and only Best Actor award. Lloyd C. Douglas's *The Robe* (1942) reached the screen in 1953. Bearing only a slight resemblance to the story line of *Ben-Hur*, the novel traces what might have happened to Jesus' robe after the Crucifixion and how the story of the Crucifixion affected people who came in contact with Jesus' discarded garment.

And we shouldn't forget the book that inspired the "What Would Jesus Do?" (WWJD) movement, Charles M. Sheldon's *In His Steps*. Sheldon's book has been described as "having the largest sale of any book ever printed except the Bible." Prior to the WWJD movement, it was estimated that *In His Steps* had sold "about 2,000,000 copies in America, and possibly 4,000,000 copies in other countries, especially England."[8] To date, however, *Left Behind* has surpassed them all in sheer publishing power.

IT'S BEEN DONE BEFORE (SORT OF)

The left behind premise is not unique to the *Left Behind* series. The first end-time Christian novel that I was able to find was the 1937 publication of Forrest Loman Oilar's *Be Thou Prepared, for Jesus is Coming*. Oilar includes the entire left behind scenario in one volume, including the millennial reign and the subsequent Great White Throne Judgment. Like LaHaye, Oilar wrote his novel as an evangelistic tract "to bring to the unbeliever, 'the Jew first, and also to the Gentile' a warning against false doctrines and to show the hope that is yet in store for him if he accepts the true gospel."[9] *Left Behind* and *Be Thou Prepared* are remarkably similar. Ernest Angley followed a similar script with his 1950 *Raptured: A Novel*.

One of the most interesting post-rapture novels is Salem Kirban's *666*, first published in 1970. By 1976, it had gone through fourteen printings with over 500,000 copies sold. Like Oilar's *Be Thou Prepared*, there are a number of striking similarities with *Left Behind*. The rapture takes place when the main characters are on an airplane; their wives were believers who were taken in the rapture; the rapture is explained away by those who are left behind; those who do not bow down and worship the beast are martyred by having their heads cut off by a guillotine.

Science fiction writers developed a left behind scenario in hundreds of novels spanning the last century. Pat Frank's *Alas, Babylon*[10] was a huge bestseller that depicts a small Florida town's struggle to survive after a nuclear war. The ones "left behind" have to use their wits, Robinson Crusoe style, to carve out a new civilization. *A Canticle for Leibowitz*[11] depicts a post-nuclear-war future that plunges the world into "a new dark age in which the Catholic church revives its old role as preserver of ancient knowledge."[12] In the nuclear black comedy *Dr. Strangelove or: How I Learned to Stop Worrying and Love the Bomb*, a left behind plot is proposed by Dr. Strangelove: "When they go down into the mine [after the effects of a worldwide nuclear holocaust], everyone else will be alive. They will have no shocking memories, and the prevailing emotion should be one of nostalgia for those *left behind*, combined with a spirit of bold curiosity for the adventure ahead."

Of course, what's unique about *Left Behind* is the particular theological perspective—a "rapture" of Christians from the earth that is the first event in a series of incidents that sets off a period of Great Tribulation for those left behind. Those left behind are not doomed to survive in a post-apocalyptic world. Their goal will be to learn what happened to friends and family after the sudden disappearance of millions from around the world. It's the pretribulational Rapture that makes *Left Behind* a unique publishing milestone. Without it, there is no title or story line.

IS IT RIGHT TO FIGHT?

As you read through *End Times Fiction*, you will notice that I disagree with Tim LaHaye on a number of theological points. These are not designed as personal attacks. Christians should thoughtfully and prayerfully contend for what's true and right but "with grace, seasoned, as it were, with salt, so that you may know how you should respond to each person" (Col. 4:6). The Bible requires that Christians "always [be] ready to make a defense to everyone who asks [us] to give an account for the hope" that is in us, "yet with gentleness and reverence" (1 Peter

3:15). We are to be "ready in season and out of season; [to] reprove, rebuke, exhort, with great patience and instruction" (2 Tim. 4:2).

Paul "reasoned with" the Jews from the Scriptures in their own synagogues, "explaining and giving evidence that the Christ had to suffer and rise again from the dead" (Acts 17:3). He followed a similar procedure with "some of the Epicurean and Stoic philosophers" in Athens (17:18). Jude called on us to "contend earnestly for the faith which was once for all delivered to the saints" (Jude 3). We have an obligation, therefore, to ask whether the theological position advocated by Tim LaHaye and Jerry Jenkins in *Left Behind* "was once for all delivered to the saints."

Some people might be critical of my attempts to scrutinize the theology of *Left Behind* with the rejoinder that Christians should not fight with one another. Let me say that Tim LaHaye understands the need and obligation to defend what he believes the Bible teaches. In his *Rapture Under Attack* (1998), LaHaye shows that he is not opposed to answering some of his critics against charges of "false teaching," "cultish beliefs," and even "heresy." The very nature of the book's title and its polemical style demonstrates that he does not object to scrutiny and debate between Christians of goodwill. Therefore, it is neither unbiblical nor unloving to address doctrinal disputes by appealing to the Bible. When Paul believed that Peter was in error, the Bible says that Paul "opposed him to his face, because he stood condemned" (Gal. 2:11). Those in Berea held Paul to the standard of biblical integrity by "examining the Scriptures daily, to see whether" the things he was saying "were so" (Acts 17:11). None of us should be held to any less of a standard.

LaHaye has not stepped back from controversy and confrontation with those with whom he disagrees when it comes to artistic integrity and contractual disputes. He has filed a breach-of-contract suit against Namesake Entertainment. Namesake owns the film rights to at least the first volume in the *Left Behind* series. Also named in the suit is Cloud Ten Pictures, a Toronto production company run by brothers Peter and Paul Lalonde. The Lalonde brothers are also in the end-times book and movie business. While "all expressed regret at the spectacle of Christians fighting other Christians in court," LaHaye's lawyer, Christopher Ruddy, "said his client 'is determined to have his day in court, and he deserves it.'"[13]

Even though Tim LaHaye and I disagree on prophecy issues, we agree on the basics of the Christian faith that put both of us in the Evangelical camp. We believe that the Bible is the very Word of God, that Jesus Christ is God in human flesh who died to pay the penalty for our sin, that Jesus rose from the dead, ascended to heaven, and presently sits at His Father's right hand where He will come again "to judge the quick and the dead." We also agree on the state of our nation, the Christian origin of our nation's founding, and the need to make a difference in the world. To demonstrate that we do not disagree on everything, he quotes me favorably in his newest nonfiction book, *Mind Siege*, written with David Noebel.[14]

The impact that *Left Behind* is having on Christians and non-Christians requires a thorough study of the theology upon which it is based. What if LaHaye and Jenkins are wrong? As one critic of the series writes, "If LaHaye and Jenkins are wrong, millions are set up for disappointment, which will invariably lead many away from the faith."[15]

IT'S ALL ABOUT EVANGELISM

Tim LaHaye wrote the following to me in a March 13, 1998, letter: "It is very exciting what God is doing with our *Left Behind* Series. Just yesterday, while in Canada on an open mike show out of Buffalo, we had a mother call to say that her 14-year-old son was so transformed that he led his unsaved father to Christ by warning him, 'when the rapture occurs, Mom and I will be taken and you will be left behind.' Very honestly, that is why we write these books and why we are hoping it is made into a movie in 1999."[16] In interviews, LaHaye always mentions the evangelistic impact of *Left Behind*. His sincerity on this point cannot be questioned.

Hal Lindsey's *Late Great Planet Earth* took the same evangelistic approach. In fact, I was first introduced to the gospel through a recounting of Lindsey's prophecy blockbuster. I had never heard such exciting things before. But it wasn't too long after I started to read the Bible for myself that I could not reconcile what Lindsey claimed the Bible was saying with what the Bible actually said. The April 7, 1997, issue of *Newsweek* carried a story by religion editor Kenneth L. Woodward in which he described Lindsey's *Late Great Planet Earth* as a "pseudo-Biblical doomsday book."[17] After a thorough study of the Bible, I had to agree. I soon learned that many others agreed with me.

Late Great Planet Earth was popular because it reads like a work of fiction and it predicts the immediate prophetic future. The future is on everyone's mind—from horoscopes and tarot card readers to psychics and prophetic prognosticators of all stripes and religions. But just as there were people who came to Christ via *Late Great Planet Earth,* there were also others who became hard-core skeptics by first embracing the theology outlined by Lindsey then later discovering a considerable number of holes in his thesis. Onetime *Late Great Planet Earth* admirer Michael Shermer relates the following story: "At Glendale College I challenged my philosophy professor, (and now my friend) Richard Hardison, to read *The Late Great Planet Earth,* believing he would see the light. Instead, he saw red and hammered out a two-page, single-spaced typed list of problems with Lindsey's book. I still have the list, folded and tucked neatly into my copy of the book."[18]

We are never told how many people are turned off by a constant rehearsing of end-time speculations that never come to pass. The reports we read only recount the successes. We almost never hear about how secularists use the works of modern-day prophetic speculators to discredit the Bible.[19] This is like the famed baseball player Babe Ruth, who is known for his prodigious home run records before Roger Marris and Hank Aaron broke them, but not for his record strikeouts. We tend only to remember the success stories.

FICTIONAL NONFICTION

Tim LaHaye declares that *Left Behind* is "the first fictional portrayal of prophetic events that is true to the literal interpretation of Bible prophecy." This is a bold claim. If he is wrong, then millions of Christians are believing a myth in the name of the literal interpretation of the Bible. It's my opinion that *Left Behind* is not only a work of fiction, but the theological premise upon which it is based is also a work of fiction.

The theology behind *Left Behind* is a rehash of Lindsey's first edition of *Late Great Planet Earth,* which is based upon sections of Merrill F. Unger's lecture notes that were eventually published as *Beyond the Crystal Ball* in 1973.[20] One can see this by comparing *Late Great Planet Earth* with *Beyond the Crystal Ball* and Unger's discussion of the role Russia plays in Bible prophecy.[21] The prophetic system upon which all of these prophecy writers depend is a nineteenth-century theological invention that changes with historical circumstances. When the "pieces of Lindsey's prophetic puzzle began to disintegrate in the early 1990s" with the breakup of the former Soviet Union, "he tried in vain to salvage his teachings by" editing "erroneous conclusions out of subsequent editions of *The Late Great Planet Earth.* His 'updated' version, along with several newer books he has written, promote an altogether different scenario. Now, instead of the U.S.S.R. attacking Israel, the southern former Soviet republics (predominately Muslim) 'will soon unite with their "Islamic brethren" in the Middle East to attack Israel.'"[22] LaHaye bases the prophetic scenario of *Left Behind* on Lindsey's original view, before the collapse of the former Soviet Union.

THE THEOLOGY BEHIND *LEFT BEHIND*

Before *Left Behind*, LaHaye had written several nonfiction prophecy books. They have since been retooled to tie them into the popularity of the series. *Revelation Illustrated and Made Plain* has been republished in a revised and updated edition and retitled *Revelation Unveiled* (1999). The back cover copy reports that it is "the biblical foundation for the bestselling *Left Behind* series."

LaHaye takes a topical approach in his revised but still outdated *The Beginning of the End*, first published in 1972. The revision took place during the Gulf War in 1991. LaHaye makes liberal use of Hal Lindsey's Rosh = Russia hypothesis (Ezek. 38–39) to develop the first prophetic scenario found in *Left Behind*.

Because the pretribulational Rapture doctrine has been coming under attack from numerous writers and scholars, some from within his own prophetic camp, LaHaye wrote *No Fear of the Storm: Why Christians Will Escape All the Tribulation* (1992). It was republished as *Rapture Under Attack* (1998). Although the first edition of this book was written before *Left Behind* (1995), it carries all the prophetic points of LaHaye's earlier books. It concentrates on the main tenet of *Left Behind*: the need for a pretribulational Rapture that removes all Christians from the earth so God can deal specifically with the nation of Israel. In essence, if there is no pretribulational Rapture, then no one is left behind.

LaHaye's latest book on prophecy is *Are We Living in the End Times?* (1999), which was written specifically

1. To provide a basic companion outline of the end-time events and scriptural verification of the personages fictionalized in the Left Behind series;

2. To show that we have more reason than any generation before us to believe Christ may return in our generation.[23]

Are We Living in the End Times? covers all the major prophetic material in LaHaye's system that is being developed in *Left Behind.* It is the supposed nonfiction behind the fiction.

Published midway through the *Left Behind* series is LaHaye's *Prophecy Study Bible.* Dr. LaHaye is the general editor, and the cover leads with, "Co-author of the best selling 'Left Behind' series." It is dedicated to "the millions of readers of the LEFT BEHIND series of end-time novels." Editors Tim LaHaye, Edward Hindson, Thomas Ice, and James Combs establish their interpretive standard: "While we recognize that the Scriptures contain symbolic language, allegories, and figures of speech, wherever possible, we have interpreted the prophecies of the Scripture in the same way past prophecies were fulfilled—literally."[24]

There is a major problem with this claim made by the editors of the *Prophecy Study Bible*—the presence of contradictory interpretations. LaHaye will make a case for one interpretation in *Are We Living in the End Times?*, and an author will take the opposite position in the *Prophecy Study Bible.* As I point out, there are even contradictory interpretations among the various authors of the *Prophecy Study Bible* and LaHaye himself.

PUTTING TIM LAHAYE TO THE TEST

The following chapters put LaHaye's claim of literalism to the test. Each chapter opens with a few sections of descriptive dialogue from

Left Behind, specifically chosen to define the theology behind the fictional story from the authors' point of view. This same method is used by LaHaye and Jenkins in their nonfiction companion volume, *Are We Living in the End Times?* These theological vignettes are the interpretive keys to help the reader understand what LaHaye (mainly) and Jenkins are saying the Bible teaches about future events that take place after the Rapture and during the Tribulation period. Of course, since Christians living today won't be around to witness the Tribulation period, there is no way to test the accuracy of the authors in terms of history. This is a significant point that will be made several times in *End Times Fiction.*

When Christians witness to non-Christians, they often appeal to fulfilled prophecy as a way to show the reliability and accuracy of the Bible. For example, Micah 5:2 states that the Messiah is to be born in Bethlehem. Matthew 2:1 tells us that Jesus was born in Bethlehem. Of course, this is just one of many messianic prophecies that have been fulfilled. Floyd Hamilton calculates that there "are in the Old Testament 332 distinct predictions which are literally fulfilled in Christ."[25] The fulfillment of prophecy can be ascertained by an appeal to the Bible and history. But this is not the case when it comes to LaHaye's approach. No Christian living today, if LaHaye's view of the Rapture is true, will ever be able to put LaHaye's system to the test by an appeal to history because none of the events outlined by LaHaye takes place until after the Rapture.

METHODOLOGY

After the opening dialogue from *Left Behind,* I've included a theological exchange to summarize the argument for each chapter. These have been taken from letter writers, friends, debate opponents, and general questioners who have written or called me to inquire about prophetic issues. Although not all of the accounts happened as written, each of them is based on the hundreds of questions I've received and debates I've participated in over the years.

Most important, I tackle the prophetic topics outlined by LaHaye and Jenkins in *Left Behind* from a biblical perspective. My goal in writing *End Times Fiction* is to apply the theological principles of the authors as they relate to Bible prophecy and ask this fundamental question: Are they consistent with their own principles? Since LaHaye has written numerous nonfiction books on prophecy, I use these works as the basis for my critique. I don't want to be accused of basing my examination of *Left Behind* solely on the fictional story line.

Keep in mind that *End Times Fiction* covers only those topics discussed in the *Left Behind* series. There is no discussion of the Millennium, the Last Rebellion, the Great White Throne Judgment, or the Eternal State since these events take place after the time period outlined in the projected twelve-book series. In addition, I do not respond to every doctrinal issue raised in the series or every prophetic theme addressed by LaHaye. For example, LaHaye assumes that all children under "the age of accountability," including preborn babies, will be taken up in the Rapture. The Bible does not address this issue, but this single topic—with the weight of study that it deserves—would necessitate a book-length treatment. This issue alone should serve as a reminder to Christians that what a person believes about Bible prophecy has consequences.

LaHaye covers a lot of prophetic ground in the *Left Behind* series; if I responded to all of it, *End Times Fiction* would turn into a multivolume series of its own. The most difficult aspect of writing this book was choosing what *not* to cover. If there is further interest in this topic, and if time permits, a sequel may be in order.

1

THE RUSSIAN PEARL HARBOR

Buck was stunned when he read Ezekiel 38 and 39 about a great enemy from the north invading Israel with the help of Persia, Libya, and Ethiopia. More stark was that the Scriptures foretold of weapons of war used as fire fuel and enemy soldiers eaten by birds or buried in a common grave.[1]

"May I speak to Gary DeMar?"

"This is Gary."

"Mr. DeMar, this is Robert Hebblewhite. I heard you on an Iowa radio station discussing Tim LaHaye's *Left Behind* series. You said some things that concerned me."

"Thanks for taking the time to call. I appreciate that you came directly to me for clarification. What particular concerns do you have?"

"First of all, you said that Dr. LaHaye claimed to interpret the Bible literally, but in reality he did not."

"That's true. It's very easy to prove if you have your Bible. Very early in *Left Behind*, LaHaye and Jenkins describe a battle with modern-day Russia. If you recall, one of the main characters of the

1

book, Buck, says he immediately recognized the fulfillment of this prophecy when he turned to Ezekiel 38 and 39 and read the prophecy."

"Yes. I remember. I did the same thing. And this is why I've called. The battle is described by Ezekiel just like Dr. LaHaye outlines it in *Left Behind*. What an amazing experience it must have been for Ezekiel to see our future."

"Where are the jet planes?"

"Excuse me?"

"The jet planes . . . missiles . . . and atomic weapons? You said that Ezekiel described this modern battle just like it's outlined in *Left Behind*. I don't see any of these things. Maybe you and I are using different Bible translations. I have about fifteen translations in my library. I've even checked the Hebrew. I can't find what *Left Behind* describes in the Hebrew or in these English translations. I even have a copy of Tim LaHaye's *Prophecy Study Bible*. No jet planes."

"Ezekiel was describing this future and highly technological battle in terms that he and his readers could understand."

"If the prophecy was written for a time more than 2,500 years removed from Ezekiel's day, why didn't God, the true Author of the Bible, describe the battle in terms that *we* could relate to? Have you read the first chapter of Ezekiel? It's a vision of 'glowing metal . . . burnished bronze . . . wings spread out . . . like burning coals of fire . . . like bolts of lightning . . . sparkling beryl . . . wheels within wheels . . . rising wheels . . . the gleam of crystal . . . like the sound of an army camp.'[2] If God wanted to describe the unexplainable, especially a high-tech battle, then why didn't He use this kind of language in Ezekiel 38 and 39? Instead, we read about horses, bows and arrows, spears, and clubs."

"I see what you mean."

"If you have some time, let me outline for you why I believe Tim LaHaye does not follow his own interpretive guidelines."

"I would appreciate it. Thank you."

According to Tim LaHaye, the "great enemy from the north" is modern-day "Russia." The failed invasion attempt against Israel includes jet planes, "exploding missiles," and "atomic and explosive" devices. If LaHaye is true to his claim of literalism, then the Russian attack described in *Left Behind* should be a literal representation of the battle in Ezekiel 38–39. There should be a one-to-one correspondence between Ezekiel's description of the battle and what LaHaye and Jenkins describe. This conclusion is based on LaHaye's own interpretive methodology:

> The best guide to Bible study is "The Golden Rule of Biblical Interpretation." To depart from this rule opens the student to all forms of confusion and sometimes even heresy.
>
> When the plain sense of Scripture makes common sense, seek no other sense, but take every word at its primary, literal meaning unless the facts of the immediate context clearly indicate otherwise.[3]

LaHaye insists that the interpreter is to "take every word at its primary, literal meaning unless the facts of the immediate context clearly indicate otherwise." We learn from LaHaye that the prophecies found in Ezekiel 38–39 "are among the most specific and easy to understand in the prophetic word."[4] But do we find descriptions of jets, missiles, and atomic weapons in these chapters? Buck supposedly saw all of these very modern weapons when he first read the two chapters in Ezekiel, even though no commentator had ever seen such weaponry in centuries of biblical exposition. Can such a modern-day battle scenario be found in Ezekiel 38–39 if, as LaHaye maintains, every word should be interpreted in terms of "its primary, literal meaning unless the facts of the immediate context clearly indicate otherwise"? Where in the immediate context are we led to a modern-day interpretive solution? Let's put LaHaye's interpretive standard to the test by a study of the Bible.

AN ANCIENT BATTLE WITH ANCIENT WEAPONS

The battle in Ezekiel 38–39 is clearly an ancient one or at least one fought with ancient weapons. *All* the soldiers were riding horses (38:4, 15; 39:20). The horse soldiers were "wielding swords" (38:4), carrying "bows and arrows, war clubs and spears" (39:3, 9). The weapons were made of wood (39:10), and the abandoned weapons served as fuel for "seven years" (39:9). But LaHaye describes a highly technological future when the Antichrist rises to power to rule the world: "A wave of technological innovation is sweeping the planet . . . The future wave has already begun. We cannot stop it . . . [T]he Antichrist will use some of this technology to control the world."[5]

How does this assessment of the immediate future square with the seven-year tribulation period when Israelites "take wood from the field" and "gather firewood from the forests" (39:10)? Where are the forests in Israel today? There is nothing in the context that would lead the reader to conclude that horses, war clubs, swords, bows and arrows, and spears mean anything other than horses, war clubs, swords, bows and arrows, and spears. And what is the Russian air force after? Gold, silver, cattle, and goods (38:13). In what modern war can anyone remember armies going after cattle? How much cattle does Israel have? Certainly not enough to feed the Russians, whose military might is dwindling at a rapid pace.[6]

What happened to LaHaye's "Golden Rule of Biblical Interpretation"? He told us that not to follow this rule would lead to "all forms of confusion and sometimes even heresy." To help readers of the *Left Behind* series "gain a clearer understanding of end-time prophecy,"[7] LaHaye and Jenkins have written the nonfiction prophecy guide *Are We Living in the End Times?* This book is interspersed with excerpts from the *Left Behind* series. The authors apply nonfiction analysis to the fictional account. In many cases, however, the analysis is incomplete. For example, in the twelve-page discussion of the battle described in Ezekiel 38–39, Jenkins and LaHaye never tell us how they were able to turn horses, war clubs, swords, bows and arrows, and spears into "war planes," "intercontinental ballistic missiles," "nuclear-equipped MiG fighter-bombers,"[8] and "chunks of burning, twisted, molten steel smashing to the ground"[9] while maintaining a "literal interpretation" where "every word" is to be taken "at its primary, literal meaning."

PLAYING WORD GAMES

LaHaye writes that one way we know that Ezekiel 38–39 "can only mean modern-day Russia" is because of "etymology," that is, by studying the origin of words. The Hebrew word *rosh* that is found in Ezekiel 38:2 and 39:1 is said to be a people-group that refers to modern-day Russia. Part of the argument rests on the belief that *rosh* sounds like Russia. Those who hold this view translate Ezekiel 38:2 this way: "Son of man, set your face toward Gog of the land of Magog, *the prince of Rosh*, Meshech, and Tubal." The key phrase is "prince of Rosh," what LaHaye would have us to understand as the "leader of Russia" when this future battle takes place. A more accurate translation, the one followed by the King James Version, based on the way *rosh* is used elsewhere in the Old Testament, would read this way: "Son of man, set your face toward Gog of the land of Magog, the *chief* prince of Meshech and Tubal."

Even scholars who would agree with LaHaye on many other prophetic points admit that the Hebrew word *rosh* does not refer to Russia. For example, Charles Ryrie disagrees with the translation found in the New American Standard Bible (NASB). He writes: *"The prince of Rosh"* is better translated as "the chief prince of Meshech and Tubal [Ezek. 38:2]."[10] Even the editors of the NASB understand that "the prince of Rosh" is not a certain or even a usual translation. They include a marginal note that reads, "Or, *chief prince of Meshech"* (39:1). Meshech and Tubal are not linked with a place called Rosh in any other place in the Bible (Gen. 10:2; 1 Chron. 1:5; Isa. 66:19;[11] Ezek. 27:13; 32:26). This means that it is very unlikely that in these two cases alone *rosh* takes on an entirely different meaning from the way it is used elsewhere in the Old Testament. This is why Hebrew scholar E. W. Hengstenberg can write, "Rosh, as the name of a people, does not occur in all the Old Testament."[12]

The Rosh = Russia interpretation is not unique to LaHaye. Hal Lindsey popularized the interpretation in his *Late Great Planet Earth* in 1970.[13] LaHaye follows Lindsey's view to the letter:

> The name *Moscow* comes from the tribal name Meshech, and Tobolsk, the name of the principal state, comes from Tubal. The noun *Gog* is from the original tribal name, Magog, which gradually became *Rosh*, then *Rus*, and today is known as Russia. In the very interesting book *The Late Great Planet Earth*, my friend Hal Lindsey presents a lengthy discussion of the identity of these nations. I was so impressed by the accuracy of his sources and his readable style that I obtained permission to quote him at length, with numbered footnotes indicating his sources.[14]

The Rosh = Russia interpretation was introduced to a broad spectrum of Christians interested in Bible prophecy in the first edition of the

Scofield Reference Bible in 1909 and in the revised 1917 edition. Scofield writes, "The reference to Meshech and Tubal (Moscow and Tobolsk) is a clear mark of identification (i.e., with Russia)."[15] He goes on to tell his readers that "all agree" that Russia heads the northern (European) alliance against Israel in "the last days." All do not agree. The views of Scofield, Lindsey, and LaHaye are not supported by most Bible-believing Christian historians, archaeologists, commentators, and linguists. Edwin M. Yamauchi, professor of history at Miami University in Oxford, Ohio, is an authority on the subject, and he disagrees completely with Lindsey's analysis. He writes that the Hebrew word *rosh* "can have nothing to do with modern 'Russia.' This would be a gross anachronism, for the modern name is based upon the name *Rus,* which was brought into the region of Kiev, north of the Black Sea, by the Vikings only in the Middle Ages."[16] Other evangelical scholars agree with Dr. Yamauchi:

> There is no evidence from the ancient Near East that a country named Rosh ever existed. Some would understand *rosh* as modern Russia. Proponents of this view usually appeal to etymology based on similar sounds (to the hearing) between two words. Such etymological procedures are not linguistically sound, nor is etymology alone a sound hermeneutical basis on which to interpret a word. The word "Russia" is a late eleventh-century A.D. term. Therefore, the data does [*sic*] not seem to support an interpretation of *rosh* as a proper name of a geographical region or country.[17]

Rosh is a common Hebrew word that is used more than six hundred times in the Bible. It is most often translated as "chief," "head," or "beginning." For example, Rosh Hashanah marks the beginning of the Jewish new year. It is described as a "high holy day" because it is the chief or head holy day of the year. It literally means "head of the year" or "beginning of the year." Rosh Hodesh, the beginning of the new month in the Jewish calendar, is celebrated during the morning worship time in a synagogue (1 Sam. 20:5). There are priests in Israel, and there are *"chief* priests." The word for "chief" is *rosh* (2 Kings 25:18; 1 Chron. 27:5; 2 Chron. 19:11; 24:6; 26:20; 31:10; Ezra 7:5; Jer. 52:24). Michael was called one of God's chief princes (Dan. 10:21).

Any concordance will show that the Hebrew word *rosh* is never used as a proper name that refers to a nation.[18] To make this common word mean something different in just two out of six hundred usages is an attempt to make a text fit a particular theology. And even if it could be shown that *rosh* is a people-group or nation, this does not mean that it refers to modern-day Russia.

AN INVASION FROM THE NORTH

LaHaye tries to establish that the "remote parts of the north" (Ezek. 38:6, 15; 39:2) must refer to Russia because Russia is north of Israel. It is true that Russia is north of Israel; it is also true that a number of nations are north of Israel and that the Bible often uses north as a designation for a geographical area that includes the north as well as the northeast. For example, Babylon was east of Israel, but Jeremiah 4:6 warned that the disaster that came upon Judah came "from the north" (Jer. 1:13–15; 3:18; 6:1, 22; 10:22; Zech. 2:6–7). The same was true when Israel was overrun by the Assyrians (Zeph. 2:13) and Persians (Isa. 41:25; Jer. 50:3). Is the Bible mistaken? Not at all. "From the perspective of the Holy Land, the invaders came down from the north, even if their place of origin was actually to the east. Ezekiel is giving the *direction* of the invasion, not the place of the invader's origin."[19] Archaeologist Barry Beitzel states that "the Bible's use of the expression 'north' denotes the direction from which a foe would normally approach and not the location of its homeland."[20] The same holds true for any invading army that was north and west of Israel. The invaders, too, would have to bring a land army into Israel from the north since the Mediterranean Sea is directly west of Israel.

IN THE LATTER YEARS

Ezekiel 38:16 sets the time frame for the battle of Gog and Magog "in the last days." In many cases, the Hebrew word often translated "last days" means nothing more than "in future days," "a later time," or "in days to come." J. A. Thompson concludes, "The phrase *in the latter days* need not be interpreted eschatologically, but merely in the sense of 'in the future.'"[21] There are "former days" (Deut. 4:32), the past, and there are "future days" (4:30), an expectation of things to come.[22] The future fulfillment was confirmed when Moses described what would happen after he died: "I know that after my death you will act corruptly and turn from the way which I have commanded you; and evil will befall you in the latter days, for you will do that which is evil in the sight of the LORD, provoking Him to anger with the work of your hands" (Deut. 31:29). Moses wasn't skipping over thousands of years of history to describe what would happen in our future. The mention of "the latter days," the same Hebrew word that appears in Ezekiel 38:16, actually referred to the period of the judges: "The anger of the LORD burned against Israel, and He said, 'Because this nation has transgressed My covenant which I commanded their fathers, and has not listened to My voice, I also will no longer drive out before them any of the nations which Joshua left when he died'" (Judg. 2:20–21).

Daniel interpreted Nebuchadnezzar's dream, explaining to him what would happen in "the latter days" (Dan. 2:28), that is, after his death. The events of Daniel 2 were fulfilled in the future, the "latter days" of the Babylonian kingdom, when the Medes and Persians overthrew Belshazzar, Nebuchadnezzar's son (5:22–30). The Greeks overthrew the Medes and Persians, and Rome overthrew the Greeks.

During the time of Jesus' ministry, Rome was in power, the fourth kingdom in Nebuchadnezzar's dream (2:40–43).

God promised to "restore the fortunes of Moab *in the latter days*" (Jer. 48:47, emphasis added). He made a similar promise to Elam. "'But it will come about in the last days that I shall restore the fortunes of Elam,' declares the LORD" (Jer. 49:39). We learn that the fulfillment for Elam's fortunes is found in the New Testament era, the period that Joel describes as being in the future (Joel 2:28–32) and what Peter defines as "the last days," that is, what was taking place in his day:

This [the outpouring of the Spirit at pentecost and people coming to Christ] is what was spoken of through the prophet Joel:

> *"And it shall be in the last days," God says,*
> *"That I will pour forth of My Spirit upon all mankind;*
> *And your sons and your daughters shall prophesy,*
> *And your young men shall see visions,*
> *And your old men shall dream dreams." (ACTS 2:16–17)*

The writer to the Hebrews told us, "God, after He spoke long ago to the fathers in the prophets in many portions and in many ways, *in these last days* has spoken to us in His Son" (Heb. 1:1–2, emphasis added). The "last days" were operating in the first century and referred to the close of the old covenant era.

And who was included in this "last days" blessing? "Parthians and Medes and *Elamites*, and residents of Mesopotamia, Judea and Cappadocia, Pontus, and Asia, Phrygia and Pamphylia, Egypt and the districts of Libya around Cyrene, and visitors from Rome, both Jews and proselytes, Cretans and Arabs" (Acts 2:9–11, emphasis added). Both "Jews and proselytes" from "every nation under heaven" were included (2:5). That meant descendants of Moab and Elam.

In the many uses of "last days," "end of days," and "latter days," we can conclude that the phrases can mean the future or the new covenant era after the death, resurrection, and ascension of Jesus. Because of what we know about the nature of the warfare in Ezekiel 38–39, we know that the battle of Gog and Magog was prophesied to take place sometime in the future when battles were still fought with ancient weapons.

LAHAYE GOES SYMBOLIC

Any commentator writing prior to the invention of gunpowder could interpret Ezekiel's descriptive battle literally since wars were still fought with clubs, spears, and bows and arrows up until the eighteenth century. To account for an invasion that would use supermodern weapons such as jets and "atomic and explosive" devices, the battle of Gog and Magog must be interpreted symbolically, a methodology that LaHaye, at first reading, seems to reject.

Those who see a symbolic battle claim that Ezekiel could describe distant future events only in terms that he and his readers understood. So horses could mean "horse power,"[23] wooden weapons are actually rifles made from very dense wood,[24] and arrows are really guided missiles. This is not to say that the word "sword" cannot be used symbolically or that parts of the Bible cannot be interpreted symbolically. The Bible tells us to take up "the sword of the Spirit" (Eph. 6:17), the "word of God is living and active and sharper than any two-edged sword" (Heb. 4:12), and a sharp sword comes out of Jesus' mouth (Rev. 19:15). Faith is described as a "shield" (Eph. 6:16). Children are compared to a quiver full of arrows (Ps. 127:5). Even so, there doesn't seem to be any indication in the "immediate context" of Ezekiel 38–39 that these implements of war are being used symbolically, that is, that they stand for sophisticated modern weapons. And even if they are symbols, it is a great leap in logic to assume that they symbolize twenty-first-century weaponry.

FOR SUCH A TIME AS THIS

If the battle described in Ezekiel 38–39 does not refer to modern-day Russia, then when and where in biblical history did this conflict take place? Many older commentators placed the battle sometime during the reign of Antiochus Epiphanes IV, "whose armies were overthrown by Israelite forces about 400 years after Ezekiel prophesied."[25] Instead of looking to the distant future or finding fulfillment in a historical setting outside the Bible where we depend on unreliable secular sources, we would do well to look to the Bible itself for fulfillment. James B. Jordan believes that "it is in [the book of] Esther that we see a conspiracy to plunder the Jews, which backfires with the result that the Jews plundered their enemies. This event is then ceremonially sealed with the institution of the annual Feast of Purim."[26]

Establishing the immediate historical and theological context for Ezekiel 38–39 is important to make the case that the battle has already taken place. In Ezekiel 34, God promises Israel that He will bring them back to their land and make a new covenant with them (Ezek. 36). In Ezekiel 37 we read about the vision of the valley of dry bones which is a picture of the restoration of God's people back to their land from exile. Following this, "Ezekiel describes the attack of Gog, Prince of Magog, and his confederates. Ezekiel states that people from all over the world attack God's people, who are pictured dwelling at peace in the land. God's people will completely defeat them, however, and the spoils will be immense. The result is that all nations will see the victory, and 'the house of Israel will know that I am the Lord their God from that day onward' (Ezek. 39:21–23) . . . Chronologically this all fits very nicely. The events of Esther took place during the reign of Darius, after the initial rebuilding of the Temple under Joshua [the high priest] and Zerubbabel and shortly before rebuilding of the walls by Nehemiah."[27]

The slaughter of Israel's enemies in Ezekiel 39:1–6 fits with the number of deaths listed in Esther 9:10, 15–16 (75,310) and the time it would take to bury the casualties, an average of 10,000 bodies each month for seven months. With modern-day earthmoving equipment, placing the bodies in massive common graves, the task could be accomplished today in about two weeks. We are told the number of the dead, yet we are not told how many men made up the total army. But we can imagine that the horse soldiers came "like a storm . . . like a cloud covering the land" (Ezek. 38:9), especially as they kicked up dust and other debris.[28]

Note the recurrence of the word *sword* in these verses. In Esther 9:5 we read that "the Jews struck all their enemies with the *sword*, killing and destroying." We learn from Ezekiel 38:21 that God calls "'for a *sword* against him [Gog] on all My mountains' . . . 'Every man's *sword* will be against his brother.'" In both instances, swords, not jet fighters, are the weapons of choice.

Ezekiel 38:5–6 tells us that Israel's enemies came from "Persia, Ethiopia [lit. Cush], and . . . from the remote parts of the north," all within the boundaries of the Persian Empire of Esther's day. From Esther we learn that the Persian Empire "extended from India to Ethiopia [lit. Cush], 127 provinces" in all (Est. 8:9). "In other words, the explicit idea that the Jews were attacked by people from all the provinces of Persia is in both passages."[29] The parallels are unmistakable.

In Esther 9:19 we see that Jews were living peacefully in "unwalled towns" (KJV) when Haman conspired against them. Israel's antagonists in Ezekiel were said to "go up against the land of unwalled villages" (38:11). The Hebrew word used in Esther and Ezekiel for "unwalled" is identical. Why mention "unwalled villages" if the Ezekiel battle is future? To say that Jerusalem is unwalled today means little since no modern city is behind a wall!

The chief antagonist of the Jews in the book of Esther was Haman, "the son of Hammedatha the Agagite" (Est. 3:1).[30] "According to Ezekiel 39:11 and 15, the place where the army of Gog is buried will be known as the Valley of Hamon-Gog, and according to verse 16, the nearby city will become known as Hamonah."[31] This all seems remarkably coincidental unless Ezekiel was predicting what was fulfilled in Esther.

Finally, how do we reconcile the Jews seizing the plunder in Ezekiel (38:12–13; 39:10) and not laying "their hands on the plunder" in Esther (9:12, 15)? The fact that both mention plunder is significant in seeing a parallel between the two accounts. Ezekiel described one aspect of what was done with the plunder. It was taken for a national cause, probably to assist in rebuilding the post-exile temple. Esther's account made it clear that the plunder was not to be taken and used by individuals: "they did not lay their hands on the plunder." The king granted the Jews as a *people*—as an exiled nation—the unconditional right "to plunder their spoil" (Est. 8:11).

The above interpretation has two things going for it over the invasion theory of modern-day Russia. First, the narrative can be read whereby every word can be taken "at its primary, literal meaning" without resorting to allegorizing. Lindsey, quoted by LaHaye in his *The Beginning of the End,* has to admit, "'Horses, swords, armor, bucklers, and shields' could be symbolic terms of implements of warfare that in our day would represent tanks, M-16s, machine guns, rockets, bazookas, etc."[32] Neither Lindsey nor LaHaye tells us how such an interpretation does not violate the "Golden Rule of Biblical Interpretation." If God wanted to picture a futuristic battle that included sophisticated and nearly impossible-to-describe weaponry,

He could have used phrases such as "glowing metal" (Ezek. 1:4, 27), "burnished bronze" (1:7), "wings . . . spread out" (1:11, 23–24), "like burning coals of fire" (1:13), "like torches darting back and forth" (1:13), "like bolts of lightning" (1:14), "sparkling beryl" (1:16), "wheels within wheels" (1:16–17), "rising wheels" (1:19), "the gleam of crystal" (1:22), and "like the sound of an army camp" (1:24).[33]

Second, the Bible itself gives us the interpretation. By comparing Scripture with Scripture, without the aid of external historical sources, which are often unreliable, or prophetic speculation that is revised as historical circumstances change, the average Christian can interpret the Bible.

CONCLUSION

The first prophetic scene in *Left Behind* that sets off a series of events leading to a pretribulational Rapture cannot be supported by an appeal to the literal interpretation of the Bible. There is no way that Buck or any first-time reader could ever have concluded that a modern-day war was being prophesied by Ezekiel if he had followed LaHaye's "Golden Rule of Biblical Interpretation." Following a literal interpretation of the Bible and comparing Scripture with Scripture show that the Gog and Magog battle is an ancient one.

2

THE RAPTURE OF THE CHURCH

Local television stations from around the world reported bizarre occurrences . . . CNN showed via satellite the video of a groom disappearing while slipping the ring onto his bride's finger. A funeral home in Australia reported that nearly every mourner disappeared from one memorial service, including the corpse.[1]

"We have Gary DeMar and Dave Hunt on the phone. They have agreed to debate the topic of Bible prophecy. Dave and Gary have debated a number of times over the years, so they are familiar with the issues. Dave, why don't you go first? From your perspective, what is the single doctrine that sets you and Gary apart?"

"I would have to say that it's the pretrib Rapture."

"Could you briefly explain it?"

"The Rapture and the Second Coming are two distinct events. One occurs at the beginning of the seven-year Tribulation period when Jesus comes for His church, and the other at the end when Jesus returns with His church to rescue Israel."

"Gary, is the pretrib Rapture a sticking point for you?"

"Yes, and a whole lot more. But I have one question for Dave. Can he show me one verse that teaches a *pretribulational* Rapture?"

"Dave?"

"Certainly. First Thessalonians 4:16–17 [KJV] is a good starting point: 'For the Lord himself shall descend from heaven with a shout, with the voice of the archangel, and with the trump of God: and the dead in Christ shall rise first: then we which are alive and remain shall be caught up together with them in the clouds to meet the Lord in the air: and so shall we ever be with the Lord.'"

"Gary, your response?"

"It's no surprise that Dave turns to this passage, since 1 Thessalonians 4 is considered the key Rapture passage. If the Rapture's not taught here, it's not taught anywhere. The issue in this debate is not whether those in Christ are being caught up; it's *when* they are being caught up and what follows this event. There is no mention of a Tribulation period following being caught up. A careful reader will note that there is no mention of the reign of Anti-christ, a rebuilt temple, or Armageddon, all the elements that assume a pretrib Rapture. There is no single verse in the entire Bible that supports a pretrib Rapture."

The story line of *Left Behind* is based upon a doctrine called the Rapture. To be more precise, it is based upon a particular view of the Rapture, a *pretribulational* as opposed to a posttribulational, midtribulational, partial, or prewrath Rapture. The Rapture, a word that is not found in English translations of the Bible, supposedly is an event where all Christians, both living and dead, will be "caught up" to meet Jesus in the sky and then be taken to heaven. Jesus' return to "rapture" His church is invisible and secret. No one will know the event has taken place until after the fact. Advocates of a Rapture do not agree when the event occurs. All agree that the timing of the

Rapture is tied to the seven-year Tribulation period. The pretribula-
tionist believes that the Rapture takes place *before* (pre) the Tribulation; the posttribulationist believes the Rapture takes place *after* (post)
the Tribulation; the midtribulationist believes the Rapture takes place
in the *middle* of the Tribulation, and advocates of the newest rapture
position, the pre-wrath Rapture, teach that Christians are raptured
just before God pours out His wrath on an unbelieving world near the
end of the Tribulation period. The partial rapture view, a minority
position, claims that only those Christians who are watching and
waiting for Christ's return will be raptured.

There is no single verse or group of verses that specifically
describes any of these five Rapture positions. In terms of pretribula-
tionalism, since that's the Rapture position advocated by LaHaye, we
should expect to find at least *one* verse that describes Jesus coming for
His *church* to take Christians to heaven *prior* to a seven-year period of
Tribulation, and then Jesus returning with His church seven years after
the Rapture to defeat Antichrist and set up a kingdom in Jerusalem
that will last for a thousand years. Of course, there is no such verse or
group of connected verses that mentions these very necessary doctrinal
elements. There is no such phrase as "the rapture of the church" or "the
catching away of the church" found anywhere in the Bible. Even
LaHaye admits that no one passage teaches a pretrib Rapture:

> One objection to the pre-Tribulation Rapture is that not one pas-
> sage of Scripture teaches the two aspects of His Second Coming
> separated by the Tribulation. This is true. But then, no one passage
> teaches a post-trib or mid-trib Rapture, either.[2]

> No single verse specifically states, "Christ will come before the
> Tribulation." On the other hand, no single passage teaches He will
> *not* come before the Tribulation, or that He will come in the

middle or at the end of the Tribulation. Any such explicit declaration would end the debate immediately.[3]

Arguing that the other Rapture positions don't have a verse to support them does not make LaHaye's position right. It's possible that
the entire end-time scenario in which all the Rapture positions have
a stake is without biblical foundation. We will consider this possibility in later chapters. At this point, readers of *Left Behind* should be
aware that the pretrib Rapture is the keystone to the entire multivolume series. If there is no pretrib Rapture, then no one is left
behind. One would think that this necessary doctrine would have at
least one or two very closely associated verses that, when harmonized,
would describe the elements necessary for the pretrib Rapture
hypothesis to make sense to the "casual reader."[4]

At the same time LaHaye gives the impression that the pretrib
Rapture doctrine is self-evident to anyone who reads the New
Testament, he has to admit that the doctrine was not discovered until
the nineteenth century. All attempts to find a pretrib Rapture any earlier than around 1830 do not stand up to historical scrutiny. It was only
in the nineteenth century, LaHaye tells us, when "the Bible was available and being read by millions in the English-speaking world" and
"prophecy was in the air," that the discovery took place.[5] If it took nearly
nineteen hundred years to discover the pretrib Rapture, why didn't it
take that long to discover the many other doctrines that Christians
believed and confessed without the aid of an English translation of the
Bible? There was no English translation of the Bible until the late four-
teenth century. How did the Apostles' Creed, the Nicene Creed, and
the Athanasian Creed, to name only a few doctrinal standards, ever get
written without the aid of an English translation of the Bible? There
have been countless commentaries published on the Bible throughout
the centuries by men who were intimately familiar with all the biblical

languages—Hebrew, Aramaic, and Greek—and they were never able to find the doctrine.[6] Even pretrib advocate H. A. Ironside, for whom LaHaye has the highest regard,[7] admitted the novelty of the position:

> [U]ntil brought to the fore through the writings and the preaching and teaching of a distinguished ex-clergyman, Mr. J. N. Darby, in the early part of the last century [i.e., the nineteenth century], it is scarcely to be found in a single book or sermon through the period of sixteen hundred years! If any doubt this statement, let them search, as the writer has in measure done, the remarks of the so-called Fathers, both pre- and post-Nicene; the theological treatises of the scholastic divines; Roman Catholic writers of all shades of thought; the literature of the Reformation; the sermons and expositions of the Puritans; and the general theo-logical works of the day. He will find the "mystery" conspicuous by its absence.[8]

Thomas Ice, cofounder with LaHaye of the Pre-Trib Research Center and an editor of LaHaye's *Prophecy Study Bible*, claims that a "certain theological climate needed to be created before premillennialism[9] would restore the Biblical doctrine of the pretrib Rapture. Sufficient development did not take place until after the French Revolution." But like LaHaye and John Walvoord, Ice has to admit that "neither pre nor posttribs have a proof text for the time of the Rapture." The doctrine, therefore, "is the product of a deduction from one's overall system of theology, both for pre and posttribbers."[10]

This is a remarkable admission for a doctrine that is so crucial to a theological position said to be fundamental for a proper understanding of the Bible. How is it possible that:

- so many well-meaning Christians believe in a pretrib Rapture when even pretrib advocates tell us that not one passage of

Scripture teaches the two aspects of Jesus' second coming separated by the Tribulation;

- the Old Testament doesn't teach a pretrib Rapture;

- no one up until around 1830 taught a pretrib Rapture; and

- the doctrine, supposedly "so clearly revealed in the Scriptures," became "utterly lost" immediately after the close of the New Testament canon?[11]

Marvin Rosenthal, a prominent and respected evangelist to the Jewish people, states that he could no longer hold to a belief in a pretrib Rapture because he determined, after his personal study, that the Bible did not teach it. Rosenthal turned to John Walvoord, whom LaHaye describes as the "dean of all living prophecy experts,"[12] hoping to find clear *biblical* support for the position. Walvoord's *The Rapture Question* includes a list of fifty arguments in support of a pretrib Rapture. Rosenthal was shocked to discover that no biblical text explicitly supported the doctrine:

> Not once, among fifty arguments, does this godly Christian leader cite one biblical text that explicitly teaches pretribulation rapturism—not once. This was not an oversight. The reason for the omission of any pretribulation Rapture texts is clear. There are none. Walvoord's own comment helps substantiate that fact. He wrote, "It is therefore not too much to say that the Rapture question is determined more by ecclesiology [the doctrine of the church] than eschatology [the doctrine of the last things]" . . . There simply is no explicit exegetical evidence for pretribulation rapturism.[13]

By all accounts, *there is not one explicit verse to support a position that millions of Bible-believing Christians hold with unbending devotion.* In

21

the first edition of *The Rapture Question*, Walvoord, like LaHaye, had to confess that evidence for either a pretribulational or a posttribulational Rapture was not explicitly taught in the Bible. "[Walvoord] deleted this statement in later editions of the book."[14]

If all of this is true, then how do proponents of a pretrib Rapture find biblical support for their position? LaHaye and other advocates of a pretrib Rapture use a number of verses to promote the doctrine, but they view five passages as fundamental. If the doctrine is not taught in these passages, then it certainly is not taught in the rest of the Bible.

1 THESSALONIANS 4:13–18

The starting point for any discussion of a pretribulational Rapture is found in a passage that John F. Walvoord describes as "one of the crucial revelations in regard to the Rapture of the church."[15]

> We do not want you to be uninformed, brethren, about those who are asleep, that you may not grieve, as do the rest who have no hope. For if we believe that Jesus died and rose again, even so God will bring with Him those who have fallen asleep in Jesus. For this we say to you by the word of the Lord, that we who are alive, and remain until the coming of the Lord, shall not precede those who have fallen asleep. For the Lord Himself will descend from heaven with a shout, with the voice of the archangel, and with the trumpet of God; and the dead in Christ shall rise first. Then we who are alive and remain shall be caught up together with them in the clouds to meet the Lord in the air, and thus we shall always be with the Lord. Therefore comfort one another with these words. (1 Thessalonians 4:13–18)

Tim LaHaye writes that the pretrib Rapture "is taught clearly in 1 Thessalonians 4:13–18, where the apostle Paul provides us with most of the available details."[16] Once again, why didn't anyone see this prior to the nineteenth century if the pretrib Rapture "is taught clearly" in this passage? For centuries, Christian writers have understood that 1 Thessalonians 4:13–18 is describing the general resurrection of believers when Jesus returns,[17] as the Apostles' Creed states, "to judge the living and the dead." Nothing is said about Jesus coming again to rapture His church in a separate invisible event. The text describes the raising of those who are "in Christ," both living and dead (1 Thess. 4:16). No mention is made of the church being raptured before, in the middle of, or after a Tribulation period. In fact, 1 Thessalonians mentions the "church" only once in the entire book, and its reference is to the "church of the Thessalonians" (1:1), not to the church in general.

In *The Bible and the Future*, Anthony A. Hoekema points out several flaws in the claim that this passage teaches a pretrib Rapture:

> What this passage clearly teaches is that at the time of the Lord's return all the believing dead (the "dead in Christ") will be raised, and all believers who are still alive will be transformed and glorified (see 1 Corinthians 15:51–52); then these two groups will be caught up to meet the Lord in the air. What these words do not teach is that after this meeting in the air the Lord will reverse his direction and go back to heaven, taking the raised and transformed members of the church with him. The passage does not breathe a word of this. To be sure, verse 17 ends with the words, "and so we shall always be with the Lord." But Paul does not say *where* we shall always be with the Lord. The idea that after meeting the Lord in the air we shall be with him for seven years in heaven and later for a thousand years in the air above the earth is pure inference and nothing more. Everlasting oneness with Christ in glory is the clear teaching of this passage, not a pretribulational Rapture.[18]

LaHaye lists five specific events that he says take place in 1 Thessalonians 4:13–18 in his *Are We Living in the End Times?*, and not one item in his list mentions anything about the church being raptured prior to a Tribulation period or Jesus returning after a seven-year period with His church to defeat Antichrist. And yet he states that "no one can argue that the rapture of the church" is taught in this passage.[19] Christians who do not believe the Bible teaches a *pretrib* Rapture do not deny that Jesus will return at some future unknown date to raise both the living and the dead who are "in Christ." First Thessalonians 4:13–18 says He will; that much is clear. But nothing in this passage supports a pretrib or any-trib version of this event.

TITUS 2:13

Looking for the blessed hope and the appearing of the glory of our great God and Savior, Christ Jesus.

LaHaye claims that "the blessed hope" is a synonym for the pretrib Rapture while "the appearing of the glory of our great God and Savior, Christ Jesus" is a description of the Second Coming. All the events described in the projected twelve-volume *Left Behind* series—the Great Tribulation, the rise of Antichrist, the rebuilding of the temple, and all the events in the book of Revelation from chapters 4 through 19—are made to fit between the blessed hope and the glorious appearing. Although LaHaye defines his version of the Rapture as "a blessed hope," the Bible never does.[20]

LaHaye's pretrib logic works like this. The rapturing of Christians prior to a Great Tribulation, according to LaHaye, is a hopeful event. The Bible mentions "the blessed hope" in Titus 2:13. The pretrib Rapture, therefore, must be "*the* blessed hope" since it is a hopeful event. But so is salvation by grace through faith a hopeful event, as is the resurrection of the dead. These and many more events in the Christian's life are hopeful events (Acts 22:6; 28:20; Rom. 5:2; Gal. 5:5; Eph. 4:4; Col. 1:5, 23, 27; Titus 1:2). Titus 2:13 is the only place in the entire Bible where the phrase "the blessed hope" appears, and there is no mention of the church being raptured or caught up. As was the case with 1 Thessalonians 4:13–18, none of the required events defining a pretrib Rapture and subsequent Tribulation can be found in this passage.[21]

The belief that Titus 2:13 describes two comings separated by a Tribulation period must be read into the text. Nothing in the immediate context even hints at a rapture of the church as an event separate from the general resurrection. In fact, there is no mention of a resurrection in this passage. Paul was awaiting our "blessed hope," *which is* "the appearing of the glory of our great God and Savior, Jesus Christ." (Notice it's the "glory" that appears.) Even John Walvoord believes that Titus 2:13 describes only one event, not two events separated by a seven-year Tribulation period: "As Paul expressed it, 'while we wait for the blessed hope—the glorious appearing of our Great God and Savior, Jesus Christ' (v. 13)."[22]

Other commentators follow the same approach. Ronald A. Ward explains that "the blessed hope and appearing," because there is only one article present, "is a single idea."[23] New Testament Greek scholar R. C. H. Lenski concurs that "our blessed hope is 'the epiphany [appearing] of the glory' of Jesus."[24] Edward Hindson, an associate editor of LaHaye's *Prophecy Study Bible* and an editor of the *Liberty Bible Commentary*, states, "The Greek construction here is fantastic for the construction makes the 'blessed hope' and 'glorious appearing' to be one and the same thing."[25] So then, there is disagreement even among pretrib advocates on the meaning of this text.

A careful study of Titus 2:13 will show that there is no two-stage coming of Jesus, no mention of a rapture of the church followed by a Tribulation period. Therefore, Titus 2:13 cannot be used to support the scenario outlined in *Left Behind*. The blessed hope is most likely the resurrection: "Blessed be the God and Father of our Lord Jesus Christ, who according to His great mercy has caused us to be born again to a living hope through the resurrection of Jesus Christ from the dead" (1 Peter 1:3).

1 CORINTHIANS 15:51–57

Behold, I tell you a mystery; we shall not all sleep, but we shall all be changed, in a moment, in the twinkling of an eye, at the last trumpet; for the trumpet will sound, and the dead will be raised imperishable, and we shall be changed. For this perishable must put on the imperishable, and this mortal must put on immortality. But when this perishable will have put on the imperishable, and this mortal will have put on immortality, then will come about the saying that is written, "DEATH IS SWALLOWED UP in victory. O DEATH, WHERE IS YOUR VICTORY? O DEATH, WHERE IS YOUR STING?" The sting of death is sin, and the power of sin is the law; but thanks be to God, who gives us the victory through our Lord Jesus Christ.

Support for the pretrib Rapture in *Left Behind* begins with a discussion of 1 Corinthians 15:51–57. The fictional character Pastor Vernon Billings of New Hope Village Church recorded a message on videotape to be viewed by those left behind "after the disappearance of God's people from the earth."[26] LaHaye and Jenkins use the Billings character and his recorded sermon as an effective device to profile the biblical support to explain what supposedly happened to millions of Christians "in the twinkling of an eye":

26

That you are watching indicates you have been left behind. You are no doubt stunned, shocked, afraid, and remorseful. I would like you to consider what I have to say here as instructions for life following Christ's rapture of his church. That is what has happened . . .

Let me show you from the Bible exactly what has happened. You won't need this proof by now, because you will have experienced the most shocking event of history. But as this tape was made beforehand and I am confident that I will be gone, ask yourself, how did he know? Here's how, from 1 Corinthians 15:51–57.[27]

This section of Scripture falls into the same category as 1 Thessalonians 4:13–18. Again, no one denies that Christians are going to be raised; the dispute is over when the event takes place and what happens afterward. The passage makes no mention of a secret rapture or Jesus coming for His church before a future Great Tribulation and then later returning with His church after the Great Tribulation. Nowhere in this passage will you find a discussion of the Great Tribulation, the rise of Antichrist, God's redemptive program for the Jews, or an earthly millennial reign of Christ. All of these events must be read into 1 Corinthians 15:51–57. The chapter deals with the general resurrection, not a rapture of the church. In the book of Acts, which is the only inspired historical account of the early church, we read that the apostles preached the doctrine of the resurrection to both Jews and Gentiles in Jerusalem (2:31), Pisidian Antioch (13:14–37), Athens (17:18), and Rome (23:3–6). Not once did anyone mention a two-stage coming of Christ separated by a Tribulation period. Paul was "on trial for the hope and resurrection of the dead" (Acts 23:6), not the rapture of the church.

The topic of discussion in 1 Corinthians 15 is the reality of Christ's resurrection and what it means to believers: "If there is no resurrection of the dead, not even Christ has been raised; and if Christ has

27

not been raised, then our preaching is vain, your faith also is vain . . . Then those also who have fallen asleep in Christ have perished" (15:13–14, 18). Not once in this entire chapter is there any discussion of two comings of Jesus separated by a Tribulation period. Notice the sequence of events:

- Christ's resurrection: "But each in his own order: Christ the first fruits" (15:23).

- The believer's resurrection: "After that those who are Christ's at His coming" (15:23).

- The consummation: "Then comes the end, when He delivers up the kingdom to the God and Father, when He has abolished all rule and all authority and power" (15:24).

Following LaHaye's sequence, we should expect to find after the resurrection of believers, the seven-year period containing the events raptured saints escape in the *Left Behind* series. Not once in 1 Corinthians 15 is there any discussion of what happens to those "left behind" because *no one* is left behind. John 5:28–29 states that believers and unbelievers will be raised at the same time, not separated either by seven years or by a thousand years. Believers will undergo "a resurrection of life" while those who committed evil deeds will undergo "a resurrection of judgment." This is plain in the parable of the tares (unbelievers) and wheat (believers). According to the Bible, both "grow together until the harvest" (Matt. 13:30). And contrary to what pretrib advocates maintain, the *tares* are dealt with first: "In the time of the harvest I will say to the reapers, 'First gather up the tares and bind them in bundles to burn them up; but gather the wheat into my barn'" (13:30). First the tares, then the wheat. C. I. Scofield, author of the notes in the *Scofield Reference Bible*, reverses the order: "At the end of this age (v. 40) the tares are set apart for burning, but *first the wheat is gathered* into the barn (John 14.3; 1 Thess. 4.14–17)."[28] Why is Scofield's view so important? Almost every modern-day advocate of the pretrib Rapture, LaHaye included,[29] is indebted to Scofield in some way. In order to make his prophetic system work, Scofield must reverse the clear order of events in Matthew 13:30.

Even though there is no mention of a two-stage coming in 1 Corinthians 15 and Matthew 13:24–30 that allows for a seven-year Tribulation period sandwiched between two comings, LaHaye and Jenkins have written a multivolume series to fill in events that the Bible nowhere discusses in relation to these and other supposed pretrib Rapture passages.

THE RAPTURE IN REVELATION

A glaring inconsistency is found in LaHaye's defense of an any-moment, pretrib Rapture when he turns to the book of Revelation. He declares that the "first-century church believed in the imminent return of Christ, possibly during their lifetime."[30] He means that first-century Christians believed that Jesus could come at any moment to rapture the church. However, later in the same book he writes, "Chapter 1 [of Revelation] is the introduction; chapters 2 and 3 *cover the church age*, using seven historical churches to describe the entire age. (For example, the church in Ephesus is the only one that refers to apostles because the first-century church alone included apostles.)"[31] How could Christians believe that Jesus could come at any moment when the Bible supposedly teaches that He would not come until the last of the seven representative churches appears? This destroys LaHaye's doctrine of the any-moment rapture of the church since the Rapture could not have taken place until nineteen hundred years later when the Laodicean church age began.[32] This view also destroys LaHaye's insistence on literalism since the seven churches are alleged to *represent* seven distinct periods of the church age. Where in Revelation are we told that the seven *literal* churches represent seven historical ages of the church throughout history?

New Testament Greek scholar William Hendriksen offers the following evaluation of the seven churches/seven ages view:

> The notion that these seven churches describe seven successive periods of Church history hardly needs refutation. To say nothing about the humorous—if it were not so deplorable—exegesis which, for example, makes the church of Sardis [A.D. 1520 to the Tribulation], which was dead, refer to the glorious age of the Reformation; it should be clear to every student of Scripture that there is not one atom of evidence in all the sacred writings which in any way corroborates this thoroughly arbitrary method of cutting up the history of the Church and assigning the resulting pieces to the respective epistles of Revelation 2 and 3.[33]

In order to find the Rapture in Revelation, LaHaye has to identify a place where the church is taken to heaven prior to the Great Tribulation and then returned with Jesus to defeat Antichrist. LaHaye sees the pre-trib Rapture of the church in Revelation 4:1–2: "After these things I looked, and behold, a door standing open in heaven, and the first voice which I had heard, like the sound of a trumpet speaking with me, said, 'Come up here, and I will show you what must take place after these things.' Immediately I was in the Spirit; and behold, a throne was standing in heaven, and One sitting on the throne."

Of course, only John was taken *temporarily* into heaven, like Paul before him (2 Cor. 12:2). LaHaye insists that this is the rapture of the church, even though Revelation 4:1–2 says nothing about the church being taken to heaven: "Inasmuch as John was the last remaining

apostle and a member of the universal Church, his elevation to heaven
is a picture of the Rapture of the Church just before the Tribulation
begins."[34] He attempts to bolster his argument by noting that this is
also a logical place to insert the pretrib Rapture since the church "is
not on the earth during the Tribulation."[35] LaHaye continues,

> There are sixteen references to the Church in Revelation 1–3,[36]
> whereas chapters 6–18, which cover the Tribulation, do not men-
> tion the Church once. The natural conclusion drawn from this is
> that the Church that was so prominent during its two thousand-
> year history (as predicted in chapters 2–3) is not mentioned in
> chapters 4–18 because those chapters describe the Tribulation,
> which the Church does not endure.[37]

LaHaye's thesis is based on his unproven assumption that Revelation
2–3 covers "the church age, using seven historical churches to describe
the entire age." Once again, LaHaye abandons his "Golden Rule of
Biblical Interpretation." The three chapters of Revelation deal with
seven *literal* churches (1:20), assemblies of Christians in Asia Minor
that were founded and operated in the first century: (1) the church
in Ephesus (2:1); (2) the church *in* Smyrna (2:8); (3) the church *in*
Pergamum (2:12); (4) the church *in* Thyatira (2:18); (5) the church *in*
Sardis (3:1); (6) the church *in* Philadelphia (3:7); and (7) the church
in Laodicea (3:14). After chapter 3, Revelation addresses the "saints"
(5:8; 8:3, 4; 11:18; 13:7, 10; 14:12; 16:6; 17:6; 18:24; 19:8), individuals who make up the seven churches in Asia Minor and elsewhere.

Is there biblical evidence for this interpretation? Yes. "To the
church of God which is at Corinth, to those who have been sanctified
in Christ Jesus, *saints by calling,* with all who in every place call upon
the name of our Lord Jesus Christ, their Lord and ours" (1 Cor. 1:2,
emphasis added; cf. 6:1–6; 14:33). Was Paul describing two groups

of people? No! The saints in that context constituted believers who made up the church. Of course, we know that the early church in Israel was made up mostly of Jews. Therefore, it makes sense that the 144,000 (12 x 12 x 1,000) of Revelation 7:4 were first-century believers who represented "the firstfruits of the gospel from Jewish converts in Israel."[38]

Let's continue by applying LaHaye's logic to other New Testament books. The word *church* appears just once in the book of Hebrews (12:23), The word *church* is not mentioned "in Mark, Luke, John, 2 Timothy, Titus, 1 Peter, 2 Peter, 1 John, 2 John, or Jude, and not until chapter 16 of Romans. Unless we are prepared to relegate large chunks of the NT to a limbo of irrelevance to the Church, we cannot make the mention or omission of the term 'church' a criterion for determining the applicability of a passage to saints of the present age."[39] If counting words is to be heavily relied upon,[40] then LaHaye refutes his own argument. He finds the Antichrist all over the book of Revelation, but the word itself does not appear anywhere. In addition, there is no mention of a rebuilt temple or Jesus reigning from Jerusalem, and yet LaHaye insists that the temple in Revelation 11:1 is a rebuilt temple and that Jesus will set up an earthly throne in Jerusalem during the thousand years of Revelation 20.

LaHaye believes that Revelation 4–19 describes the time of a yet-future Great Tribulation when Israel, not the church, is in view. The pretrib Rapture of the church is a theological necessity for LaHaye—"the product of a deduction from one's overall system of theology"—so God can once again deal with national Israel for seven years. But word counts leave us with something of a problem since the word *Israel* appears only once after the supposed rapture of the church—and not until Revelation 7:4! One would think that if the church is in view in the first three chapters because the words *church* and *churches* are used nearly twenty times, then shouldn't we expect to find the word *Israel* used more than once after chapter 3 if this entire seven-year period is about God's dealings with a future national Israel? Moreover, LaHaye believes that Israel is to reign on the earth with Jesus during the thousand years of Revelation 20, but the word *Israel* does not appear there either.

Once again we are left wondering how the keystone doctrine of *Left Behind* is not found in the most comprehensive prophetic book in the Bible. George Eldon Ladd's comments are to the point: "There is no reference in 4:1 to the rapture of the church; the language is addressed exclusively to John and refers to his reception of the revelations of the book."[41]

JOHN 14:1-4

Let not your heart be troubled; believe in God, believe also in Me. In My Father's house are many dwelling places; if it were not so, I would have told you; for I go to prepare a place for you. And if I go and prepare a place for you, I will come again, and receive you to Myself; that where I am, there you may be also. And you know the way where I am going.

LaHaye has the same problem with John 14:1–4 as he has with the other passages he uses to support a pretrib Rapture. Where is the Tribulation period that—supposedly—immediately follows the Rapture? If this passage refers to the general resurrection, then it matches 1 Thessalonians 4:13–18, Titus 2:13, and 1 Corinthians 15:51–57 where Jesus returns at some unknown future date. These passages do not include the events that define the Great Tribulation, the period of time fictionalized in the *Left Behind* series. It may even be a stretch to apply John 14:1–4 to the general resurrection.

D. A. Carson, professor of New Testament at Trinity Evangelical Divinity School, offers several possible interpretations of John 14:1–4:

But the language used of Jesus' "coming back" and "being with" his disciples refers at various places in these chapters to different things: sometimes to Jesus' return to his disciples after his resurrection, sometimes to Jesus' "coming" to them by the Spirit after he has been exalted to the glory of the Father, and sometimes to his "coming" at the end of the age.[42]

"Receive you to Myself" (14:3) does not refer to a rapture since the Greek word for "receive" differs considerably from *harpadzo* (1 Thess. 4:17), the Greek word that means "rapture of the church," according to LaHaye.[43] There is no mention of returning with Jesus to the earth, something that is required of a pretrib Rapture. If Jesus was speaking of the general resurrection in John 14:1–4, then the parallel is with 1 Thessalonians 4:17, where those who are raised "shall always be with the Lord." The "place" that Jesus prepares is a place of permanence. But for advocates of a pretrib Rapture, just seven years later, these raptured Christians leave their heavenly home to return with Jesus to the earth. Note that these passages do not mention this return trip to earth.

None of the above passages describes a pretribulational Rapture. The elements necessary for such a doctrine are not present. LaHaye admits that "many details of the Second Coming must be pieced together from various passages of Scripture, no matter what view you take."[44] An important doctrine like the pretrib Rapture should not have to be "pieced together"; it should be evident even to the most casual Bible reader.

RETURNING WITH HIS CHURCH

LaHaye believes in a two-stage coming of Jesus: coming *for* His church in the Rapture and *with* His church in the Second Coming. In support for the idea that Jesus returns with His church after the

Tribulation, appeal is made to Revelation 19:11, 13–14 where Jesus, "clothed with a robe dipped in blood" and riding a "white horse," is seen coming, followed by the "armies which are in heaven." This heavenly army is said to be, according to LaHaye, "the angelic hosts, the Old Testament saints, the Church, and the Tribulation saints."[45] This is highly unlikely. At this point in Revelation, it would have been the perfect place to see the word *church* appear again if LaHaye is right about his contention that the absence of the word *church* after Revelation 3 means the church has been raptured.

The "armies which are in heaven" most certainly refers to angelic beings. At the time of Jesus' arrest, He told His captors that He had at His "disposal more than twelve legions of angels" (Matt. 26:53). A legion is a military designation for six thousand troops. Earlier in Matthew's gospel, Jesus addressed the issue of judgment: "The Son of Man is going to come in the glory of His Father with *His angels;* and will then recompense every man according to his deeds" (16:27, emphasis added; cf. 13:40–42, 49–50; Mark 8:38; Luke 9:26; 2 Thess. 1:7). This idea is repeated, using almost the same language, in Matthew 25:31: "When the Son of Man comes in His glory, *and all the angels with Him,* then He will sit on His glorious throne" (emphasis added). Jude described a past judgment-coming where "the Lord came with many thousands of His holy ones, to execute judgment" (Jude 14–15). This is a direct quotation from Deuteronomy 33:2, which describes God coming "from the midst of ten thousand holy ones." In each and every case, the references are to heavenly beings, not a raptured church. It's impossible to force these texts to fit any of the Rapture positions since the events are in the past.

Pretrib advocates appeal to 1 Thessalonians 3:13 as a clear reference to the church returning with Jesus after the Tribulation period, "at the coming of our Lord Jesus Christ with all His saints." A better translation is "holy ones" since the language parallels Deuteronomy 33:2

and Jude 14. It's most likely, since 1 Thessalonians 3:13 is almost identical to Matthew 16:27 and 25:31, that angelic beings are in view here. Paul is describing a judgment-coming of Jesus that would take place in the first century against those "who both killed the Lord Jesus and the prophets, and drove us out" (1 Thess. 2:15; see Acts 17:1–11). God's "wrath" (1 Thess. 2:16) will come upon these persecutors of God's people at the coming of Jesus in judgment against them (2:19). At the same time that God's wrath is being poured out on them because of the "distress and affliction" (3:7) that they brought on God's church, He will establish the hearts of the redeemed "unblamable in holiness before our God and Father at the coming of our Lord Jesus with all His Saints" (3:13).

CONCLUSION

LaHaye takes Bible passages that refer to the general resurrection and applies them to a pretrib Rapture of the church. The resurrection of the dead, not the rapture of the church, is the hope of the church. Paul was on trial for the "resurrection of the dead" (Acts 24:21), not the rapture of the church. Paul was emphatic: "But if there is no resurrection of the dead, not even Christ has been raised; and if Christ has not been raised, then our preaching is vain, your faith also is vain" (1 Cor. 15:13–14). No such defense was made for a supposed pretribulational, midtribulational, posttribulational, partial, or prewrath Rapture. Paul's goal was to "attain to the resurrection from the dead" (Phil. 3:11), not the rapture of the church. The Christian message hinges on the reality of the Resurrection, not the rapture of the church. The pretrib Rapture doctrine obscures and distorts this message.

3

FINDING SEVEN YEARS OF TRIBULATION

Bruce pulled up the first blank sheet on a flip chart and showed a time line he had drawn. "I'll take the time to carefully teach you this over the next several weeks, but it looks to me, and to many of the experts who came before us, that this period of history we're in right now will last for seven years. The first twenty-one months encompass what the Bible calls the seven Seal Judgments, or the Judgments of the Seven-Sealed Scroll. Then comes another twenty-one month period in which we will see the seven Trumpet Judgments. In the last forty-two months of this seven years of tribulation, if we have survived, we will endure the most severe tests, the seven Vial Judgments. The last half of the seven years is called the Great Tribulation."[1]

"Mr. DeMar, there's an Associated Press reporter on the phone. He wants to talk to you about the *Left Behind* series. Do you have time to speak with him?"

"Yes, I have some time. Put him through."

"Hello, Mr. DeMar. This is Zachary Taylor. I'm a reporter for the

Associated Press. You were recommended to me as someone who could explain some of the theology behind the *Left Behind* books and movie. This topic is really out of my league. I'm not at all familiar with this end-time stuff."

"What do you need to know?"

"I'm curious about this 'seven-year Tribulation period' that keeps coming up. I've actually read through the book of Revelations . . ."

"Revelation . . ."

"Pardon me?"

"It's the book of Revelation, not Revelation*s*. A lot of people make that mistake."

"I appreciate the correction. I would like to get this story right. Like I was saying, I've read through the book of Revelation, and not once did I come across a 'seven-year Tribulation period.'"

"Of course you didn't. There is no seven-year Tribulation period mentioned in Revelation."

"Now I'm confused."

"You should be."

The *Left Behind* series outlines a future prophetic scenario called the Tribulation period, a seven-year span of time that immediately follows the rapture of the church, with only the second half of the seven-year period being the Great Tribulation. Immediately a problem appears. If people who are left behind know the "day and hour" of the Rapture, then they know the "day and hour" of the Second Coming since it occurs *exactly* seven years after the Rapture. And yet Jesus said, "But of that day and hour no one knows, not even the angels of heaven, nor the Son, but the Father alone" (Matt. 24:36). This is not the only problem with LaHaye's Tribulation period scenario.

NO SEVEN YEARS IN THE BOOK OF REVELATION

The seven-year Tribulation period of *Left Behind* is based on a single verse in the book of Daniel: "And he will make a firm covenant with the many for *one week,* but in the middle of the week he will put a stop to sacrifice and grain offering" (Dan. 9:27, emphasis added). For LaHaye, Revelation is a panoramic prophetic unfolding of this last "week" of Daniel's prophecy that works out to be a seven-year time period divided into two segments of three and one-half years. If there is a link with Daniel 9:27, one would expect Revelation to make some reference to seven years as well. Although there are lots of sevens in Revelation (the number appears more than fifty times), and lots of seven things, everything from seven churches (1:4), spirits (3:1), candlesticks (2:1), and stars (1:16) to seven mountains (17:9), heads (12:3), kings (17:10), and plagues (21:9),[2] there is no mention of seven years. In fact, "seven years" appears only once in the entire New Testament (Luke 2:36), and this verse has nothing to do with a Tribulation period.

As was the case with the pretrib Rapture, here is another key doctrine that has no verse supporting it in the most important prophetic book in the Bible. It's legitimate, therefore, to ask why Revelation does not mention seven years since the time is critical to LaHaye's *Left Behind* scenario. There are two forty-two-month periods (11:2; 13:5),[3] two 1,260-day periods (11:3; 12:6), and one "a time and times and half a time" (12:14), each adding up to three and one-half years. If these are counted consecutively, then they add up to seventeen and one-half years. If the years run concurrently, then each of these time periods is describing the same three and one-half years. LaHaye does not explain how he gets seven years out of these five references. Which of the three and one-half years goes with the first half of the Tribulation, and which of the three and one-half years goes with the second half?

The paragraph from *Left Behind* that introduces this chapter describes the "first twenty-one months" and then "another twenty-one month period" of the first half of the seven-year Tribulation period. But Revelation has no mention of either one or two twenty-one-month periods of time. In his *Prophecy Study Bible*, LaHaye describes the division this way: "John in Revelation divides [the Tribulation] into two periods of three and one-half years each or 1,260 days each, a total of seven years."[4] Where in Revelation does it say this? There is no such specific breakdown of time periods found anywhere in the Bible. Even so, LaHaye includes four charts in his *Prophecy Study Bible* depicting this division—but with no scriptural support.

LaHaye attempts to find his needed seven years in Revelation 11:2–3 where we read of a forty-two-month period (11:2) and a 1,260-day span of time (11:3). He combines these two time periods to get his needed seven years. He says that the "forty-two months," during which the Holy City will be "tread under foot" (11:2), "cannot happen in the first half of the Tribulation."[5] It follows then that the "forty-two months" of 11:2 make up the second half of the seven-year period. Confused? It gets even more confusing as we try to describe what LaHaye insists is "the most logical view of second-coming Scriptures when taken for their plain, literal meaning whenever possible."[6] How is it possible that the period of "twelve hundred and sixty days" (11:3), which equals "forty-two months" and comes *right after* 11:2, takes place in time, according to LaHaye, *before* the events of 11:2? If the "twelve hundred and sixty days" of 11:3 refer to the first half of the seven-year Tribulation period, then why don't the "two witnesses" of Revelation 11 appear earlier? We should expect to find three and one-half years in Revelation 4 where LaHaye says the Rapture takes place and the first half of the seven-year Tribulation period begins. We don't. In fact, all the three-and-one-half-year periods appear more than halfway through Revelation. LaHaye has to do a lot of juggling to get his five halves to add up to one seven-year period. If the above paragraph lost you, don't worry, you're not alone.

John F. Walvoord, whom LaHaye describes as "the most knowledgeable living prophecy scholar in the world today,"[7] disagrees with LaHaye and concludes that the "twelve hundred and sixty days" of 11:3 refer to the same period of time as the "forty-two months" of 11:2, putting both in the second half of LaHaye's seven-year Tribulation period. Walvoord states,

> [From the fact that the two witnesses in Revelation 11:1–13] pour out divine judgment upon the earth and need divine protection lest they killed, it implies that they are in the latter half of the seven years when awful persecution will afflict the people of God, as this protection would not be necessary in the first three and one-half years. The punishments and judgments the witnesses inflict on the world also seem to fit better in the great tribulation period.[8]

The Tribulation period in Revelation is three and one-half years long. Since it takes place just before Jerusalem's destruction in A.D. 70, we should look for three and one-half years of tribulation in this particular time frame. Kenneth L. Gentry, the leading authority on the date when Revelation was written, shows how Revelation's time frame fits with first-century history:

> Now from the time of this official imperial engagement in the Jewish War (early Spring, A.D. 67) until the time of the Temple's destruction and Jerusalem's fall (early September, A.D. 70) is a period right at the symbolic figure of 1260 days (or 42 months or 3 ½ years). Indeed, counting backward from early September, A.D. 70,

we arrive 42 months earlier at early March—in the Spring of 67! Surely the figure cannot be dismissed as sheer historical accident. Though the time-frame undoubtedly carries with it the foreboding spiritual connotation associated with a broken seven (3 ½ is one-half of the perfect number 7), nevertheless, we are also driven to recognize the providence of God in these historical affairs. In keeping with divinely ordained symbol, in fulfillment of divinely inspired prophecy, it did, as a matter of fact, take Rome 3 ½ years to trample Israel and the city of Jerusalem totally.[9]

The historical and biblical facts point to a period of three and one-half years of tribulation just before the destruction of Jerusalem in A.D. 70.

DANIEL'S SEVENTIETH WEEK

Since Revelation does not mention a seven-year Tribulation period, LaHaye must go elsewhere to find the needed seven years. He attempts to manufacture the period from the book of Daniel which does not mention seven *literal* years.

> *Seventy weeks have been decreed for your people and your holy city, to finish the transgression, to make an end of sin, to make atonement for iniquity, to bring in everlasting righteousness, to seal up vision and prophecy, and to anoint the most holy place. So you are to know and discern that from the issuing of a decree to restore and rebuild Jerusalem until Messiah the Prince there will be seven weeks and sixty-two weeks; it will be built again, with plaza and moat, even in times of distress. Then after the sixty-two weeks the Messiah will be cut off and have nothing, and the people of the prince who is to come will destroy the city and the sanctuary. And its end will come with a flood;*

even to the end there will be war; desolations are determined. And he
will make a firm covenant with the many for one week, but in the
middle of the week he will put a stop to sacrifice and grain offering;
and on the wing of abominations will come one who makes desolate,
even until a complete destruction, one that is decreed, is poured on the
one who makes desolate. (DAN. 9:24–27)

Though this passage does not directly describe a period of seven years, it does so in symbolic terms. A full seventy weeks of time is prophesied, making up a total of 490 years. Nearly all conservative Bible scholars agree that the "seventy weeks" (7 + 62 + 1 = 70) equal 490 years with each "week" representing seven years (7 x 70 = 490). Once again, LaHaye has to abandon his literalism and adopt a symbolic interpretation, which I believe is legitimate in this case, in order to make his system work. A disagreement arises over the last week, the last seven years, and when it takes place.

LaHaye separates the final seven years from the other 483 years of the prophecy and inserts an indeterminate period called the "church age" between the two time periods. It looks something like this: 483 years—a gap in time called "the church age" that is nearly 2,000 years in length—7 years that make up a future Great Tribulation. The church age continues to push the final seven years into the future until the rapture of the church. The pretrib Rapture, if you recall, removes the church from the earth and sets the seventieth week's time clock ticking. LaHaye says that this seven-year period is the basis of the seven-year Tribulation, which Revelation never mentions.

In addition to a gap in time, LaHaye finds the Antichrist in these verses, which he ties to the Beast of Revelation 13: "Verse 27 [of Daniel 9] tells us that the evil prince that shall come (Antichrist) will 'make a covenant' with Israel to begin that seven-year period, then break it in the middle of the seven years by desecrating the rebuilt temple in Jerusalem."[10]

Keep in mind the following as we study LaHaye's position in terms of what Daniel 9:24–27 says:

- Neither Daniel 9:24–27 nor Revelation uses the word *Antichrist.*

- The "prince" of Daniel 9:26 is not described as evil.

- There is no record in Revelation or Daniel 9:27 of the Antichrist making a covenant with Israel.

- There is no record in Revelation or Daniel 9:27 of the Antichrist breaking a covenant.

- There is no mention of a rebuilt temple anywhere in the New Testament, including Revelation.

LaHaye continues by arguing that "483 of the 490 years 'decreed' for Daniel's people have already elapsed; the 'divine counter' stopped just before the death of Jesus, with seven years still left to go. That remaining seven-year period is what we call the Tribulation."[11] J. Barton Payne, author of the massive *Encyclopedia of Biblical Prophecy,*[12] sums up the chronology and timing of events in Daniel 9:24–27 by following a more literal approach that finds serious problems with LaHaye's position:

The most noteworthy feature of Daniel's prophecy is the inspired prophetic calendar that accompanies it. Daniel predicted a lapse of "seventy weeks [of years]," or 490 years, for the accomplishing of the redemptive work (Dan. 9:24). The beginning point would be indicated by the commandment to restore Jerusalem (v. 25), an event that was accomplished, a century after Daniel, in the reign of the Persian, Artaxerxes I (465–424 B.C.), under Nehemiah (444 B.C.). . . . Daniel then went on to predict that from this commandment, to the Messiah, would be "seven weeks, and three score and two weeks" (9:25), or 69 weeks of years, equaling 483 years. From 458 B.C. this brings one to A.D. 26, the very time which many would accept for the descent of the Holy Spirit upon Jesus Christ and the commencement of His incarnate ministry. Verses 26 and 27 then describe how, in the midst of the final week (that is, of the last seven year period, and therefore in the spring of A.D. 30), He would bring to an end the Old Testament economy by His death. There could hardly have been a more miraculously accurate prediction than was this! The 490 years then conclude with the three and a half years that remained, during which period the testament was to be confirmed to Israel (cf. Acts 2:38).[13]

According to Payne and contrary to LaHaye, the remaining seven years follow immediately after the 483 years and encompass three and one-half years of Jesus' earthly ministry to the Jews ("the lost sheep of the house of Israel" [Matt. 15:24]) and three and one-half years of the early church's ministry to the Jews (Acts 1–9). Daniel 9:24 states that "seventy weeks have been decreed for your people [the Jews] and your holy city [Jerusalem]." Paul was converted soon after Stephen's death, the same year Jesus was crucified. Paul wrote that he met with Peter "three years later" in Jerusalem "to become acquainted with Cephas [Peter]" (Gal. 1:18). At that same time Peter was given instructions that the gospel was to go to the Gentiles (Acts 10–11). Paul's meeting with Peter and Peter's instructions concerning the Gentiles occurred three and a half years after the Crucifixion, marking the end of the seventy weeks "for Israel." This has been the standard interpretation for centuries, except for minor differences in details.[14]

45

John Nelson Darby, C. I. Scofield, and others changed this very straightforward interpretation by placing an unspecified period of time between the first sixty-nine weeks and the final week of Daniel's seventy weeks. In this view, the seventieth week does not follow immediately after the sixty-ninth week. LaHaye, following Darby and the *Scofield Reference Bible*, teaches that the seventieth week is still future, and it's not Jesus who makes a "firm covenant with the many for one week" (Dan. 9:27)—*it's the Antichrist!* It's not Jesus who "will put a stop to sacrifice and grain offering"—*it's the Antichrist!* But this interpretation is contrary to the New Testament's own commentary on Daniel 9:27.

A MORE BIBLICAL INTERPRETATION

Philip Mauro, who once taught the same view advocated by LaHaye, shows how Jesus' redemptive work as outlined in the Gospels is the fulfillment of the seventieth-week prophecy: "[T]he 'one week' (the last of the 70, of which 69 had been previously accounted for) would witness the confirming of the new covenant with many (see Matt. 26:28, noting the words 'covenant' and 'many'), whereby the sacrifices and oblation of the old covenant were caused to cease (see Heb. 10:9), and the things predicted in verse 24 [of Daniel 9] were fulfilled."[15]

Those who separate the seventieth week from the sixty-nine weeks maintain that sacrifices and grain offerings did not stop when Jesus was crucified as required by the language of Daniel 9:27. From God's covenantal and judicial perspective, they did stop. Jesus put an end to them through His shed blood. That was why He could cry out on the cross, "It is finished!" (John 19:30). The book of Hebrews carries an identical message: "[Jesus], having offered one sacrifice for sins for all time, sat down at the right hand of God" (10:12).

LaHaye contends that the Antichrist makes a covenant with the

Jews. Where in Scripture does it say that? God is the One who "confirms," "makes firm," or "establishes" covenants (e.g., Gen. 6:18; 9:9, 11; 17:2, 19, 21). Jesus used the language of covenant making at the Last Supper, just before His crucifixion: "For this is My blood of the *covenant,* which is poured out for *many* for forgiveness of sins" (Matt. 26:28, emphasis added; cf. Mark 14:24; Heb. 9:28). This is "the new covenant in My blood," Jesus told His disciples (Luke 22:20). Now read Daniel 9:27: "He will make a firm *covenant* with the *many* for one week" (emphasis added). How can this refer to the Antichrist when Jesus used the words *covenant* and *many*? Where in the Bible do we read the words *covenant* and *many* being used by the Antichrist? Nothing in Revelation, a book that supposedly describes a future seven-year Great Tribulation, mentions the Antichrist making a covenant with the Jews and then breaking it. The New Testament's fulfillment of the seventieth week of Daniel 9:27 is found in the redemptive work of Christ. Scripture could not be any more clear.

PRINCE OF LIFE OR PRINCE OF DEATH?

LaHaye's argument hinges on the identity of the "prince" in Daniel 9:26 and the "he" in verse 27. LaHaye assumes that the "prince" of verse 26 is the Antichrist. This is impossible. The Messiah is identified as "the Prince" in verse 25, and the Hebrew word translated "prince" in verses 25 and 26 is the same word. The "Messiah" is mentioned again in conjunction with the "prince" in verse 26.[16] Jesus is described as "the Prince of life" (Acts 3:15) and "a Prince and a Savior" (Acts 5:31). The word *Antichrist* does not appear anywhere in Daniel 9:24–27, and the word *prince* is never used anywhere in Daniel to identify him. Jesus, as the Prince just mentioned, comes with His "people" (armies of Rome) to "destroy the city [of Jerusalem] and the

sanctuary [temple]" in A.D. 70 (Matt. 22:2–14, especially v. 7). Therefore, it is the Messiah—not the Antichrist—"who will make a firm
covenant with the many for one week."

BUYING SOME TIME

We've seen so far that there is no seven-year span of time mentioned in
Revelation and no suggestion of an antichrist in Daniel 9:27. Now
we'll see that there is no gap in time between the first 483 years and the
final 7 years of Daniel 9:24–27. To make his system work, LaHaye
must insert gaps in time in several critical places. We've seen him insert
a gap between Revelation 3:22 and 4:1. He does it in Daniel 2 between
the feet and the toes of Nebuchadnezzar's visionary statue. He inserts a
gap between Revelation 12:5 and 6. And he does it in Daniel 9:27
between the first sixty-nine weeks and the final week. Is there any justification for these gaps? When God gives a specific number of days or
years for an event or a prophecy to be fulfilled, there is never an inter-
ruption in the sequence.[17]

Let's look at how the Bible presents the seventy-year time period
of Daniel 9:24–27. Because Israel refused to honor the Jubilee years—
seventy in all—God sent the nation into captivity for seventy years so
the land could enjoy its long overdue sabbath rest (Lev. 25:1–13,
18–22): "Then the land will enjoy its sabbaths all the days of the desolation, while you are in your enemies' land; then the land will rest
and enjoy its sabbaths. All the days of its desolation it will observe the
rest which it did not observe on your sabbaths, while you were living
on it" (Lev. 26:34–35, 43; 2 Chron. 36:21–23; Jer. 25:12; 29:10).

Is there *any* indication of a gap in this seventy-year period? No!
The near end of this period of judgment and captivity under the
Babylonians leads Daniel to study the Bible for confirmation of the
terms of captivity: "I, Daniel, observed in the books the number of

the years which was revealed as the word of the LORD to Jeremiah the prophet for the completion of the desolations of Jerusalem, namely, seventy years" (Dan. 9:2). The seventy-year period of captivity as described in Jeremiah 29:10 is a *pattern* for the "seventy weeks" in Daniel 9:24–27. This means that "'the seventy weeks' prophecy must be interpreted with regard to *history* in as realistic a way as Daniel did for the prophecy of Jeremiah."[18] From this alone we can conclude that since the seventy years of captivity were consecutive *with no gap in time*, the "seventy weeks" must also be consecutive, seeing that nothing in the text makes us think otherwise. "Had there been a gap in Jeremiah's prophecy (Jer. 29:10) Daniel could never have understood the years of the captivity."[19] Daniel bases his prayer for restoration to the land on the certainty of the reestablishment promised by God when the seventy years were completed (Jer. 29:10). God made a covenant. What right do we have to conclude that God would somehow change the way time is ordinarily kept when we come to the use of another period of "seventy" in the same chapter (Dan. 9:2, 24)?

If LaHaye's method is legitimate, could God have placed a gap between the sixty-ninth and seventieth years of Israel's captivity, adding, say, a hundred years, and maintained that this would have done nothing to destroy the integrity of God's promise of only seventy years of captivity? What if God came back to the captives and said, "I didn't actually *add* any years; I just *postponed* the final year by means of a gap of one hundred years. The gap consisting of one hundred years, which you assume to be additional years, should not be calculated in the overall accounting." This would mean that 170 years would have passed. Using "gap logic," God could still maintain that Israel was in captivity only seventy years. Let's call this what it is: nonsense.

What would we think of such a deal? Could God ever delay keeping His promise in such a way and still be called a covenant-keeping God? No! And yet this is exactly what LaHaye and other pretrib advocates do with the "seventy weeks of years" (490 years) of Daniel's prophecy. A gap of nearly two thousand years supposedly does nothing to change the integrity of a prophecy specifying the passage of only 490 years. The notable Old Testament scholar E. W. Hengstenberg describes the period of seventy weeks of years

> as one that will continue uninterruptedly from its *commencement* to its *close,* or completion, both with regard to the entire period of seventy [weeks of years], and also as to the several parts (7, 62, and 1) into which the seventy are divided. What can be more evident than this? *Exactly* seventy weeks in all are to elapse; and how can anyone imagine that there is an interval between the sixty-nine and the one, when these together make up the seventy?[20]

If we can find no gaps in the sequence of years in the various examples cited here, then how can a single exception be made for the "seventy weeks" in Daniel 9:24–27? Once again, LaHaye has no basis for justifying a future seven-year Tribulation period.

To further solidify the position that the seventy weeks of years are to be interpreted as a unit, Milton Terry, an authority on Bible interpretation, notes that while "weeks" is a plural noun, it is connected "with a verb in the singular (*is decreed*). The seventy [weeks] are conceived as a unit, a round number, and are most naturally understood as so many sevens of years."[21]

DESOLATIONS ARE DETERMINED

A careful reading of Daniel 9:27 will show that the destruction of Jerusalem does not take place within the seventieth week: "After the sixty-two weeks . . . desolations are *determined* [i.e., 7 + 62 weeks]"

(9:26, emphasis added). Sometime within the seventieth week, desolations will be determined for the city of Jerusalem and the temple. Disowning "the Holy and Righteous One," asking "for a murderer to be granted" to them, and putting "to death the Prince of life" (Acts 3:14–15) "determined" that the "city and the sanctuary" would become desolate (Dan. 9:26). Stuart Olyott offers a helpful summary of this argument in his brief commentary on Daniel's prophecy:

> Daniel is seeing this in the sixth century B.C., but it did not happen until A.D. 70, when Titus and his Roman legions fulfilled this prophecy exactly. The destruction of Jerusalem did not immediately follow Calvary, but it was an event which was determined by the fact that the Jews rejected Christ. It did not happen in the seventieth "week," but was determined in the seventieth "week." Our Lord made it clear, both in His Olivet discourse and as He walked to the cross, that His rejection by the Jews would mean the destruction of their city and temple (MATT. 23:34–24:38; LUKE 23:27–31).[22]

The destruction of the temple took place when Titus and his Roman armies (Matt. 21:33–46; 22:1–14; 24:1–34) laid siege against the city in A.D. 70. This corresponds to what Jesus said to the Pharisees: "Behold, your house *is being left to you desolate!*" (Matt. 23:38, emphasis added). The temple was being left to them desolate when Jesus spoke to them around A.D. 30, but its actual desolation did not take place until forty years later. The events would happen within a "generation" (Matt. 23:36; 24:34). In principle, it was an accomplished fact when Jesus turned His back on the temple and walked out (Matt. 24:1), leaving His disciples to ask "when" the actual destruction would take place (24:3).

CONCLUSION

Contrary to what LaHaye states, there is no seven-year Tribulation period or Antichrist making a covenant with the Jews and then breaking it found in Revelation. There is no gap in time in Daniel's seventy weeks' prophecy. When all of the elements of prophecy are put together, we find that there is no need for gaps, postponements, a seven-year Tribulation period, another rebuilt temple, or an antichrist making a covenant with the Jews and then breaking it. To get these things, Tim LaHaye has to skip over nearly two thousand years of church history, turn three and one-half years into seven, minimize the importance of the destruction of Jerusalem in A.D. 70, create a new doctrine called the pretrib Rapture, and turn a reference to the Messiah into a reference to Antichrist.

4

TIMING THE TRIBULATION

A covenant had been struck. God's chosen people, who planned to rebuild the temple and reinstitute the system of sacrifices until the coming of their Messiah, had signed a deal with the devil.

Only two men on the dais knew this pact signaled the beginning of the end of time. One was maniacally hopeful; the other trembled at what was to come.

At the famed Wall, the two witnesses wailed the truth. At the tops of their voices, the sound carrying to the far reaches of the Temple Mount and beyond, they called out the news: *"Thus begins the terrible week of the Lord!"*

The seven-year "week" had begun.

The Tribulation.[1]

"This morning we're going to discuss Bible prophecy. I've been asked by your Sunday school teacher to spend a couple of weeks on the Great Tribulation. But before we begin, I would like to ask a question: When is the Great Tribulation? That's hard to say since we don't know when the Rapture will occur. I believe the Tribulation period is near because the signs leading up to the time of the Rapture are near: wars, earthquakes, famines, plagues. It's going to happen soon."

"What do you mean by *near* and *soon*?"

"Well, I believe that we're living in the last days. *Near*, like in any day now or at least in my lifetime. We can't go on much longer."

"Let me understand what you're saying. You believe that the Rapture is near. And by *near* you mean that the Rapture could take place in our lifetime. Would these words qualify as synonyms for *near*? *Soon . . . at hand . . . around the corner . . . close . . . shortly . . . approaching . . . impending?*"

"Yes. You could add *imminent* and *any moment.*"

"I want to be sure I'm not putting words in your mouth. Do you understand what I mean when I say, 'This class is nearly over . . . The time for the bell to ring is near . . . This class will end shortly'?"

"Sure."

"If someone were to say, 'There are twenty reasons why Jesus is coming soon,' you would understand him to mean that Jesus' coming is near at hand. Close at hand. Not two thousand years in the future."

"Yes. I think that's pretty clear."

"Good. Now turn to the book of Revelation, the first chapter, verses 1 and 3. What do these verses tell us about the timing of the events in Revelation?"

"Well, verse 1 says that the things revealed to John 'must shortly take place.' Verse 3 says, 'The time is near.'"

"But two thousand years have passed. How is it possible that the majority of prophetic events in Revelation have not taken place when the Bible tells us that the things revealed to John '*must* shortly take place . . . for the time *is* near'? Why don't *near* and *shortly* mean 'anytime' or at least 'in my lifetime' to those who first read the prophecy in Revelation? To say it another way, Why didn't *shortly* and *near* mean to the first century what they mean to us today?"

"No one has ever raised the question before. I'm not sure I have an answer."

A quick reading of the book of Revelation will show that there is no mention of a seven-year Tribulation period, a rebuilt temple, or a signed treaty. The "two witnesses" in Revelation 11 never utter the words "Thus begins the terrible week of the Lord," and they do not "wail" at the "Wall," an allusion to the Wailing Wall that stands in Jerusalem today. Uninformed readers of *Left Behind* will assume that these things are in Revelation because the books are convincingly written and no alternative position is mentioned. Most readers assume that Revelation is describing a period of time in our future because LaHaye and Jenkins write as if their view is self-evident in the Bible. But what will an informed investigation reveal?

TIMING IS EVERYTHING

The most important factor in determining when a prophecy is to be fulfilled is the time element. The first chapter and verse of Revelation begin with a very clear time indicator: "The Revelation of Jesus Christ, which God gave Him to show to His bond-servants, *the things which must shortly take place*" (1:1, emphasis added). Two verses later we read, "Blessed is he who reads and those who hear the words of the prophecy, and heed the things which are written in it; *for the time is near*" (1:3, emphasis added). The first readers of the Revelation scroll would have immediately applied the prophecy to themselves. There is nothing to indicate a distant future interpretation.

In the final chapter of Revelation we read that the events described in the previous chapters are to happen "shortly" (22:6), "for the time is near" (22:10) for those who first received the prophecy.

Because the events were so near, John was told, "Do not seal up the words of the prophecy" (22:10). Centuries before John transcribed Revelation, Daniel was told to seal up the book until "the time of the end" (Dan. 12:4 KJV). The fulfillment of Daniel's prophecy was at least six hundred years away; therefore, it was to be sealed because its fulfillment stepped over several generations. Jesus would come and break the sealed prophecy. The prophecy revealed to John was to remain open, however, because the time was near for those who first read it.

According to LaHaye, we are to "take every word at its primary, literal meaning unless the facts of the immediate context clearly indicate otherwise."[2] If *near* and *shortly* are interpreted literally, then they mean what they usually mean. In fact, on the front cover flap of *Are We Living in the End Times?*, LaHaye says that his book will show that there are "20 reasons [why Jesus is] coming soon." How are we to understand LaHaye's use of *soon,* other than "near at hand," "close," "nearby," "approaching," "impending"? If this is what he wants to convey to his readers by the use of *soon,* then how could nearly two thousand years have passed without the fulfillment of the events in Revelation since the words *shortly, near,* and *quickly* were used?

Near (*engus*) and *shortly* (*tachos*) are used hundreds of times in the New Testament, and they mean what they mean in everyday speech. That's why the translators chose these very clear English words to represent their Greek equivalents. While there is often debate over how some words should be translated and interpreted based on their use in certain contexts, there is no debate over how these two Greek words should be translated. Nothing in the context of Revelation indicates that these words should have specialized and unique meanings.

Every time *near* is used in the New Testament, it always means "close" in terms of distance (Mark 2:2; Luke 15:1; John 11:18; Acts 1:12) or "close" in terms of time (Matt. 24:32; Luke 21:30). *Shortly* is used in a similar way (Acts 25:4; Phil. 2:19, 24; 3 John 14). Thus, the events of Revelation were near—close, at hand, impending, right around the corner—for those who first read and heard the prophecy. If literalism is the standard, there is no other way to interpret these time words.

Even the context shows that the events described in Revelation were about to take place in John's day. John, as the secondary author of Revelation (1:1), described himself to the first readers as their "brother and fellow partaker in the tribulation" (1:9), a tribulation that was going on while John was writing. Jesus had predicted that John and his fellow Christians would be delivered "to tribulation" (Matt. 24:9) before their generation passed away (24:34). Notice the use of the second person plural in Matthew 24:9: "They will deliver *you* to tribulation, and will kill *you*." That is a perfect match to John's statement. Later in Revelation we learn that John was to be kept "from the hour of testing, that hour which *is about to come* upon the whole world [or Roman Empire], to test those who dwell upon the earth [or lands of Israel]" (Rev. 3:10, emphasis added).[3] The hour of testing was "about to come," that is, it was near for John. In the middle of Reve-lation, its first readers were told that the "third woe is coming quickly" (11:14). On ten separate occasions in Revelation, at the beginning (1:1, 3; 2:16; 3:11), in the middle (11:14), and at the end (22:6, 7, 10, 12, 20), the nearness of a series of prophetic events was on the immediate horizon.

Seven literal, historical churches are described. The context of Revelation 2–3 does not intimate that the churches, contrary to what LaHaye believes (see previous chapter), represent seven church ages spanning two millennia. The seven churches existed in Asia Minor in the first century. The message was "to the seven churches that are in Asia" (1:4). The Christians in those churches made up the primary audience, and a number of first-century concerns were addressed. Reference was made to "the deeds of the Nicolaitans" (2:6, 15); the "synagogue of Satan" (2:9; 3:9); "tribulation" (2:9, 10); the martyrdom of "Antipas," who was said to have been "killed among you" (2:13); the "teaching of Balaam" (2:14); and eating "things sacrificed to idols" (2:14, 20; cf. Acts 15:29). In addition, Jesus described and judged the seven churches in terms of their conduct at the time Revelation was written: "I know your deeds and your toil and perseverance" (2:2); "I know your tribulation and your poverty" (2:9); "I know where you dwell" (2:13); "I know your deeds" (2:19; 3:1, 8, 15).

A picture of the era described in Revelation was beginning to develop that included tribulation for the early church (Acts 4:1–31; 5:17–32; 7:54–60), the threat of false doctrine (Acts 20:29–31), Jewish persecution (Acts 22–23), and the rise of apostasy (Gal. 1:6–10; 2 Tim. 2:17; 1 John 4:1). The happenings were close at hand for John and his first-century readers. The claim by John fits very well with the time reference words *near, shortly,* and *quickly.* If we "take every word at its primary, literal meaning" and assess "the facts of the immediate context," there is no justification to skip over two thousand years of church history to engage in speculative methods of interpretation.

LaHaye's *Prophecy Study Bible* offers no notes on the meaning of *shortly* and *near* under Revelation 1:1, 3. There is no discussion of these significant time words in his *Revelation Unveiled* commentary, in what is said to be "the biblical foundation for the bestselling Left Behind series." LaHaye states only, "Again we see that the emphasis of the book is on future events."[4] The question is, How far in the future? *Soon* and *near* refer to the immediate future!

THE TEMPLE AND TIME

In Revelation 11:1, John was told to "measure the temple of God, and the altar, and those who worship in it." All historians agree that the temple was destroyed in A.D. 70. LaHaye assumes that Revelation 11:1 is describing a third temple, another rebuilt temple. He believes that John wrote Revelation around A.D. 95, more than twenty years after the temple was destroyed. Of course, this doesn't make sense since nearly two thousand years have passed after Revelation tells us that the events were to happen "shortly" (1:1) and the "time is near" (1:3). According to LaHaye, John was to measure the temple that would exist during the seven-year Tribulation period. This view presents several problems, however.

First, the New Testament makes no mention of a rebuilt temple. Numerous passages describe the temple's destruction, but not one verse describes its reconstruction. As we found with the pretrib Rapture and the seven-year Tribulation period, those who hold to the position advocated by LaHaye have to admit, "There are no Bible verses that say, 'There is going to be a third Temple.'"[5]

Second, only the Old Testament describes a rebuilt temple (2 Chron. 36:22–23; Ezra 1:2–3; 3:8–10). This second temple, built during the restoration period around 537 B.C. (Ezra 6:13–15; Zech. 4), was to replace Solomon's temple destroyed by the Babylonians (Dan. 1:1). The postexilic rebuilt temple was desecrated by Antiochus Epiphanes in 168 B.C., partially restored by Judas Maccabaeus in 164 B.C., desecrated again by the Roman general Pompey in 63 B.C., and left in a state of disrepair for nearly forty years. Herod, in the eighteenth year of his reign (20–19 B.C.), undertook the restoration of the second temple. In this temple an angel of the Lord appeared to Zacharias (Luke 1:5–23), Jesus' parents brought Him to fulfill the law of Moses (Luke 2:21–38), He sat listening and questioning the teachers (Luke 2:41–52), and He drove out the moneychangers (John 2:13–25). By the time of Jesus' public ministry, "forty-six years" had been spent on the restoration project (John 2:20). It was completed in A.D. 64 and destroyed six years later.

Third, Jesus predicted that the temple that was standing in His day would be destroyed, with "not one stone left upon another"

(Matt. 24:2; Mark 13:2; Luke 21:6). Nothing in the context of the Olivet Discourse implies that Jesus was describing the destruction of a future temple or that a future temple would be built. Even so, without offering a single verse in support, LaHaye writes, "That there will be a third temple is predicted by the prophet Daniel, the apostles Paul and John, and none other than the Lord Jesus Himself. They all taught that Israel's third temple will be rebuilt either before the Tribulation begins or soon thereafter, for it is seen when it is desecrated. Obviously, since Israel does not now have a temple, the third temple must be rebuilt for such an event to occur."[6]

If LaHaye could offer a verse in support of this bold claim, he would have done so. Instead, he bases his argument on deduction: there has to be a rebuilt temple because "it is seen when it is desecrated." The desecration took place in A.D. 70 when those people living at that time saw it: "Therefore when you," that is, those to whom Jesus was speaking, "see the abomination of desolation which was spoken of through Daniel the prophet, standing in the holy place (let the reader understand), then let those who are in Judea flee to the mountains" (Matt. 24:15–16).

Fourth, how could John measure what no longer existed if Revelation was written twenty-five years after the temple's destruction? The temple described in Revelation 11:1–2 is not in heaven, since "it has been given to the nations . . . to be tread under foot . . . for forty-two months" (11:2). No one will be doing any treading underfoot of anything in heaven. It's not a visionary temple of the future like the one described in Ezekiel 40 since *John* was told to measure it. Unlike John, Ezekiel did not have access to the temple he saw. The temple was measured by "a man whose appearance was like the appearance of bronze" (Ezek. 40:3; cf. Rev. 1:15; 2:18). LaHaye's *Prophecy Study Bible* describes the person who measures the temple in Ezekiel as "a high-ranking angel . . . or possibly a pre-incarnate appearance of the 'angel of the Lord,' Jesus Christ."[7] But in his *Revelation Unveiled*, LaHaye contradicts his *Prophecy Study Bible* note when he attempts to refute those who maintain that the temple in Revelation 11:1–3 is the temple that was destroyed in A.D. 70: "One problem with their reasoning is that we have Biblical precedent for God's commanding His servant Ezekiel (Ezek. 40–44) to measure the Temple long after it had been destroyed by the armies of Nebuchadnezzar six hundred years before Christ."[8]

Thomas Ice, an editor and contributor to LaHaye's *Prophecy Study Bible*, makes the same mistake: "Ezekiel, during a similar vision of a temple (Ezek. 40–48), was told to measure that same temple."[9] Once again, Ezekiel was not the one who measured the temple. John, unlike Ezekiel, could measure the temple *because it was still standing!* Its destruction was only a few years away; Revelation was written prior to the destruction of the temple in A.D. 70. The only way to get around the obvious is not to interpret Revelation 11:1–3 literally. G. K. Beale takes this approach in his massive commentary on Revelation: "That the temple in Jerusalem is spoken of in Revelation 11:1–2 as still standing is sometimes taken as evidence of a pre-A.D. 70 date . . . But this assumes a literal reading of 11:1–2—and that it refers to the first-century Herodian temple. The literal reading should be questioned in the light of the symbolism throughout the book and in chapter 11 in particular (e.g., vv. 3–7)."[10]

Such a view goes against everything LaHaye believes. But Beale's point is important. If Revelation 11:1–2 is interpreted literally, it refers to Herod's temple, and Revelation was written before its destruction.

LOOKING FOR SUPPORT OUTSIDE THE BIBLE

When it comes to Bible interpretation, two methods of investigation are internal evidence (using the Bible's testimony) and external evidence (using noninspired sources). Of course, if there is a contradiction between internal and external evidence, internal evidence always wins out: "Let God be found true, though every man be found a liar" (Rom. 3:4).

The claim of those who argue for a late date for the writing of Revelation hinges on one sentence of one man who wrote more than one hundred years after the destruction of the temple and a number of historical arguments based on inferences. In his *Revelation Unveiled*, LaHaye appeals to "the known statements of Irenaeus and other early church fathers"[11] for support of his contention that Revelation was written around A.D. 95 during the reign of Domitian. Yet LaHaye does not describe the content of these "known statements," and he puts forth a weak historical argument.

AN ARGUMENT OF CONFUSION

There are major problems with an appeal to this second-century writer. First, the opinions of Irenaeus are not authoritative, inspired, or infallible. The Bible is the standard, not the opinions of men. If John was told to measure the temple, and the temple was destroyed in A.D. 70, then John must have been told to measure the temple before it was destroyed. It does not matter if fifty people in the second century say otherwise. Irenaeus could be mistaken, misunderstood, or misinformed.

Second, the late-date argument hinges on a single ambiguous sentence written by Irenaeus around A.D. 180. A study of the passage makes it difficult to know whether he was saying that John "was seen . . . toward the end of Domitian's reign," that he was still alive in A.D. 95, or that the "apocalyptic vision . . . was seen . . . toward the end of Domitian's reign."[12] Scholars cannot be dogmatic one way or the other because of the grammatical construction of the Greek text.

LaHaye never discusses the scholarly debate over what Irenaeus wrote. He leaves the false impression that Irenaeus's statement is so clear that no one could ever dispute a composition date for Revelation of A.D. 95. Kenneth L. Gentry Jr., an authority on the dating of the book of Revelation, offers the following conclusion in his *Before Jerusalem Fell: Dating the Book of Revelation*, the most comprehensive study of the subject: "[T]he Irenaean evidence for a late date for Revelation tends to render any confident employment of him suspect. The difficulties with Irenaeus in this matter are many and varied, whether or not his witness is accepted as credible. A bold 'thus saith Irenaeus,' cannot be conclusive on this matter."[13]

Other historical sources cited by LaHaye are equally ambiguous. Gentry offered this analysis of the historical record in *Beast of Revelation*, refuting LaHaye's claim, "All the external evidence points to the writing of Revelation by John when he was banished to the Isle of Patmos during the reign of Roman emperor Domitian (A.D. 91–96)."[14]

> I cannot see how the external evidence can be used with much credence by late date advocates. Irenaeus's statement is grammatically ambiguous and easily susceptible to a most reasonable re-interpretation, which would eliminate him as a late-date witness. An appeal to Origen and Clement of Alexandria for support is more in the mind of the modern reader than in the script of the ancient text. The important references from both of these two fathers wholly lack the name "Domitian." Victorinus is a sure witness for the late date, but requires incredible implications. Eusebius and Jerome provide us with conflicting testimony. We have weighed the evidence in the balance and found it wanting.[15]

Once again, although history is instructive and helpful, it is not authoritative. It's remarkable that LaHaye seems to depend more on a debatable historical record than on the clear statements in God's revealed Word.

AN ARGUMENT OF INFERENCES

Trying to muster further support for a late date for Revelation, LaHaye makes the following argument: "Christ's message to the first-century church of Ephesus was they 'had forsaken their first love.' If Revelation were written in A.D. 64 or 65, . . . that would mean the early church became cold in their zeal for Christ just thirty years after His ascension, while Peter and Paul were still alive!"[16] Paul warned the elders in the church at Ephesus of this very possibility: "I know that after my departure savage wolves will come in among you, not sparing the flock; and from among your own selves men will arise, speaking perverse things, to draw away the disciples after them" (Acts 20:29–30). He issued this warning while he and Peter were still alive. Paul said "after my departure," not two millennia in the future.

LaHaye next turns to the church of Laodicea that describes itself as being "rich," "wealthy," and in "need of nothing" (Rev. 3:17). "That was impossible in A.D. 64–66," LaHaye contends. "The entire city had been destroyed by an earthquake in A.D. 62 and would not have had time to rebuild by then. Thirty or more years later, in A.D. 95, yes, but no city in those days could rebuild to its original level of prominence in just three or four years after such a devastating earthquake."[17] This is an argument from silence. The Roman historian Tacitus wrote in his *Annals* that Laodicea "arose from the ruins by the strength of her own resources, and with no help from [the Roman government]."[18] Apparently there was a great deal of wealth available even after the earthquake. In addition, it's possible that the *church* in Laodicea was not much affected by the earthquake. "Perhaps by the grace of God, the Christians were in areas less affected by the quake, as Israel was in an area of Egypt unaffected by the plagues (Ex. 8:22; 9:4, 6, 24; 10:23; 11:27). Would this token of God's providence lead the Laodiceans to a too proud confidence in their standing as in Revelation 3:17? Perhaps a roughly analogous situation is found with the situation at Corinth, which Paul set about to correct (1 Cor. 4:6–8)."[19] James described a similar attitude among those to whom he addressed his letter (James 2:1–13).

LaHaye's arguments cannot survive serious scrutiny and investigation. If he admits that the time texts should be interpreted literally, that the temple in Revelation 11 was still standing, and that there is no gap between Revelation 3 and 4, the entire basis for the *Left Behind* story line ends up being a work of fiction in every sense.

TIMING IN THE GOSPELS

LaHaye teaches that Jesus described a future seven-year Tribulation period in the Olivet Discourse (Matt. 24; Mark 13; Luke 21). But as is true of the book of Revelation, there is no mention of a Rapture, a seven-year Tribulation period, or a gap in time in the Gospels. To make the Olivet Discourse match Revelation, LaHaye inserts a time gap between Matthew 24:3 and the verses that follow. He also assumes that the temple has been rebuilt somewhere between verses 4 and 15. Yet Matthew 24 relates nothing about a rebuilt temple— only its destruction is noted. Even LaHaye has to admit that the temple of Matthew 24 was destroyed in A.D. 70:

> History records that our Lord's words [in Matthew 24:1–2] were fulfilled *to the letter in A.D. 70.* In that year the Roman army under the command of Titus destroyed the city of Jerusalem. Fires raged through the city and in the temple area itself. After the flames burned themselves out, the soldiers saw large amounts of gold had

melted and flowed into the crevices of the blocks of the temple. In order to recover the precious metal, the Romans had to take the buildings apart, stone by stone. And so Jesus' prophecy was fulfilled literally; not one stone was left upon another.[20]

After acknowledging the A.D. 70 destruction of the temple, LaHaye then skips over nearly two thousand years of history and picks up with the events described in verses 7 and 8, events that he says lead up to a pretrib Rapture. He never explains where the Rapture passage is found. Like the problems with his timing of the events in Revelation, there are serious problems with LaHaye's timing of the events found in the Olivet Discourse.

A FIRST-CENTURY AUDIENCE

Throughout the Olivet Discourse, Jesus continually used the second-person plural ("you"). LaHaye's *Prophecy Study Bible* concludes that the word "'you' must be taken generically as 'you of the Jewish nation.'"[21] This is odd since he admits that the "you" of Matthew 23 refers to Jesus' first-century audience. Matthew 24 doesn't indicate that "you" refers to anyone else other than the audience to whom Jesus was speaking. If Jesus had a future audience in mind, He could have eliminated all confusion by using "them" and "they" instead of "you" throughout the chapter. Once again, LaHaye violates his "Golden Rule of Biblical Interpretation" in order to manufacture the needed prophetic elements to make his system work.

LaHaye states, "History records that our Lord's words [in Matthew 24:1–2] were fulfilled to the letter in A.D. 70." Notice what Jesus said in 24:2: "Do *you* not see all these things? Truly I say to *you*." Obviously the "you" in verse 2 refers to the disciples to whom Jesus was speaking. Why all of a sudden does the meaning of "you" change in the following verses?

- "See to it that no one misleads you" (24:4).

- "And you will be hearing of wars and rumors of wars; see that you are not frightened" (24:6).

- "They will deliver you to tribulation, and will kill you, and you will be hated by all nations on account of My name" (24:9).

- "Therefore when you see the abomination of desolation which was spoken of through Daniel the prophet" (24:15).

- "Pray that your flight may not be in the winter, or on a Sabbath" (24:20).

- "Then if anyone says to you" (24:23).

- "Behold, I have told you in advance" (24:25).

- "If therefore they say to you" (24:26).

- "Even so you too, when you see all these things, recognize that He is near, right at the door" (24:33).

- "Truly I say to you, this generation will not pass away until all these things take place" (24:34).

There is no indication that Jesus switched audiences from His first-century disciples in verse 2 to a distant future general "Jewish nation" audience in verses 4 through 34. "You" means those to whom Jesus was speaking throughout the chapter. For someone who claims to interpret the Bible literally, turning the obvious meaning of "you" into a designation for a future audience is highly irregular and contrary to all the rules of biblical interpretation.

A FIRST-CENTURY GENERATION

Jesus told His first-century audience that "*this* generation will not pass away until *all* these things take place" (Matt. 24:34, emphasis added). That is, the generation that was in existence when Jesus addressed His disciples would not pass away until all the events that preceded verse 34 came to pass. "This" refers to: "this day" (Matt. 6:11); "this news" (9:26); "this city" (10:23); "this man" (12:24); "this age" (12:32). Why should "this" be understood differently when it is used with "generation"? If Jesus had a future generation in mind, He would have said, "*That* generation."

Every time "this generation" is used in the New Testament, it means, without exception, the generation to whom Jesus was speaking. The following is a list of every occurrence of "this generation" used in the Gospels:

- "But to what shall I compare *this generation?*" (Matt. 11:16).

- "The men of Nineveh shall stand up with *this generation* at the judgment, and shall condemn it because they repented at the preaching of Jonah; and behold, something greater than Jonah is here" (Matt. 12:41; cf. Luke 11:29).

- "The Queen of the South shall rise up with *this generation* at the judgment and shall condemn it" (Matt. 12:42).

- "Then [the unclean spirit] goes, and takes along with it seven other spirits more wicked than itself, and they go in and live there; and the last state of that man becomes worse than the first. That is the way it will also be with *this evil generation*" (Matt. 12:45; cf. v. 39).

- "Truly I say to you, all these things shall come upon *this generation*" (Matt. 23:36; cf. Luke 11:49–51).

- "Truly I say to you, *this generation* will not pass away until all these things take place" (Matt. 24:34; cf. Mark 13:30; Luke 21:32).

- "Why does *this generation* seek for a sign? Truly I say to you, no sign shall be given to *this generation*" (Mark 8:12).

- "To what then shall I compare the men of *this generation*, and what are they like?" (Luke 7:31).

- "For just as Jonah became a sign to the Ninevites, so shall the Son of Man be to *this generation*" (Luke 11:30).

- "The Queen of the South shall rise up with the men of *this generation* at the judgment and condemn them, because she came from the ends of the earth to hear the wisdom of Solomon; and behold, something greater than Solomon is here" (Luke 11:31).

- "The men of Nineveh shall stand up with *this generation* at the judgment and condemn it, because they repented at the preaching of Jonah; and behold, something greater than Jonah is here" (Luke 11:32).

- "But first He must suffer many things and be rejected by *this generation*" (Luke 17:25).

These verses describe events within the lifetime of that present generation. D. A. Carson, one of the most respected Bible commentators writing today, concludes, "[This generation] can only with the greatest difficulty be made to mean anything other than the generation living when Jesus spoke."[22] LaHaye insists on literalism. Why not in this instance? William Sanford LaSor writes in *The Truth About Armageddon*, "If 'this generation' is taken literally, all of the predictions were to take place within the life-span of those living at that time."[23] An honest assessment of Scripture can lead to no other conclusion.

Instead of following the literal approach, LaHaye states that "this generation" refers "to the future generation that will live to see all the signs listed in the previous verses fulfilled in their lifetime."[24] Of course, Matthew 24:34 does not say this. Based on the use of "you" and the way "this generation" is always used in the New Testament, LaHaye's interpretation is without merit.

Some want to maintain that Jesus was saying, "This Jewish race will not pass away until all these things take place." This is impossible since the Greek word for "race"[25] is not used in Matthew 24:34. In addition, the logic is all wrong. The Jewish race would have to pass away once all "these things take place." LaHaye is correct that the best translation is "generation." His mistake is on the timing.

CONCLUSION

But how is it possible that the events in Revelation and Matthew 24, Mark 13, and Luke 21 refer to events leading up to and including the destruction of the temple and the city of Jerusalem in A.D. 70? It doesn't seem possible if the prophetic scenario outlined by LaHaye is followed. If the time indicators are interpreted literally (as they are elsewhere in the New Testament), no other interpretation *is* possible. To follow LaHaye's methodology, "near," "soon," and "quickly" must mean their opposite. This is hardly a literal approach. The same is true of "this generation" in Matthew 24:34. For LaHaye, "this generation" must have a unique meaning different from the way the phrase is used elsewhere in the New Testament. Since Jesus said "this generation"—the generation to whom He was speaking—"will not pass away until all these things take place," then we must take Him at His word.

5

SIGNS OF TRIBULATION

"God's people are in for dark days. Everybody is. I've been thinking and praying about what we're supposed to do as a church between now and the Glorious Appearing."

Chloe wanted to know all about that, so Bruce showed her from the Bible why he believed Christ would appear in seven years, at the end of the Tribulation. "Most Christians will be martyred or die from war, famine, plagues, or earthquakes," he said.[1]

"I see you are reading one of the books in the *Left Behind* series."

"They're great for passing time when I have to fly. The fact that the author got the idea for the series while on an airplane adds something to the story line for me."

"What do you like about the books?"

"They're easy to read and inspirational. I especially like the way that LaHaye and Jenkins incorporate sound biblical teaching throughout. Also, they're so up to date. It's like reading today's news stories about famines, earthquakes, plagues, and wars."

"What's so up to date about famines, earthquakes, plagues, and wars? We've always had them. There's nothing unusual about them."

"They're signs of the end times. Jesus said, 'And you will be hearing of wars and rumors of wars . . . There will be famines and earthquakes.'"

"But there were famines, earthquakes, wars, and plagues in the first century. Every century has had its share of these calamities. In fact, Luke told us in Acts 11 that there was 'a great famine all over the world' in his day. The historical record of that time describes numerous wars throughout the Roman Empire. Earthquakes were also common. The New Testament mentions three earthquakes. Population centers were always dealing with plagues, which often followed war and famine. In fact, you can't study the history of the world without being confronted with the monumental effects of plagues. Remember the Carly Simon song 'You're So Vain'? The principle applies to prophecy: 'We're so vain. We think these prophecies are about us.' We just can't believe they were about other people in another time."

"I'm not sure I understand what you're saying. Are you claiming that these are not signs of the end of the age?"

"Famines, earthquakes, plagues, and wars are not signs if they are common to every generation. They are signs only when they happen within a specified time frame. Jesus said that they were signs to the generation that was alive when He gave the prophecy. Did you notice that Jesus said, 'And *you* will be hearing of wars'?"

"'You,' as in 'you and me.'"

"'You,' as in whoever Jesus' audience was when He gave the prophecy. Do *you* remember the first thing I said to *you*? 'I see *you* are reading one of the books in the *Left Behind* series.' Was I speaking to someone else? You didn't think so."

"Can you prove that Jesus was describing events in the first century?"

"Sure . . . If you believe the Bible is the best interpreter of the Bible."

"I'm interested. Can you do it in an hour? That's when our plane lands."

"Let me take you verse by verse through Matthew 24. This is the only way to do it right."

———————

The signs of the Tribulation period are found in the Olivet Discourse in Matthew 24, Mark 13, and Luke 21. As we study Matthew's version, consider these verses from the perspective of those who first heard Jesus' words. What would they have thought Jesus was talking about? Keep in mind that LaHaye insists that these prophetic events take place after the Rapture and define a future Tribulation period.

MATTHEW 24:1–2

Jesus came out from the temple and was going away when His disciples came up to point out the temple buildings to Him. And He answered and said to them, "Do you not see all these things? Truly I say to you, not one stone here shall be left upon another, which will not be torn down." (MATT. 24:1–2)

When Jesus' disciples heard His prediction of "desolation" for the temple and city (Matt. 23:29–39), they "came up to point out the temple buildings to Him," as if to say, "Lord, You can't mean *this* temple!" But Jesus confirmed His earlier prediction of judgment by declaring that "not one stone here shall be left upon another, which will not be torn down." Notice that Jesus said, "Not one stone *here* shall be left upon another." Jesus was not describing what would happen to some future rebuilt temple. He was speaking about the destruction of the very temple that stood before them at that time. As was mentioned in the previous chapter, LaHaye agrees that "history records that our Lord's words were fulfilled *to the letter in A.D. 70.*" Probably stunned at that point, the disciples asked Jesus a three-part question.

MATTHEW 24:3

As He was sitting on the Mount of Olives, the disciples came to Him privately, saying, "Tell us, when will these things happen, and what will be the sign of Your coming, and of the end of the age?" (MATT. 24:3)

The disciples clearly equated the destruction of the temple with Jesus' "coming" in judgment, which would result in "the end of the age." In Matthew 24:34, Jesus told His disciples that their generation would see the events leading up to and including the judgment on Jerusalem and the destruction of the temple. "The end of the age" (not the end of the "world" as some translations have it) refers to the expiration of a period of time that specifically applied to Israel in Jesus' day (Dan. 9:24–27; Matt. 15:24; Luke 24:27, 44). The old covenant age came to an end and was made "obsolete" because of the work of Christ (Heb. 8:13). This resulted in the "age to come" (Matt. 12:32), which incorporated believing Jews and Gentiles into the blessings of the "new covenant in [Jesus'] blood" (Luke 22:20; cf. Jer. 31:31; Acts 10; Rom. 9–11; 1 Cor. 11:25; 2 Cor. 3:6; Eph. 2; Heb. 8:8, 13).

Jesus replaced the sacrificial system of bulls and goats with Himself as the "Lamb of God" (John 1:29), the physical temple with "the temple of His body" (John 2:13–22), a sanctuary built with hands with the "true tabernacle" (Heb. 8:2; 9:11, 24), and God's earthly, sinful high priest with Himself as the "perfect High Priest" (Heb. 2:17; 3:1; 5:1–10; 7:26–28). That was why Paul could write that "the ends of the ages" had come in his day (1 Cor. 10:11; cf. Heb. 1:1–2). The "end of the age" refers to the last days of the old covenant world that were passing away (1 Cor. 2:6). The destruction of the temple was the observable sign that the end was a reality and the new covenant had dawned.

The use of "end of the age" does not necessarily refer to the distant future, as Thomas Ice, LaHaye's colleague in the Pre-Trib Research Center, demonstrates:

> Sometimes Christians read in the Bible about the "last days," "end times," etc., and tend to think that all of these phrases all of the time refer to the same thing. This is not the case. Just as in our own lives, there are many endings. There is the end of the work-day, the end of the day according to the clock, the end of the week, the end of the month, and the end of the year. Just because the word "end" is used does not mean that it always refers to the same time. The word "end" is restricted and precisely defined when it is modified by "day," "week," "year," etc. So it is in the Bible, that "end times" may refer to the end of the current church age or it may refer to other times.[2]

In Matthew 24:3, Jesus was referring to the "end of the age," not the end of the world or the end of the so-called church age.

After the disciples asked Jesus the questions about when He would come in judgment to destroy the temple, He addressed the issue of signs and the importance of not being misled by them. Like today, the people in Jesus' day saw signs as a way of predicting the end of an era. These common signs would not be the key they would need to determine when Jesus would come in judgment. The key would be found in a number of uncommon signs that had theological significance only for those who knew the Scriptures.

MATTHEW 24:4-8

Jesus answered and said to them, "See to it that no one misleads you. For many will come in My name, saying, 'I am the Christ,' and will mislead many. You will be hearing of wars and rumors of wars; see that you are not frightened, for those things must take place, but that is not yet the end. For nation will rise against nation, and kingdom against kingdom, and in various places there will be famines and earthquakes. But all these things are merely the beginning of birth pangs." (MATT. 24:4–8)

First, Jesus was clearly addressing His first-century audience: "See to it that no one misleads *you* . . . See that *you* are not frightened." The conclusion is obvious: Jesus warned the generation of disciples who asked the question about the coming judgment, not some unnamed generation in the distant future.

Second, Jesus warned His disciples to beware of false messiahs. One such false messiah, Judas of Galilee, "rose up in the days of the census, and drew away some people after him" (Acts 5:37). Simon claimed to be called "the Great Power of God" (Acts 8:9–11; also see 5:36; 13:6). The Jewish historian Flavius Josephus (A.D. 37–101) told about "a certain impostor named Theudas [who] persuaded a great number to follow him to the river Jordan which he claimed would divide for their passage."[3] Alexander Keith, in his study of the first-century destruction of Jerusalem, wrote that "Dositheus, the Samaritan, pretended that he was the lawgiver prophesied of by Moses."[4] There were so many impostors preying on the gullibility of the people that under the procuratorship of Felix (Acts 23:24), "many of them were apprehended and killed every day. They seduced great numbers of the people still expecting the Messiah; and well therefore might our Saviour caution his disciples against them."[5]

Jesus next warned of "wars and rumors of wars" and the rising of "kingdom against kingdom." The *Annals of Tacitus*, covering the historical era from A.D. 14 to the death of Nero in A.D. 68, describes the era with phrases such as "disturbances in Germany," "commotions in Africa," "commotions in Thrace," "insurrections in Gaul," "intrigues among the Parthians," "the war in Britain," and "the war in Armenia." Wars were fought from one end of the empire to the other in the days of the apostles.

Jesus told His disciples that famines would be another sign prior to Jerusalem's destruction in A.D. 70. "Now at this time some prophets came down from Jerusalem to Antioch. And one of them named Agabus stood up and began to indicate by the Spirit that there would certainly be a great famine all over the world. And this took place in the reign of Claudius. And in the proportion that any of the disciples had means, each of them determined to send a contribution for the relief of the brethren living in Judea" (Acts 11:27–29). The famine was so great that the church as far away as Corinth participated in relief efforts (1 Cor. 16:1–5; Rom. 15:25–28). The entire Roman Empire was affected.

In Matthew 24:7 Jesus also spoke of earthquakes that would take place in their generation. A great earthquake occurred at the time of Jesus' crucifixion (Matt. 27:54) and another one at His resurrection (28:2). The Bible records "a great earthquake" that shook "the foundations of the prison house" (Acts 16:26). According to historical accounts, they were not rare for that time period. Rather, a staggering number of earthquakes assaulted the Roman Empire in the first century. There were earthquakes in Crete, Smyrna, Miletus, Chios, Samos, Laodicea, Hierapolis, Colosse, Campania, Rome, and Judea. The cities of Pompeii and Herculaneum were almost destroyed by an earthquake in A.D. 62, seventeen years before they were wiped off the face of the earth by a volcanic eruption from Mount Vesuvius.

MATTHEW 24:9

Then they will deliver you to tribulation, and will kill you, and you
will be hated by all nations because of My name. (MATT. 24:9)

Jesus continued His warnings to His disciples by telling them that
their generation would experience tribulation, falling away and
betrayal, false prophets, and increased lawlessness. Once again, Jesus
clearly identified His audience: "Then they will deliver *you* to tribulation, and will kill *you*, and *you* will be hated."

No one can doubt that tribulation followed the church soon after
pentecost. Jesus told His disciples that those who hated Him would hate
them as well (Matt. 23:34; John 13:18). From its inception the church
underwent relentless tribulation from Roman and Jewish religious and
civil officials. Peter and John were arrested and put in jail (Acts 4:3).
They were warned not to speak to any man in the name of Jesus (Acts
4:17). They were "flogged" after their second arrest (Acts 5:40).

The tribulation worsened with the deaths of Stephen (Acts
7:54–60) and James (12:2), the brother of John. Soon "a great tribulation[6] began against the church in Jerusalem, and they were all scattered
throughout the regions of Judea and Samaria, except the apostles" (Acts
8:1). It was not too long before the crowds turned against the disciples:
"Jews came from Antioch and Iconium, and having won over the
crowds, they stoned Paul and dragged him out of the city, supposing
him to be dead" (Acts 14:19). Paul wrote, "Five times I received from
the Jews thirty-nine lashes. Three times I was beaten with rods, once I
was stoned . . . I have been on frequent journeys, in dangers from rivers,
dangers from robbers, dangers from my countrymen, dangers from the
Gentiles . . . dangers among false brethren" (2 Cor. 11:24–26).

Throughout the New Testament, we see that Jesus' disciples were
delivered up to tribulation, and some were killed (Matt. 24:9). The

apostle John wrote that he was a "fellow partaker in the tribulation" (Rev. 1:9). Paul described the tribulation endured by Christians in Thessalonica: "We ourselves speak proudly of you among the churches of God for your perseverance and faith in the midst of all your persecutions and afflictions which you endure" (2 Thess. 1:4). The "persecutions and afflictions" directed at the church brought on God's righteous judgment (1:5). God would "repay with affliction those who afflict you" (1:6).

In Mark's account of the Olivet Discourse, we learn that the disciples would be delivered "to the courts," "flogged in the synagogues," and made to "stand before governors and kings" (13:9). Jesus used similar words in Matthew 10:17–18 when He sent the Twelve out as witnesses to Israel: "Beware of men; for they will deliver you up to the courts, and scourge you in their synagogues; and you shall even be brought before governors and kings for My sake, as a testimony to them and to the Gentiles." Acts records the fulfillment of Jesus' prediction of religious and political tribulation in the period *before* the destruction of Jerusalem (4:1–22; 5:17–40; 8:1–3; 12:1–9; 14:19–20; 16:22–23; 22:30–23:11). The existence of religious and political tribunals is indicative of what life was like in first-century Judea. Later, John would write, "Do not marvel, brethren, if the world hates you" (1 John 3:13). Jesus had warned His disciples, "If the world hates you, you know that it has hated Me before it hated you" (John 15:18).

MATTHEW 24:10

At that time many will fall away and will betray one another and hate one another. (MATT. 24:10)

There is no doubt that the first-century church had to contend with betrayal and apostasy from within, as Jesus had said (Matt. 24:10).

Those who once proclaimed the name of Christ went on to do harm to the church. Paul stated, "All who are in Asia turned away from me, among whom are Phygelus and Hermogenes" (2 Tim. 1:15). Demas, who was said to have "loved this present world," deserted Paul (2 Tim. 4:10). The apostasy did not seem to be an isolated event: "At my first defense no one supported me, but all deserted me; may it not be counted against them" (2 Tim. 4:16). There were also Judaizers who were constantly distorting Jesus' message and preaching doctrines that opposed "the gospel of Christ" (Gal. 1:6–10).

MATTHEW 24:11

Many false prophets will arise, and will mislead many. (MATT. 24:11)

Jesus' warning against false prophets soon proved true as well. Peter wrote that "false prophets also arose among the people, just as there will also be false teachers among you, who will secretly introduce destructive heresies, even denying the Master who bought them, bringing swift destruction upon themselves" (2 Peter 2:1). Paul described the Judaizing teachers as "false apostles, deceitful workers, disguising themselves as apostles of Christ" (2 Cor. 11:13). The church at Ephesus was warned that "savage wolves will come in among *you*, not sparing the flock; and *from among your own selves* men will arise, speaking perverse things, to draw away the disciples after them" (Acts 20:29–30, emphasis added).

Some false prophets were singled out for condemnation, such as Hymenaeus and Philetus, who led people into "further ungodliness" and spread their doctrine "like gangrene" (2 Tim. 2:16–17). Paul condemned them for "saying that the resurrection has already taken place" (2 Tim. 2:18). The apostle John wrote that "many false prophets have gone out into the world" (1 John 4:1). He also wrote that "many deceivers have gone out into the world, those who do not acknowledge Jesus Christ as coming in the flesh. This is the deceiver and the antichrist" (2 John 7). He indicated that the deceivers rose up in the midst of the church in his day: "They went out from us, but they were not really of us; for if they had been of us, they would have remained with us; but they went out, in order that they might be shown that they all are not of us" (1 John 2:19). All of these Bible passages give us solid scriptural evidence that the words of Jesus were fulfilled in the days of the apostles. There is no need for LaHaye to project what happened in the first century into a future concentrated period of affliction called the Great Tribulation.

MATTHEW 24:12

Because lawlessness is increased, most people's love will grow cold. (MATT. 24:12)

The last warning Jesus gave in Matthew 24:9–12 was that there would be increased lawlessness. The New Testament writers constantly addressed the sensual living that was prevalent in their time. The worldliness destroyed relationships within the church and tore down the body of Christ. Paul was shocked at the behavior of the members of the Corinthian church: "It is actually reported that there is immorality among you, and immorality of such a kind as does not exist even among the Gentiles, that someone has his father's wife. And you have become arrogant, and have not mourned instead, in order that the one who had done this deed might be removed from your midst" (1 Cor. 5:1–2).

MATTHEW 24:13

But the one who endures to the end, he shall be saved. (MATT. 24:13)

Here Jesus offered His disciples comfort. He told them that all those who endured the great social, religious, and political upheaval would be saved—that is, they would not die in Rome's war with the Jews. "The end" is not a reference to the end of everything or even the end of the world. Even LaHaye maintains that "the end" here refers to the end of the Tribulation period, which lasts only seven years.

Using "the end" in terms of the subject under discussion at the time is common to the Bible and in our everyday speech. When God was about to judge the land of Israel through the agency of Babylon, Ezekiel recorded God's words concerning the impending judgment: "An end! The end is coming on the four corners of the land. Now the end is upon you, and I shall send My anger against you; I shall judge you according to your ways, and I shall bring all your abominations upon you . . . An end is coming; the end has come! It has awakened against you; behold, it has come!" (Ezek. 7:2–3, 6).

MATTHEW 24:14

This gospel of the kingdom shall be preached in the whole world as a testimony to all the nations, and then the end will come. (MATT. 24:14)

Many people conclude that there is no way that the gospel could have been preached in the whole world before the destruction of the temple in A.D. 70. Our first commitment, however, is to believe what the Bible tells us. Remember Matthew 24:34, "This generation will not pass away *until all these things take place.*" One of the "all these things" is the gospel being "preached in the whole world."

The word translated "world" in 24:14 is the Greek word *oikoumene* rather than the more common word *kosmos*. This is the only place where Matthew uses the word *oikoumene*. It is best translated as "inhabited earth," "known world," or the "Roman Empire" (Acts 11:28; 17:6).

The same Greek word is used in Luke 2:1: "Now in those days a decree went out from Caesar Augustus, that a census be taken of all *the inhabited earth.*" This translation helps us understand that Jesus was saying the gospel would be preached throughout the Roman Empire before He would return in judgment upon Jerusalem. In fact, that is exactly what happened, and that is what the Bible says happened.

Paul wrote that the gospel "has come to you, just as *in all the world [7] also* it is constantly bearing fruit and increasing" (Col. 1:6, emphasis added) and that it "was proclaimed in *all creation under heaven*" (1:23, emphasis added). Paul said that the gospel was "being proclaimed throughout the whole world" (Rom. 1:8) in his day, and he was making plans to go to Spain (Rom. 15:24, 28). The gospel had nearly reached the western border of the Roman Empire in Paul's day. Paul quoted from Psalm 19:4: "But I say, surely they have never heard, have they? Indeed they have; THEIR VOICE HAS GONE OUT INTO ALL THE EARTH, AND THEIR WORDS TO THE ENDS OF THE WORLD'" (Rom. 10:18; see also 2 Tim. 4:17). Paul declared that the gospel had "been made known *to all the nations,*" a direct fulfillment of Matthew 24:14 (Rom. 16:26, emphasis added). Notice the verb tense, *"has been* made known." All the requirements of a pre-A.D. 70 fulfillment are met when we let the Bible interpret the Bible.

MATTHEW 24:15-16

Therefore when you see the abomination of desolation which was spoken of through Daniel the prophet, standing in the holy place (let the reader understand), then those who are in Judea must flee to the mountains. (MATT. 24:15–16)

By comparing this passage with the parallel passage in Luke 21:20–21, we can pinpoint the time when the abomination of desolation was to happen: "When you see Jerusalem surrounded by armies, then recognize that her desolation is at hand. Then those who are in Judea must flee to the mountains." Was Jerusalem ever surrounded by armies prior to A.D. 70? Yes! Did Christian Jews flee the city? Yes! Notice that Jesus said, "When *you* see Jerusalem surrounded by armies." The event was local and visible to those living in Jerusalem in the first century. But how could anyone escape *after* Jerusalem was surrounded? Cestius Gallus, the Roman general in charge of the siege, suddenly retreated. In doing so, his actions opened a way of escape for God's people to flee to the mountains.

An abomination in the Old Testament was anything that desecrated the true worship of God: Aaron and the golden calf (Ex. 32); Eli's evil two sons, Hophni and Phinehas (1 Sam. 2–4); the strange fire offered by Nadab and Abihu (Lev. 10:1); and the desolating sacrilege that resulted in God's departure from Solomon's temple (Ezek. 8–11). God sent Judah into captivity under the Babylonians and destroyed the temple because of her "abominations" (Ezek. 5:9). God's sanctuary had been defiled with "detestable idols and . . . abominations" (Ezek. 5:11).

At least two "abomination of desolation" theories can be applied to A.D. 70. The first theory points to Jewish Zealots who advocated the overthrow of the Roman government by force: "The zealots had got possession of the Temple at an early stage in the siege and . . . made the Holy Place (in the very words of the historian [Josephus]) 'a garrison and stronghold' of their tyrannous and lawless rule; while the better priests looked on from afar and wept tears of horror."[8]

At the outbreak of the Jewish war with Rome, the Zealots occupied the temple area. They allowed criminals, even some murderers, to roam about freely in the Holy of Holies. In the winter of A.D. 67–68, they placed a non-Levite as high priest.[9] "It was in response to this specific action that the retired priest Ananus, with tears, lamented: 'It would have been far better for me to have died before I had seen the house of God laden with such abominations and its unapproachable and hallowed places crowded with the feet of murderers' (*Wars,* 4:3:10)."[10]

The Zealots "went over all the buildings, and the temple itself, and fell upon the priests, and those that were about the sacred offices."[11] They believed that God would intervene directly to vindicate their cause against Rome. The Zealots hoped that "God would send them his supernatural help as he had done when they had been led by Moses and Joshua."[12] As history attests, that did not happen. God's purpose was judgment upon the "city and the sanctuary" (Dan. 9:26) for the nation's rejection of the promised Messiah (John 1:11).

The second, and most popular theory, is that the Romans caused the abomination that brought about the desolation when they walked about the outer court of the temple with their pagan symbols lifted high. While the sanctuary was engulfed in flames, Roman soldiers set up their legionary standards, emblazoned with emblems depicting their heathen gods, and offered sacrifices. John described the Roman desecration this way: "Leave out the court which is outside the temple and do not measure it, for it has been given to the nations; and they will tread under foot the holy city for forty-two months" (Rev. 11:2). The Romans did in fact tread underfoot the Holy City for three and one-half years.

MATTHEW 24:17–20

Whoever is on the housetop must not go down to get the things out that are in his house. Whoever is in the field must not turn back to get his cloak. But woe to those who are pregnant and to those who are nursing babies in those days! But pray that your flight will not be in the winter, or on a Sabbath. (MATT. 24:17–20)

In these verses, Jesus told His disciples that when the temple's approaching desolation became evident to them, it would be time to head for the hills. The first-century Christians had been expecting the temple's destruction. The New Testament—which is composed mostly of letters written to first-century churches—is filled with time texts emphasizing that "the end of all things is near" (1 Peter 4:7).

Matthew 24:17–20 presents a clear picture of the living conditions of first-century Israel. Most roofs in Israel were flat with an outside staircase (Mark 2:4). They were designed for occupancy (Deut. 22:8), storage (Josh. 2:6), and rest in the evening (2 Sam. 11:2). In addition, Jesus referred to the strict Sabbath laws in effect at that time. An acceptable distance for travel on the Sabbath was about three-quarters of a mile as determined by Pharisaical law (Acts 1:12), not enough travel distance to get out of harm's way during Jerusalem's destruction.

History records that those Jews who remained were slaughtered. Estimates put the number killed at more than one million! Thousands more were taken into captivity. Forty years earlier, Jesus had given the warning to flee to the mountains when Jerusalem was encompassed by armies. Those who believed the prophecy and acted upon it escaped with their lives. Those who remained suffered untold tribulation.

MATTHEW 24:21

For then there will be a great tribulation, such as has not occurred since the beginning of the world until now, nor ever will. (MATT. 24:21)

Jesus was not describing a worldwide tribulation in this verse. The geographical context is Judea: "Then let those who are in *Judea* flee to the mountains" (24:16). All one had to do to escape the impending tribulation was to leave the city and head for the mountains. Therefore, the boundary of this particular "great tribulation" did not extend beyond the city limits of Jerusalem. How could anyone on foot, carrying a nursing baby, escape if a modern-day tribulation is in view? Tanks and jet planes would thwart any attempted exodus from the city.

The tribulation is described as "great" because the crime that brought it on was great. The chief priests and religious leaders, in collusion with the Roman government in Judea, killed the "Lord of glory" (1 Cor. 2:8). Jesus' disciples described it this way: "The chief priests and our rulers delivered Him to the sentence of death, and crucified Him" (Luke 24:20). Peter declared that his fellow countrymen "disowned the Holy and Righteous One and asked for a murderer . . . [and] put to death the Prince of life" (Acts 3:14–15; cf. 1 Thess. 2:15). Today's Jews did not deliver Jesus up to death, so why should they endure "God's righteous judgment" (2 Thess. 1:5)? The outpouring of God's wrath in tribulation came upon the generation that chose Caesar as king over Jesus:

> The blood of all the prophets, shed since the foundation of the world, may be charged against *this generation*, from the blood of Abel to the blood of Zechariah, who was killed between the altar and the house of God; yes, I tell you, it shall be charged against *this generation*. (LUKE 11:50–51, emphasis added)

> When Pilate saw that he was accomplishing nothing, but rather that a riot was starting, he took water and washed his hands in front of the crowd, saying, "I am innocent of this Man's blood; see to that yourselves." And all the people said, "*His blood shall be on us and on our children!*" Then he released Barabbas for them; but after having Jesus scourged, he handed Him over to be crucified. (MATT. 27:24–26, emphasis added)

They cried out, "Away with Him, away with Him, crucify Him!" Pilate said to them, "Shall I crucify your King?" The chief priests answered, "*We have no king but Caesar.*" (JOHN 19:15, emphasis added)

The "great tribulation" is a description of what happened to Jews living in Israel in the first century. Nothing will ever compare to it because of Israel's special covenantal status. Her sin was great; therefore, her judgment was great:

> *For the iniquity of the daughter of my people*
> *Is greater than the sin of Sodom,*
> *Which was overthrown as in a moment,*
> *And no hands were turned toward her.* (LAM. 4:6)

The tribulation was so severe, and the resultant famine so great, Josephus records that at least one woman killed, cooked, and ate her own child.

The tribulation had reference to the Jews, the people of Judea (Matt. 24:16); it was not a worldwide tribulation. Luke described the tribulation period as "days of vengeance . . . For there will be great distress upon the land and *wrath to this people;* and *they* will fall by the edge of the sword, and will be led captive into all the nations; and Jerusalem will be trampled under foot by the Gentiles until the times of the Gentiles are fulfilled" (Luke 21:22–24, emphasis added; see Rev. 11:2). LaHaye says this passage refers to the first-century destruction of Jerusalem where, "according to the historian Josephus, the Romans took over 100,000 Jewish captives to Egypt and sold them as slaves to the merchants of the world."[13] If this is true, and it is, then the tribulation period is a first-century event. But LaHaye maintains that while Luke is describing events of A.D. 70, Matthew is describing a future seven-year Tribulation period.[14] This is impossible. There is no indication that Matthew and Luke are describing two different events in two time periods. The accounts are *parallel* in terms of time and place, even though Luke included some events not found in Matthew's account.[15] That was typical of Luke. Luke recorded numerous events related to the births of John the Baptist and Jesus and the early life of Jesus that are not found in Matthew's gospel (Luke 1–2). Are we to conclude that Luke was describing different events in different times? Not at all.

MATTHEW 24:22

Unless those days had been cut short, no life would have been saved;
but for the sake of the elect those days will be cut short. (MATT. 24:22)

Jesus was telling His disciples that the tribulation that was coming would be shortened "for the sake of the elect." Who were the elect? For the most part, they were Jewish Christians. The tribulation of A.D. 70 was so severe that if God had allowed the Romans to continue their devastation, not a single Jew living in Judea and its outlying districts would have survived. For the Romans, the Christian Jews were not considered a separate religious sect but simply Jews who were a part of the larger Jewish rebellion. If "no life would have been saved" referred to the entire world, then how would fleeing to the mountains help? Since Jesus offered a simple way to escape the coming judgment, the judgment was local.

MATTHEW 24:23–26

If anyone says to you, "Behold, here is the Christ," or "There He is,"
do not believe him. For false Christs and false prophets will arise and
will show great signs and wonders, so as to mislead, if possible, even

the elect. Behold, I have told you in advance. So if they say to you, "Behold, He is in the wilderness," do not go out, or, "Behold, He is in the inner rooms," do not believe them. (MATT. 24:23–26)

Jesus had spoken of false prophets in 24:11, but in all likelihood, He was indicating that there would be streams of false prophets. He told His disciples that shortly after His ascension, false christs and prophets would appear, "but that is not yet the end" (24:6). Then as the time for the destruction of Jerusalem drew near, and as the time for that generation was about to pass away, more false prophets would arise.

Just as Jesus prophesied, false prophets did arise toward the end of that generation. In fact, Paul was thought to be "the Egyptian who some time ago stirred up a revolt and led the four thousand men of the Assassins out into the *wilderness"* (Acts 21:38, emphasis added). This incident is reminiscent of Jesus' words about those who claimed that He might be "in the *wilderness"* (Matt. 24:26, emphasis added). Those who had rejected their Messiah at the "time of [their] visitation" (Luke 19:44), the same people who wanted to make Jesus king to overthrow the tyrants of Rome (John 6:15), were still looking for a political savior right up until the time of Jerusalem's destruction. Josephus wrote,

> A false prophet was the occasion of these people's destruction, who had made a public proclamation in the city that very day, that God commanded them to get upon the temple, and that there they should receive miraculous signs of their deliverance. Now, there was then a great number of false prophets suborned by the tyrants to impose upon the people, who denounced this to them, that they should wait for deliverance from God.[16]

In times of trouble, people look for any glimmer of hope for securing deliverance. The Israelites' true hope was to embrace Jesus as the

Messiah. Those who did were saved from "the wrath to come" (Matt. 3:7; 1 Thess. 1:10).

CONCLUSION

This section of the Olivet Discourse clearly shows that Jesus was describing events in the first century. From persecution and tribulation to earthquakes and famines, Jesus' prophetic words were fulfilled to the letter. It is these signs that Jesus said were "the beginning of birth pangs" (Matt. 24:8). Events would escalate to the point of wholesale destruction. Since all of these early signs are common to every generation, Jesus continually made it clear throughout the discourse that He was addressing His first-century audience. Those of their generation would see the abomination of desolation, suffer persecution, flee to the mountains, and be alive when the temple was finally toppled. As history attests, the temple was destroyed, not one stone was left upon another. The accuracy of Jesus' predictions is so precise that liberal scholars maintain that the Gospel accounts had to have been written after the fact. Tim LaHaye acknowledges that the temple was destroyed as Jesus predicted, but he then creates an elaborate fictional future scenario that repeats everything Jesus said would take place within the span of that contemporary generation.

6

THE GLORIOUS APPEARING

"That last half of the seven years is called the Great Tribulation, and if we are alive at the end of it, we will be rewarded by seeing the Glorious Appearing of Christ."

Loretta raised her hand. "Why do you keep saying, 'If we survive'? What are these judgments?"

"They get progressively worse, and if I'm reading this right, they will be harder and harder to survive. If we die, we will be in heaven with Christ and our loved ones. But we may suffer horrible deaths. If we somehow make it through the seven terrible years, especially the last half, the Glorious Appearing will be all that more glorious."[1]

"Ladies and gentlemen, we just received word from Hartsfield International Airport that there are thunderstorms in the Atlanta area. Incoming flights will have to maintain a holding pattern until the storms dissipate. This will mean a delay of about thirty minutes."

"Of course, that's airplane time. We should be up for at least an hour. This gives me a chance to ask a few more questions. I can see now how Matthew 24 describes events in the first century, at least up through verse 26. But you can't really believe that the description of the coming of the Son of Man, the sun going dark, and the stars falling from the sky have already happened."

"What is our governing time indicator?"

"Matthew 24:34 . . ."

"That's right. *This* generation will not pass away until *all these things take place.*' Jesus could not have been more clear."

"But the language seems so 'end of the worldish.'"

"What's our governing interpretive principle?"

"The best interpreter of the Bible is the Bible."

"Many Christians are surprised to learn that the prophetic language of Matthew 24 is not unique. Jesus quoted directly from the Old Testament. In order to understand how Jesus meant for His words to be interpreted, we must study their Old Testament context."

"But how could Jesus have come when no one saw Him?"

"How could Jehovah have come when no one saw Him?"

"I'm not sure I understand!"

"The Old Testament mentions a number of comings by Jehovah that took place in Israel's history. Jesus borrowed this Old Testament language and applied it to Himself in His description of the judgment that was to come upon Jerusalem before that generation passed away."

"I've read those Old Testament comings, but it never registered that there was some relationship to the language used by Jesus in the New Testament. I would like to see how you apply these Old Testament comings to the ones described by Jesus in the Olivet Discourse, and how they might apply to the destruction of Jerusalem in A.D. 70."

"I left off with Jesus' warning not to be led astray by claims that 'He is in the wilderness' or 'He is in the inner rooms.' The very next verse describes the 'coming of the Son of Man.'"

MATTHEW 24:27

For just as the lightning comes from the east and flashes even to the
west, so will the coming of the Son of Man be. (MATT. 24:27)

In the Bible, lightning often signifies the presence of the Lord (Ex.
19:16; 20:18), the manifestation of His power (Ezek. 1:13), and the
display of His awesome judgment against His enemies (Deut. 33:2;
2 Sam. 22:15; Pss. 18:14; 144:6). That was vividly demonstrated
when Ezekiel, as the "son of man," was told to set his face toward
Jerusalem to "speak against the sanctuaries" and to "prophesy against
the land of Israel" (Ezek. 21:2). This description of an impending
judgment was against Old Testament Israel and her temple and land.
It is no accident that the language and circumstances of Ezekiel's
prophecies regarding the destruction of Jerusalem in the sixth century B.C., especially the usage of "the son of man"[2] for Ezekiel and
Jesus, are strikingly similar to the way Jesus described the impending
destruction of Jerusalem in His day. "And because of all your abominations [Matt. 24:15], I will do among you what I have not done,
and the like of which I will never do again [Matt. 24:21]" (Ezek.
5:9). God assured Ezekiel, just as Jesus assured His disciples (Matt.
24:34), that judgment "comes and it will happen" (Ezek. 21:7).

The imagery of a sword "polished to flash like lightning" is used
to describe God's judgment that will make every heart melt and all
hands feeble and all knees weak as water (Ezek. 21:7):

Son of man, prophesy and say, "Thus says the LORD." Say,
"A sword, a sword sharpened
And also polished!
Sharpened to make a slaughter,
Polished to flash like lightning!" (EZEK. 21:9–10)

This sword of judgment is "made for striking like lightning, it is wrapped up in readiness for slaughter" (21:15). The sword has power to consume "like lightning" (21:28), swiftly, without warning, and terribly. Therefore, the image of Jesus as the Son of man, coming in judgment against first-century Israel, "as the lightning comes from the east," is most appropriate.

Throughout the Old Testament, God *came* in judgment in language remarkably similar to Jesus' description of His coming to that first-century generation:

The LORD *came down to see* the city and the tower which the sons of men had built. (GEN. 11:5)

So I have *come down to deliver* them from the power of the Egyptians, and to bring them up from that land to a good and spacious land. (EX. 3:8)

He bowed the heavens also, and *came down*
With thick darkness under His feet . . .
He sent out His arrows, and scattered them,
And *lightning flashes in abundance*, and routed them. (PS. 18:9, 14)

The oracle concerning Egypt.
Behold, the LORD is riding on a swift cloud, and *is about to come to Egypt;*
The idols of Egypt will tremble *at His presence*,
And the heart of the Egyptians will melt within them. (ISA. 19:1)

So will the LORD of hosts *come down to wage war* on Mount Zion and on its hill. (ISA. 31:4)

Behold, the LORD is *coming forth from His place*.
He will *come down* and tread on the high places of the earth [land].

The mountains will melt under Him
And the valleys will be split,
Like wax before the fire,
Like water poured down a steep place. (MIC. 1:3–4)

Earlier in the Gospels, there are references to Jesus' coming to His first-century audience (Matt. 10:23). Notice how many times Jesus threatened to judge the churches of Asia Minor by His coming if they did not repent (Rev. 2:5, 16; 3:3). It makes no sense if the comings referred to in these passages were future *distant* comings.

Furthermore, Jesus stated that His coming in judgment would be before the last apostle died: "For the Son of Man is going to come in the glory of His Father with His angels, and will then repay every man according to his deeds. Truly I say to you, *there are some of those who are standing here who will not taste death until they see the Son of Man coming in His kingdom*" (Matt. 16:27–28, emphasis added; cf. John 21:1–3). This coming had to be far enough in the future that many in His audience would be dead but not so far in the future that everyone was dead. The fulfillment could not have been the Transfiguration that happened about a week later. Jesus could not have been describing the events of pentecost, since only Judas had died by then (Acts 1:18–19). The reference could not have been to any of LaHaye's future comings (for His church in the Rapture or with His church after the Tribulation), since everyone who heard Jesus deliver the prophecy is dead. The event that fits the time requirement of the text is the destruction of Jerusalem in A.D. 70.

James stated that "the coming of the Lord is at hand" (James 5:8), that is, "right at the door" (5:9). "At hand" for whom? He told his readers to "be patient." How could James have exhorted his readers to be patient if the coming he was describing was a long way off?

Jesus clearly indicated that He would be the avenger in Jerusalem's destruction: "But the king was enraged and sent his armies, and destroyed those murderers, and set their city on fire" (Matt. 22:7). The Roman armies led by Titus would act as God's agent to set the city on fire. The armies entered Jerusalem "from the east" and struck "like lightning" (cf. Luke 10:18). In the Old Testament, God sent pagan Assyria to judge the Israelites who had turned away from Him. Assyria was called the "rod of My anger and the staff in whose hands is My indignation" (Isa. 10:5). Nebuchadnezzar "came to Jerusalem and besieged it," yet the Lord "gave Jehoiakim king of Judah into his hand" (Dan. 1:1–2). In a similar way, Rome was the tool Jesus used to punish apostate Israel in A.D. 70. No future generation is in view here.

MATTHEW 24:28

Wherever the corpse is, there the vultures will gather. (MATT. 24:28)

Being familiar with the Hebrew Scriptures, Jesus' disciples would have understood exactly what He was describing. They would have recognized the words of Jeremiah that describe a judgment of those who break God's covenant: "The dead bodies of this people will be food for the birds of the sky and for the beasts of the earth" (Jer. 7:33). And stated later in Jeremiah, "[God] will cause them to fall by the sword before their enemies and by the hand of those who seek their life; and I will give over their carcasses as food for the birds of the sky and the beasts of the earth" (19:7).

Notice the similarities between what Jeremiah did and what Jesus did. God told Jeremiah to "stand in the gate of the LORD's house" and proclaim God's Word to the people (Jer. 7:2). Compare this with Matthew 23:36 and 24:1 where Jesus was preaching at the front of the temple. In the days of Jeremiah, just as in Jesus' day, the people were told not to trust in the temple and empty rituals (Jer. 7:4). The temple was meaningless without obedience: "Thus says the LORD of hosts, the God of Israel, 'Amend your ways and your deeds, and I will let you dwell in this place'" (Jer. 7:3). Without obedience, the temple had "become a den of robbers" (Jer. 7:11; compare with Matt. 21:13). Therefore, God rejected "the generation of His wrath" (Jer. 7:29; compare with Matt. 23:36; 24:34).

Because of its dead rituals, the Jerusalem of Jesus' day was a carcass, food for the scavenging birds, the Roman armies. In addition, there was a literal fulfillment of this prophecy: hundreds of thousands of people were killed during the Roman siege. (The historian Josephus noted that there were more than a million deaths.) Even the temple area was not spared. The Idumean and Zealot revolt left thousands slaughtered in and around the sanctuary. A single carcass would have rendered the city and temple area "unclean," and according to Numbers 19:11–22, anyone touching the corpse of a human being was unclean and must be cut off from Israel. As our High Priest, Jesus could no longer remain in the city because of its defilement. It had to be burned with fire for purification.

On the Mount of Olives, the disciples came to Jesus to point out the temple buildings, and Jesus condemned the temple as spiritually empty and defiled, fit only for destruction. But He promised that just as certainly as He would destroy that temple, He would raise up another perfect temple in three days—the temple of His body (John 2:19–21), not a temple of stone (cf. Eph. 2:1–2; 1 Peter 2:4–12).

MATTHEW 24:29

Immediately after the tribulation of those days the sun will be darkened, and the moon will not give its light, and the stars will fall

from the sky, and the powers of the heavens will be shaken. (MATT.
24:29)

At this point many commentators divide the events of A.D. 70 from
what they say is the distant future coming of Christ. Everything up to
24:29, so the theory goes, refers to the events leading up to the destruction of Jerusalem in A.D. 70, while the events from 24:29 and following refer to a yet future coming of Christ. This is impossible. Jesus said
that *"immediately* after the tribulation of those days," the sun and
moon would be darkened, and the stars would fall from the sky. So,
whatever these images mean, we know that they followed "immediately
after" the tribulation described in verses 15–28. Matthew uses "immediately" to indicate a straightaway continuation of events with no
pauses or gaps in time (e.g., Matt. 3:16; 4:20, 22; 8:3; 20:34; 26:74).

Jesus' disciples asked not about the end of the world (*kosmos*),
but about the end of that covenant age (*aion*). When the tribulation
of "those days" was completed, the religious and political structure of
Israel as a covenant nation came to an end before that first-century
generation passed away. Even LaHaye does not see Matthew 24:29 as
being a description of the end of the world, since a thousand-year
earthly millennium is said to follow immediately after the Tribulation
period with a renovated heaven and earth to follow.

But when in the first century did the sun and moon go dark and
stars fall from the sky? The language here is typical of Old Testament
imagery where stellar phenomena represent rulers and nations. LaHaye
admits that sun, moon, and stars are often used as symbols for something else, namely nations and political systems.

The symbolic interpretation is confirmed for us when Joseph
had a dream in which he saw "the sun and the moon and eleven
stars" bowing down to him (Gen. 37:9). Joseph related the dream "to
his father and to his brothers; and his father rebuked him and said to

him, 'What is this dream that you have had? Shall I and your mother and your brothers actually come to bow ourselves down before you to the ground?'" (37:10).

LaHaye writes that the image of the sun, moon, and eleven stars of Genesis 37:9 and the "woman clothed with the sun, and the moon under her feet," and having "on her head a crown of twelve stars" (Rev. 12:1) "is a reference to the nation of Israel."[3] LaHaye's further comments are helpful in understanding the imagery:

> These objects are light-conveying objects: The moon is a reflector, the sun, a source of light. They are *symbolic of Israel* as God's light-bearer to humankind. This Israel was in Old Testament days, for God intended her to propagate His message from the Holy Land to the entire world. Unfaithful in the dissemination of this message, the nation of Israel fell under the judgment of God.[4]

Here is something on which Tim LaHaye and I can agree. The sun, moon, and stars "are symbolic of Israel." If they are symbolic of Israel in Genesis 37:9 and Revelation 12:1, then why doesn't the same hold true in Matthew 24:29? When Israel is faithful, the sun is shining, the moon is giving off its reflective light, and the stars are positioned high in the heavens. "In Ecclesiastes 12:1, 2, we find that the expression 'while the sun, or the light, or the moon, or the stars, be not darkened' is used to symbolize *good* times. Consequently, the reverse—an expression about the sun, moon, and stars being darkened—would symbolize 'evil days,' days of *trouble*."[5] Since Jesus' prophecy in Matthew 24 deals with Israel's judgment, the sun and moon are dark, and the stars fall. Like LaHaye, I believe that the image is symbolic of Israel, but symbolic of Israel's impending *judgment*.

The Old Testament—the only Scriptures the disciples had to

interpret Jesus' words—is filled with metaphors of the darkening of sun and moon and the falling of stars. In each case, the images clearly indicate the fall of nations. Let's first look at a passage concerning the destruction of Babylon by the Medes and Persians:

> Behold, the day of the LORD is coming,
> Cruel, with fury and burning anger,
> To make the land a desolation;
> And He will exterminate its sinners from it.
> For the stars of heaven and their constellations
> Will not flash forth their light;
> The sun will be dark when it rises,
> And the moon will not shed its light. (ISA. 13:9–10)

Similar language is used to describe the destruction of Egypt:

> And when I extinguish you,
> I will cover the heavens and darken their stars;
> I will cover the sun with a cloud
> And the moon will not give its light.
> All the shining lights in the heavens
> I will darken over you
> And will set darkness on your land . . .
> When I make the land of Egypt a desolation. (EZEK. 32:7–8, 15)

Even more telling, this kind of stellar imagery was used to indicate judgment on Israel:

> Alas, you who are longing for the day of the LORD,
> For what purpose will the day of the LORD be to you?
> It will be darkness and not light. (AMOS 5:18)

"It will come about in that day," declares the Lord GOD,
"That I shall make the sun go down at noon
And make the earth dark in broad daylight." (AMOS 8:9)

Using similar language, in Matthew 24:29, Jesus told His disciples that there would come a time of intense divine judgment against Israel within that generation. By letting Scripture interpret Scripture, we are not left to speculate what Jesus meant to say: Israel would be judged before the generation to whom He was speaking passed away. To be strictly literal, as LaHaye insists, would mean that "the stars will fall from the sky."[6] But where do they "fall"? Revelation 6:13 says that "the stars of the sky fell to the earth." How is this possible since the size of a star is many times larger than the earth? A single star hitting the earth would vaporize it. If these stars are meteorites, as LaHaye claims, then once again literalism is abandoned. But even a shower of meteorites over the earth would bring unspeakable devastation. And yet we are to believe that the Antichrist will rule the world using super-sophisticated technology after these "stars" fall to the earth (Rev. 13). The more biblical approach is to follow the Bible's own interpretation of how the sun, moon, and stars apply to the temporal judgment of nations (Isa. 13:10–13; 24:16, 19–23; 34:4; Ezek. 32:6–8; Joel 2:10, 30–31; 3:15–16; Hab. 3:6–11). In none of these cases is the destruction of the earth in view even though cosmic language is used.[7]

MATTHEW 24:30

Then the sign of the Son of Man will appear in the sky, and then all the tribes of the earth will mourn, and they will see the Son of Man coming on the clouds of the sky with power and great glory. (MATT. 24:30)

This verse is often interpreted to mean the physical second coming of Christ. We must remember, however, that this verse, like all the others we have discussed thus far, is governed by the time text of Matthew 24:34: "This generation will not pass away until all these things take place." Verse 30, which describes the Son of Man coming on the clouds of heaven, simply continued Jesus' discussion with His disciples about events that would take place before their generation passed away.

Throughout the Bible, God showed Himself by the physical presence of clouds, even though He was not physically present (Ex. 13:21; 14:24; 19:9; 20:21; 24:15; 33:9; 34:5; 1 Kings 8:12). In addition, the Bible constantly refers to clouds in reference to God's judgment: the "day of the LORD . . . will be a day of clouds" (Ezek. 30:3; Joel 2:1–2); "In whirlwind and storm is His way, and clouds are the dust beneath His feet" (Nah. 1:3); and "Behold, the LORD is riding on a swift cloud, and is about to come to Egypt" (Isa. 19:1; see also Ps. 104:3–4).

Matthew 24:30 also uses clouds to describe Jesus' coming. LaHaye agrees that this verse is taken directly from Daniel 7:13: "Christ's return will be marked by the 'sign of the Son of man.' The 'clouds of heaven' reveal that Christ will come from heaven to the earth (cf. 7:1–4; 2 Thess. 1:7–9)."[8] Since LaHaye and I agree that Jesus quotes Daniel 7:13, analyzing what the passage actually says will be helpful:

> I kept looking in the night visions,
> And behold, with the clouds of heaven
> One like a Son of Man was coming,
> *And He came up to the Ancient of Days*
> *And was presented before Him.* (emphasis added)

Notice that the coming of the Son of Man is *up*, not *down*. The destination is heaven, not earth. LaHaye writes that Daniel 7:13 reveals "that Christ will come from heaven to the earth." That is not what the text says. The Son of Man "came *up* to the Ancient of Days"; the Ancient of Days is enthroned in heaven, not in the sky (Dan. 7:9). Daniel 7:13 is quoted again, along with a portion of Psalm 110:1, when Caiaphas the high priest asked Jesus if He is "the Christ, the Son of God" (Matt. 26:63). Jesus said to him, "You have said it yourself; nevertheless I tell you, hereafter[9] you shall see the Son of Man sitting at the right hand of power, and coming on the clouds of heaven" (Matt. 26:64). Nothing is mentioned, as LaHaye insists, about Jesus returning to earth "with the 'clouds of heaven' to be worshiped."[10]

LaHaye claims to interpret the Bible literally. How can his interpretation be accurate if he completely misses what Daniel 7:13 actually states? Why does LaHaye write, based on Daniel 7:13, that Jesus "will come from heaven to the earth" when the text says the opposite?

It is obvious that Jesus was speaking of His enthronement that took place at His ascension when "He was received up into heaven and sat down at the right hand of God" (Mark 16:19; see Ps. 110:1; Acts 2:3–6). Soon after that event Jesus' disciples understood His redemptive mission. This is made evident to us when Stephen, "being full of the Holy Spirit, . . . gazed intently into heaven and saw the glory of God, and Jesus standing at the right hand of God; and he said, 'Behold, I see the heavens opened up and the Son of Man standing at the right hand of God'" (Acts 7:55–56). Daniel 7:13 and Psalm 110:1 were fulfilled in the first century at Jesus' ascension.

At first reading, many assume that in Matthew 24:30 Jesus was saying that everyone on earth would see Him physically appearing in the sky; part of this assumption stems from a poor translation of the text. First of all, the text does not speak of *Jesus* appearing in the *sky.*

Rather, a word-for-word translation of the Greek reads, "Then will appear the *sign* of the Son of Man *in heaven.*" (The Greek word for "sky" and "heaven" is the same.) The "*sign* of the Son of Man" appears, and the "sign" is that Jesus is in heaven (cf. Rev. 12:1). Jesus was telling His disciples to look for the sign of His enthronement in heaven. That turned out to be His ascension, a direct reference to Daniel 7:13 and Psalm 110:1. All Christians now look to "the Jerusalem above" (Gal. 4:26). That is why Paul could write, "If you have been raised up with Christ, keep seeking the things above, where Christ is, seated at the right hand of God" (Col. 3:1). When God raised Jesus from the dead, He "seated Him at His right hand in the heavenly places, far above all rule and authority and power and dominion, and every name that is named, not only in this age, but also in the one to come" (Eph. 1:20–21).

A generation would pass before those who crucified "the Lord of glory" (1 Cor. 2:8) would understand that the earthly temple was no longer a temporal dwelling place of God. God would destroy it, not leaving one stone upon another, so the Jewish nation would "see," that is, understand that they were to set their minds "on the things above, not on the things that are on earth" (Col. 3:2). The destruction of the city of Jerusalem and the desolation of the temple pointed all eyes to focus on the New Jerusalem above.

The second confusion in the translation of Matthew 24:30 is the phrase "all the tribes of the *earth* will mourn," which is more accurately translated "all the tribes of the *land* will mourn." The Greek word for "earth" (*ge*) can also be translated as "land," "soil," or "ground." Jesus was warning His audience to flee Judea when they saw "Jerusalem surrounded by armies" (Luke 21:20). Only those near enough to the temple would be able to see the "abomination of desolation . . . standing in the holy place" (Matt. 24:15). The Olivet Discourse was clearly not a message to the world, but a warning to the tribes of Israel of the first century. Jesus told the "daughters of Jerusalem" to "weep for yourselves and for your children" (Luke 23:28–30).

The tribes of Israel mourned because they understood that judgment was a reality for them in their day as they saw their city and temple set ablaze by the invading Roman armies. They were warned to embrace Jesus as their promised Messiah, flee the city, or perish in the impending conflagration. The Jews who rejected Jesus because He was not their idea of a political savior died at the spear point of Roman soldiers. Their Savior had come, and they had crucified Him. Those who "pierced" Jesus (Zech. 12:10) experienced His covenant wrath in their day. This helps explain Revelation 1:7 where the same wording is used; those who "see" Him are "those who pierced Him" (cf. John 19:7). Nineteenth-century commentator James Glasgow explained it this way:

> *"Every eye, and those who pierced Him, shall see Him."*—The subject of the text is "the people of the land," viz. Judea; and it would be a direct misinterpretation, as well as false logic, to strain a term beyond its subject, by applying it to the final judgment of all. That all men shall see Him, we learn from other scriptures [2 Cor. v. 10]; but we must deal faithfully with the text, and not force any word in order to make out a case. Truth never requires this. That the land of Judea, in the prophetic sense, is the subject, is evident from Zech. xii. 10; from which the words are taken, both here and in John xix. 37.
>
> *"Those who pierced Him"* are obviously those who had a hand in His death. The text declares they shall see Him, employing for seeing the verb *optomai*, already noticed, as not limited to ocular seeing. Though those who pierced Him saw not His person after His ascension, yet they saw His power bringing judgment on them, and making His cause prevail in despite of their persecution, and they speedily saw their kingdom terminated.[11]

Equating "seeing" with "understanding" is a common biblical metaphor. Paul wrote, "I pray that the eyes of your heart may be enlightened, so that you will know what is the hope of His calling, what are the riches of the glory of His inheritance in the saints" (Eph. 1:18). "Eyes of your heart" is a metaphor for understanding that is borrowed from the Old Testament:

> Render the hearts of this people insensitive,
> Their ears dull,
> And their eyes dim,
> Lest they *see with their eyes*,
> Hear with their ears,
> *Understand* with their hearts,
> And return and be healed. (Isa. 6:10; JOHN 12:20)

To "see with the eyes" refers to spiritual understanding that takes place with the heart, another metaphor. To be blind is not to understand; to see is to understand and believe. The biblical writers used the expression "to open their eyes" to describe recognition and understanding (Acts 26:18; cf. 1 Kings 8:29, 52; 2 Kings 6:20; 19:16; Isa. 35:5; 42:7, 18).

Jesus' disciples saw His enthronement at His ascension (Acts 1:11); it was confirmed by Stephen at his death (Acts 7:56); and with the destruction of Jerusalem, "the house of Israel" came to know "for certain that God . . . made Him both Lord and Christ—this Jesus whom" they "crucified" (Acts 2:36). Unfortunately it was too late for so many.

MATTHEW 24:31

He will send forth His angels with a great trumpet and they will gather together His elect from the four winds, from one end of the sky to the other. (MATT. 24:31)

Some commentators apply this verse to the Rapture. This is highly unlikely since the imagery is used throughout the Old Testament to describe God calling His people to forsake their wicked ways and worship Him (e.g. Isa. 11:12; 27:12–13). Jesus was telling His disciples that after the judgment of Jerusalem and the destruction of the temple, His messengers would preach the gospel of the new covenant, and that gospel would go forth in great power "from one end of the sky to the other." This verse is telling us that the gospel was to have a worldwide impact, far beyond the confines of the land of Israel, and that it would include all the elect.

No longer was Jesus' message directed only to the "lost sheep of the house of Israel" (Matt. 10:6; 15:24), but "that He might also *gather* together into one the children of God who are scattered abroad" (John 11:52, emphasis added; see Isa. 56:8). The nations began to recognize Christ as King, not only of Israel but of the world. In context, Matthew 24:31 speaks of the spread of the gospel to the nations and their eventual discipleship (28:18–20). This helps explain why "angels" is best translated "messengers" since the Greek word *angelos* means "messenger," sometimes heavenly messengers, and sometimes earthly messengers. John the Baptist was God's "messenger" who prepared the way for Jesus (Matt. 11:10; Mark 1:2). The disciples of John are called "messengers" (Luke 7:24, 27). Jesus "sent messengers on ahead of Him" (Luke 9:52). Paul was given "a thorn in the flesh, a messenger of Satan" (2 Cor. 12:7). Rahab "received the messengers and sent them out by another way" (James 2:25). In each of these examples, the Greek word *angelos* is used.

The phrase "from the four winds" is a reference to the entire world. Indeed, the phrase "the four corners of the earth" is a common expression for the four points of the compass, that is, from around the world. Jesus was emphasizing the fact that under the new covenant,

His elect are gathered from everywhere. Jesus takes this metaphor from Deuteronomy 30:4–5: "If your outcasts are at the ends of the earth [lit., sky], from there the LORD your God will gather you, and from there He will bring you back. And the LORD your God will bring you into the land which your fathers possessed, and you shall possess it; and He will prosper you and multiply you more than your fathers." Notice that Jesus does not say that His gathered elect will be brought back to the land. Jesus later commands His disciples to go "and make disciples of all the nations" (Matt. 28:19).

The trumpet describes, in a poetic way, the call of the gospel. When Israel was in captivity, we are told that "a great trumpet" was blown and those "who were perishing in the land of Assyria and who were scattered in the land of Egypt will come and worship the LORD in the holy mountain at Jerusalem" (Isa. 27:13). It's doubtful that exiled Jews in these faraway places actually heard a trumpet blow as they made their way back to Israel. Rather, they heard God's call to return. In a similar way, God's messengers herald the gospel "to gather together His elect from the four winds, from one end of the sky to the other."

> Cry loudly, do not hold back;
> Raise your voice like a trumpet,
> And declare to My people their transgression
> And to the house of Jacob their sins. (ISA. 58:1; see also Jer. 6:17;
>   EZEK. 33:3–6; ROM. 10:18)

Matthew 24:31 draws upon Old Testament imagery to symbolize the evangelistic work about to commence, the great gathering of God's elect from around the world, both Jew and Gentile, into one people of God. Those who were once "separate from Christ," "excluded from the commonwealth of Israel, and strangers to the covenants of promise," and "who formerly were far off have been brought near by the blood of Christ" (Eph. 2:12–13). The word for "gather" (Matt. 24:31) is the Greek word *synagogue,* which was an assembly of believers. Many in Judea rejected Christ and became a "synagogue of Satan" (Rev. 2:9). The true synagogue of God is made up of believing Jews and Gentiles from around the world, "from every nation and all tribes and peoples and tongues" (Rev. 7:9; cf. Rev. 5:9; Acts 2:5). The land of Israel was no longer the center. Churches were planted throughout the Roman Empire. It is interesting and significant that the scroll of Revelation is delivered to each "angel" (messenger) of the seven churches in Asia Minor. God's message of redemption had gone global in the first century.

MATTHEW 24:32–33

Now learn the parable from the fig tree: when its branch has already become tender and puts forth its leaves, you know that summer is near; so, you too, when you see all these things, recognize that He is near, right at the door. (MATT. 24:32–33)

Many people interested in prophecy have been told that the "fig tree" that "puts forth its leaves" is Israel becoming a nation again. Hal Lindsey made this interpretation especially popular in his *Late Great Planet Earth* (1970). LaHaye, following Lindsey, states:

[W]hen a fig tree is used symbolically in Scripture, it usually refers to the nation Israel. If that is a valid assumption (and we believe it is), then when Israel officially became a nation in 1948, that was the "sign" of Matthew 24:1–8, the beginning "birth pains"—it meant that the "end of the age" is "near." It was as if the tree were planted in 1914–1918 when the first "birth pain" was felt, but it did not grow into a full-blown tree capable of budding until 1948 when Israel was granted statehood, thus fulfilling Ezekiel 37:1–8.[12]

That was LaHaye's view in 1999. In his *Prophecy Study Bible*, published in 2000, the editors conclude that "the fig tree is not symbolic of the nation of Israel."[13] So, which view of LaHaye's works should we follow? Jesus used the parable of the fig tree as an analogy. His point was that when leaves begin to sprout on a fig tree—or, for that matter, on "all the trees" (Luke 21:29)—it is a sign that summer is near. In a similar way, when Jesus' first-century audience saw certain signs, they knew that Jesus was near, "right at the door." Near to what? Near to fulfilling the promise He made about coming within a generation to destroy the temple. This is the simple and clear meaning of the text. Any other interpretation wildly stretches the Bible beyond its intended meaning.

MATTHEW 24:34

Truly I say to you, this generation will not pass away until all these things take place. (MATT. 24:34)

As we saw in Chapter 4, the phrase "this generation" always refers to the generation to whom Jesus was speaking. Following the biblical evidence, a majority of Bible commentators have interpreted "this generation" as the generation of Jesus' day. In addition, these same commentators understood that all the signs in the Olivet Discourse (Matt. 24:1–34) referred to events leading up to and including the destruction of Jerusalem in A.D. 70. I've chosen the works of Bible expositors whose works have been well respected and read by Bible-believing Christians from the sixteenth century to the present. Many of the commentaries listed below are still in print, a testimony to their sound scholarship and evangelical emphasis.

John Calvin (1563): The meaning therefore is: "This prophecy does not relate to evils that are distant, and which posterity will see after the lapse of many centuries, but which are now hanging over you, and ready to fall in one mass, so that there is no part of it which the present generation will not experience."[14]

Henry Hammond (1653): I now assure you, that in the age of some that are now alive, shall all that has been said in this chapter be certainly fulfilled.[15]

John Lightfoot (1658): Hence it appears plain enough, that the foregoing verses [Matt. 24:1–34] are not to be understood of the last judgment, but, as we said, of the destruction of Jerusalem. There were some among the disciples (particularly John), who lived to see these things come to pass. With Matt. xvi. 28, compare John xxi. 22. And there were some Rabbins alive at the time when Christ spoke these things, that lived until the city was destroyed.[16]

Philip Doddridge (1750): And *verily I say unto you;* and urge you to observe it, as absolutely necessary in order to understand what I have been saying, *That this generation* of men now living *shall not pass away until all these things be fulfilled,* for what I have foretold concerning the destruction of the Jewish state is so near at hand, tht some of you shall live to see it all accomplished with a dreadful exactness.[17]

Thomas Newton (1755): It is to me a wonder how any man can refer part of the foregoing discourse to the destruction of Jerusalem, and part to the end of the world, or any other distant event, when it is said so positively here in the conclusion, *All these things shall be fulfilled in this generation.*[18]

John Gill (1766): This is a full and clear proof, that not any thing that is said before [v. 34], relates to the second coming of Christ, the day of judgment, and the end of the world; but that all belongs to the coming of the son of man in the destruction of Jerusalem, and to the end of the Jewish state.[19]

Thomas Scott (1817): This absolutely restricts our primary interpretation of the prophecy to the destruction of Jerusalem, which took place within forty years.[20]

Robert G. Bratcher and Eugene A. Nida (1961): [T]he obvious meaning of the words 'this generation' is the people contemporary with Jesus. Nothing can be gained by trying to take the word in any sense other than its normal one: in Mark (elsewhere in 8:12, 9:19) the word always has this meaning.[21]

William L. Lane (1974): The significance of the temporal reference has been debated, but in Mark "this generation" clearly designates the contemporaries of Jesus (see on Chs. 8:12, 38; 9:19) and there is no consideration from the context which lends support to any other proposal. Jesus solemnly affirms that the generation contemporary with his disciples will witness the fulfillment of his prophetic word, culminating in the destruction of Jerusalem and the dismantling of the Temple.[22]

D. A. Carson (1984): [This generation] can only with the greatest difficulty be made to mean anything other than the generation living when Jesus spoke.[23]

There are literally hundreds of works that take a similar position. Prior to the twentieth century, Bible-believing commentators almost unanimously agreed that "this generation" refers to the generation of Jews who lived between A.D. 30 and 70. As the last two references indicate by their dates, a number of contemporary scholars have followed their lead. This means that the prophetic position taken by LaHaye on the end times in *Left Behind* is relatively new and has little if any historical support among major Bible expositors.

CONCLUSION

The texts that govern the timing of the Olivet Discourse prophecy—Matthew 23:36 and Matthew 24:34—make it clear that Jesus was speaking of the events leading up to and including the fall of Jerusalem in A.D. 70. If we abandon the clear time texts, then these signs can be applied to any generation, the very thing that Tim LaHaye and Jerry Jenkins do in their *Left Behind* series. As history attests, it's been done before. There have always been wars, false prophets, famines, tribulation, lawlessness, and persecution. If people fail to recognize the timing of these events set by Scripture and the historical context of Jesus' words, they will always be led astray by those who keep insisting that it's our generation that's living in the end times.

THE RISE AND FALL OF NEW BABYLON

"The logistics alone are incredible, the cost, the . . . everything."

"What?"

"He wants to move the U.N."

"Move it?"

Steve nodded.

"Where?"

"It sounds stupid."

"Everything sounds stupid these days," Bailey said.

"He wants to move it to Babylon."

"You're not serious."

"*He* is."

"I hear they've been renovating that city for years. Millions of dollars invested in making it, what, New Babylon?"

"Billions."[1]

"Can I help you? I see that you're interested in Bible prophecy. Is there a particular book that I can help you find?"

"Not really. I'm trying to get a handle on what prophecy writers say about the identity of Babylon in the book of Revelation. I've noticed that there's a wide difference of opinion in what I've read so far."

"In what way?"

"A number of writers say that the Roman Catholic Church is Babylon. This seems to be an old position held by the majority of Protestant Reformers. Not surprisingly a few prominent prophecy writers hold a similar position today. Here's an author who says that America is Babylon. This one takes a more symbolic approach and claims that today's end-time apostate church is Babylon. In this view, Babylon is a symbol for corrupt religion. I pulled two books from your shelves whose authors insist that the ancient political nation of Babylon will be rebuilt and become a world power. This writer believes that the reference to Babylon is spiritual and refers to the revival of Rome during the so-called Tribulation period."

"I didn't realize there were so many different interpretations. How does any reader know which one is right?"

"Now that's a good question."

Tim LaHaye claims that the literal approach to Bible prophecy demands "that the city of Babylon must be restored before the Second Coming."[2] He begins by appealing to "the law of double reference,"[3] that Babylon must be overthrown twice. There is no such law in the Bible. The Bible states clearly that Babylon "will never be inhabited or lived in from generation to generation" (Isa. 13:20); it will be swept "with the broom of destruction" (Isa. 14:23); it "will be desolate forever" (Jer. 51:26); it will be "a desolation without inhabitants" (Jer. 51:29); God will "exact full vengeance" (Jer. 51:36); "it will be a perpetual desolation" (Jer. 51:62); and it shall "sink down and not rise again" (Jer. 51:64).

Even after these repeated statements that Babylon will never be inhabited or rise again, LaHaye insists that "the law of double reference" requires that Babylon will be rebuilt and inhabited because there must be "two overthrows of Babylon"—the first occurring hundreds of years before the birth of Christ and the second during the seven-year Tribulation period.

LaHaye first appeals to Isaiah 13 to promote his belief in a "double reference" rebuilding of Babylon. There is no doubt that this chapter describes the destruction of ancient Babylon. "The day of the LORD," that is, the day of God's judgment against Babylon, was said to be "near" (Isa. 13:6). Isaiah told us that God stirred "up the Medes against" the Babylonians (13:17). We learn from Daniel that Darius the Mede conquered Babylon (Dan. 5:30–31).

Jeremiah 50–51 is LaHaye's support for his claim that there is a prophetic "double reference" that requires a "double fulfillment." Like Isaiah 13, Jeremiah 50–51 describes the same judgment. It takes place in "the land of the Chaldeans," not modern-day Iraq (50:1; 51:4). Babylon's ancient gods Bel and Marduk are mentioned for destruction (50:2; 51:44). Premodern weapons are used for the ancient nation's destruction: bows and arrows (50:9, 14; 51:4, 11, 56), horse soldiers (51:21, 27), and chariots (51:21). Once again, the Medes are listed as Babylon's conquerors (51:11, 28). There is no indication of a "law of double reference" in these passages.

LaHaye appeals to Jeremiah 51:8 to show that Babylon must fall "suddenly" and be "destroyed." Actually the Hebrew states, "Suddenly Babylon has fallen and been broken." LaHaye contends that this did not happen. The Bible says it did. The transfer of power from Babylon to the Medes happened in a single night. Babylon was indeed "broken" as a world power that very evening, never to rise again: "That same night Belshazzar the Chaldean king was slain. So Darius the Mede received the kingdom at about the age of sixty-two" (Dan. 5:30–31). You can't get much more sudden than "that same night."

To further support his belief that Babylon will be rebuilt, LaHaye appeals to Isaiah 13:19. He insists that Babylon must be destroyed in the same way as Sodom and Gomorrah. That's not what the Bible says: "Babylon . . . will be as when God overthrew Sodom and Gomorrah" (Isa. 13:19). That is, as the next verse tells us, Babylon "will never be inhabited or lived in from generation to generation" (13:20). Isaiah does not say, as LaHaye implies, that Babylon has to be destroyed by "fire and brimstone."[4] Joseph Addison Alexander (1809–60), who served as professor of ancient languages and literature at Princeton, offered a helpful interpretation of the suddenness of Babylon's fall and the steady removal of all indications that Babylon ever existed: "The . . . prophecy does not relate to any one invasion or attack exclusively, but to the whole process of subjection and decay, so completely carried out through a course of ages, that the very site of ancient Babylon is now disputed."[5]

As history attests, the ruins of Babylon were buried under the desert sands for centuries. Babylon was so completely destroyed that archaeologists had a difficult time determining the kingdom's original site. Compare Egypt with Babylon. Numerous monuments to ancient Egypt's existence rise up out of the desert sands as constant reminders of its once lofty position in the world. The same cannot be said for Babylon.

BABYLON AND THE TOURIST TRADE

When Saddam Hussein invaded Kuwait in 1990, speculation arose concerning Iraq's role as a modern Babylon. Were the military actions of Saddam Hussein a long overdue fulfillment of prophecies set forth in the book of Isaiah hundreds of years before Jesus was born? Some people thought so. Charles Dyer, whom LaHaye quotes in his *Are We Living in the End Times?*, claims that events depicted in Isaiah 13 were being fulfilled with the Iraqi invasion of Kuwait. Dyer asserts, "'The day of the Lord' described by Isaiah [in 13:6] refers to the tribulation period that is still to come. Babylon's destruction will come in the time of the tribulation—a short period of time just before the second coming of Christ."[6] Is this possible? Isaiah 13:6 explicitly states that "the day of the LORD is *near!*" that is, near for those who first read the prophecy more than twenty-five hundred years ago! LaHaye and Dyer—who insist on a *literal* interpretation of the Bible—do not understand "near" in this way. As was noted, Isaiah predicted that Babylon would be overthrown by the Medes (13:17). Since the Medes did overthrow Babylon, the use of "near" makes perfect *literal* sense.

The "day of the LORD" most often refers to a time of judgment that was on the horizon for those who first read the prophecy. The "day of the LORD" was "near" for Edom (Obad. 15; see Isa. 34:5, 8), Egypt (Ezek. 30:2–11), and Judah (Zeph. 1:4, 7, 14). The day of judgment was certainly near for Babylon in Isaiah's day: "Behold, the day of the LORD is coming . . . And her days will not be prolonged" (Isa. 13:9, 22). LaHaye and Dyer insist that the "day of the Lord" is a moniker for events related to the Great Tribulation. But Ronald Showers, a contributor to LaHaye's *Prophecy Study Bible*, takes a different approach:

> The Day of the Lord refers to God's special interventions into the course of world events to judge His enemies, accomplish His purpose for history, and thereby demonstrate who He is—the sovereign God of the universe (Isa. 2:1–2; Ezek. 13:5, 9, 14, 22–23; 30:3, 8, 19, 25–26).
>
> Evidence for this significance of the Day of the Lord is found in references in the Scriptures to past Days of the Lord. The Bible indicates that there have been several past Days of the Lord in which God exercised and demonstrated His sovereign judgment on other nations. He raised up Assyria to judge the northern kingdom

of Israel during the 700s B.C. (Amos 5:18, 20), Babylon to judge the southern kingdom of Judah during the 600s and 500s B.C. (Lam. 1:12; 2:1, 21–22; Ezek. 7:19; 13:5; Zeph. 1:7–13; 2:2–3), Babylon to judge Egypt and its allies during the 500s B.C. (Jer. 46:10; Ezek. 30:3), and Medo-Persia to judge Babylon during the 500s B.C. (Isa. 13:6, 9).[7]

Notice that Showers writes that "the day of the LORD" in Isaiah 13 refers to the judgment on "Babylon during the 500s B.C.," not during a distant future period of a seven-year great tribulation.

But what of Saddam Hussein's reconstruction of the ancient city of Babylon? This is a myth. To rebuild Babylon would entail everything Babylon was, not just a few buildings that are "designed to attract tourists. Like the Shah's celebrations at Persepolis, this was a measure of understandable if chauvinistic nationalism rather than an aspiration to imperialism. If anything from the past inspired Hussein it was the glorious role of Baghdad in the Abbasid era (A.D. 749–1258)."[8] Mimicking the past does not fulfill prophecy. The buildings are not inhabited; they are used for theater presentations. There are no thriving cities that could be described as "Babylonian." Tony Horwitz writes in the *Washington Post:* "On the day I visited, there were no other tourists, only a handful of Bedouin hustlers lurking in slivers of shade cast by free-standing pillars. One of them grasped my sleeve and unfolded his fist to reveal a tiny cuneiform tablet and a statuette of a Babylonian king. 'Very ancient, very real,' he said. And very cheap at only $10."[9]

Are we to conclude that from the sale of artifacts to a sparse tourist trade that the splendor and grandeur of ancient Babylon are returning and Iraq is becoming a vast world power that will rival Nebuchadnezzar's Babylon? Iraq is a third-rate military power that lost a war with the United States in a matter of weeks. Where are the famed

Hanging Gardens of Babylon, one of the original Seven Wonders of the ancient world?

THE BIBLE OR AN ANCIENT RABBINIC RULE?

Should we expect Babylon to be rebuilt based upon events described in the book of Revelation? Is Revelation's Babylon the same as the Babylon of the Old Testament? LaHaye says yes, but his appeal is not to the Bible. "An ancient rabbinic rule of interpretation says that when the Bible mentions an event twice, it means the event will happen twice. If this rabbinic guideline is correct, then we should be assured that Babylon will be rebuilt, for both Isaiah and the apostle John use the same double verbs to describe its destruction."[10] While "an ancient rabbinic rule of interpretation" is an interesting subject of study, there is no such rule in the Bible. The Bible is our authority, not the opinions of rabbis who have dismissed more than three hundred prophecies that point to Jesus Christ as the promised Messiah. How is it that these rabbis could be so wrong on so many prophecies but be right on an ancient rule of interpretation that is not found in the Bible?

Why doesn't LaHaye apply this "rabbinic rule of interpretation" to "Sodom" since the long-destroyed city is mentioned several times in the Bible, including Revelation (11:8)? We learn from Isaiah that "Judah and Jerusalem" are like Sodom (Isa. 1:1):

> Hear the word of the LORD,
> You rulers of Sodom;
> Give ear to the instruction of our God,
> You people of Gomorrah. (1:10)

The "rulers" and "people" are from Jerusalem and Judah, who "display their sin like Sodom" (Isa. 3:9). Sodom, as a symbol of wickedness, is used in Revelation to describe the sins of first-century Jerusalem: "And [the dead bodies of the two witnesses] will lie in the street of the great city which mystically is called Sodom and Egypt, where also their Lord was crucified" (Rev. 11:8). Sodom and Gomorrah are "exhibited as an example" (Jude 7) of what happens when God's ways are rejected. In his commentary on Revelation, LaHaye states that Sodom is "a symbol of immorality" while Egypt is "a symbol of materialism."[11] Why can't this be true for Revelation's use of Babylon?

"Jezebel" is also mentioned in Revelation (2:20), and yet nobody believes that Jezebel will be raised from the dead during a future seven-year Tribulation period. LaHaye says nothing about a "double reference" for Sodom, Jezebel, Balaam, and Balak (2:14). In fact, he writes that Jezebel is used "symbolically to convey a religious teaching" representing "false religion."[12] Revelation is filled with Old Testament images that serve as symbols, a form of interpretive shorthand: "key of David" (3:7; Isa. 22:22); "Root of David" (5:5; Isa. 11:10); "olive trees and . . . lampstands" (11:4; Zech. 4:11); "sun . . . moon . . . twelve stars" (12:1; Gen. 37:9); "six hundred and sixty-six" (13:18; 1 Kings 10:14; 2 Chron. 9:13); "first fruits" (14:4); "a new heaven and a new earth" (21:1; Isa. 65:17); "book of life" (21:27; Ps. 69:28); and "river of the water of life" (22:1; Ezek. 47:1–5, 9, 12; cf. John 4:13).

BABYLON: LITERAL OR SYMBOLIC?

As we've seen so far, LaHaye believes that the ancient kingdom of Babylon will be rebuilt. He claims this is what the Bible teaches when the Bible is interpreted literally. But his own *Prophecy Study Bible* takes a completely different approach. An article titled "The Figurative Babylon" appears in the context of Isaiah 13. Its author, Arno Froese, writes the following:

Even after Babylon no longer existed, the Bible speaks about Babylon in Revelation 17 as an entity that propels the Antichrist to power. Will ancient Babylon be rebuilt and become the center of the world's economy, finances and religion? The Bible mentions, "Mystery, Babylon the great, the mother of harlots and abominations of the Earth" (Rev. 17:5). *This verse does not refer to "Babylon" literally, but rather figuratively.* This Babylon is a different entity than the one mentioned in Jeremiah 27:6.[13]

While a literal Babylon no longer exists, the spirit of Babylon, characterized by rebellion and confusion, continues. *Babylon is a symbol* of rebellion against God, whose position in that regard passed to Media-Persia, then to Greece, and finally to Rome.[14]

Froese's analysis of Revelation's "mystery Babylon" contradicts LaHaye's strongly held position that Babylon must be rebuilt. Their positions could not be any more different: literal Babylon must be rebuilt, or the Babylon in Revelation "does not refer to 'Babylon' literally, but rather figuratively." So who is right? LaHaye insists that we can "be sure that any city mentioned seven times in two chapters, as is Babylon in Revelation 17 and 18, will be a literal city."[15] But his *Prophecy Study Bible* understands Babylon in Revelation to be symbolic. The symbolic interpretation seems to be the better approach. It fits well with the way in which Egypt, Sodom, and Jezebel are used in Revelation.

WILL THE REAL BABYLON PLEASE STAND UP?

Babylon, as described in the book of Revelation, has been interpreted in numerous ways throughout the history of the church: as a designation for first-century Rome, first-century Jerusalem, the Roman

Catholic Church,[16] a revived Roman Empire in the "last days,"[17] decadent America, and the revived political kingdom of Babylon in present-day Iraq. Since Revelation was written prior to the destruction of Jerusalem in A.D. 70 (Rev. 11:1), we should look for a first-century application, either first-century Rome or Jerusalem.[18] The time texts are critical in determining when the events in Revelation are to take place:

- The events "must shortly take place" (1:1).
- "For the time is near" (1:3).
- "I am coming to you *quickly*" (2:16).
- "I am coming *quickly*" (3:11).
- "The third woe is coming *quickly*" (11:14).
- "The things which must *shortly take place*" (22:6).
- "Behold, I am coming *quickly*" (22:7).
- "For the time is *near*" (22:10).
- "Behold, I am coming *quickly*" (22:12).
- "Yes, I am coming *quickly*" (22:20).

With the time frame established and the temple still standing, our next step is to examine the historical context using Scripture to interpret Scripture.

THE GREAT CITY

Jerusalem is described as "the great city which mystically is called Sodom and Egypt, where also their Lord was crucified" (Rev. 11:8). Of course, we know that Jesus was not crucified in either of these places. Sodom and Egypt are being used as symbols. The Jerusalem of the first century was *like* Sodom and Egypt. But in what way? If you recall, it was the men of Sodom who wanted to harm the angels who were sent to rescue Lot and his family. Most commentators agree that one of the angels was the pre-incarnate Christ. The pre-incarnate Christ warned Lot to flee to the mountains (Gen. 19:17) as He warned the Jews in His day to flee to the mountains as the impending judgment of their city drew near (Matt. 24:16). Egypt is the place where Israel—God's Son (Ex. 4:22–23; Matt. 2:15)—was persecuted. In addition to being identified as Sodom and Egypt because of its treatment of Jesus, Jerusalem is also designated "mystery Babylon" (17:5). Old Testament Babylon, like Egypt, held "God's Son" (Israel) in captivity and put many faithful Jews to death. Jerusalem, led by its religious leaders, crucified God's Son. To identify Babylon with Jerusalem, God describes it as "the great city" (16:19; 17:18). By comparing Scripture with Scripture, we can conclude that Jerusalem, the great city, is "mystery Babylon" (17:5). There is even more direct evidence for this view.

THE BLOODY CITY

The harlot (Babylon) is said to be "drunk with the blood of the saints" (Rev. 17:6). In Babylon there "was found the blood of prophets and of saints and of all who have been slain on the earth" (Rev. 18:24). Israel was also drunk with the blood of the saints. Jesus made that clear when He pronounced judgment on the "scribes and Pharisees" of His day (Matt. 23:15):

> *Consequently you bear witness against yourselves, that you are sons of those who murdered the prophets. Fill up then the measure of the guilt of your fathers. You serpents, you brood of vipers, how shall you escape the sentence of hell? Therefore, behold, I am sending you prophets and wise men and scribes; some of them you will kill and crucify, and some*

of them you will scourge in your synagogues, and persecute from city to city, that upon you may fall the guilt of all the righteous blood shed on earth, from the blood of righteous Abel to the blood of Zechariah, the son of Berechiah. (MATT. 23:31–35)

This prophecy was fulfilled not by the Romans, but by first-century Jews who persecuted their countrymen who had embraced Jesus as the Messiah. Stephen was the first Christian to have his blood shed (Acts 7:58; 22:20). Herod "had James the brother of John put to death with a sword. When he saw that it pleased the Jews, he proceeded to arrest Peter also" (Acts 12:2–3). Up until the time of Nero, Rome was somewhat protective of the church. Paul was saved from a group of forty Jews who took an oath not to eat any food until they killed him (Acts 23:12–14, 21). When Roman officials heard of the plot, soldiers were sent to "bring him safely to Felix the governor" (Acts 23:24). Paul was permitted to preach "the kingdom of God" while he awaited his trial (Acts 28:30–31). The Jews of his day would never have allowed him such freedom.

THE HARLOT CITY

Israel is described as "the faithful city" that "has become a harlot" (Isa. 1:21). The Babylon of Revelation is also said to be a "harlot" (17:1, 15; 19:2). Throughout the Bible, when Israel is unfaithful, she is characterized as a "harlot" and an "adulterer" (Ezek. 16). She played the harlot with the Egyptians and the Assyrians (Ezek. 16:26, 28). Both Israel and Judah played the harlot with the idolatrous nations surrounding them:

Have you seen what faithless Israel did? She went up on every high hill and under every green tree, and she was a harlot there. And I thought, "After she has done all these things, she will return to Me"; but she did

not return, and her treacherous sister Judah saw it. And I saw that for
all the adulteries of faithless Israel, I had sent her away and given her
a writ of divorce, yet her treacherous sister Judah did not fear; but she
went and was a harlot also. And it came about because of the light-
ness of her harlotry, that she polluted the land and committed adul-
tery with stones and trees. (JER. 3:6–9)

In a similar way, first-century Israel played the harlot with Rome. The Jews collaborated with Rome against Jesus and the saints. When given the choice to accept Jesus as their King, they cried out, "We have no king but Caesar" (John 19:15; cf. Luke 23:2). They accused Pilate of not being a "friend of Caesar" (John 19:12). Caiaphas, a high priest, turned Jesus over to the Romans to be crucified (John 18:28–32). The Jews aligned themselves with Rome against Jewish converts to Christ, claiming that "they all act contrary to the decrees of Caesar, saying that there is another king, Jesus" (Acts 17:7; also see 4:27; 16:20; 18:12; 21:11; 24:1–9; 25:1–2).

The Harlot Priesthood

The harlot of Revelation is dressed in a way that would remind anyone familiar with the Old Testament that it is Israel being described: "The woman was clothed in purple and scarlet, and adorned with gold and precious stones and pearls, having in her hand a gold cup full of abominations and of the unclean things of her immorality" (Rev. 17:4; also 18:16). She wore the garments of the high priest, which were made "of gold, of blue and purple and scarlet material and fine twisted linen," including precious stones (Ex. 28:6, 8–12). As God described Judah's sins, He made it clear:

> *Although you dress in scarlet,*
> *Although you decorate yourself with ornaments of gold,*

> *Although you enlarge your eyes with paint,*
> *In vain you make yourself beautiful.*
> *Your lovers despise you.* (JER. 4:30)

They worshiped God "in vain" (Matt. 15:9), even though they were dressed for the part.

The high priest was to wear on his forehead "a plate of pure gold" that would be a constant reminder to the people that "Aaron shall take away the iniquity of the holy things which the sons of Israel consecrate" (Ex. 28:33–38). The scarlet woman of Revelation has upon "her forehead a name written, a mystery, 'BABYLON THE GREAT, THE MOTHER OF HARLOTS AND OF THE ABOMINATIONS OF THE EARTH'" (Rev. 17:5). The "Jerusalem above" is the church's "mother" (Gal. 4:26), while the Jerusalem below has become "the mother of harlots." In addition, "The prostitute's blasphemous inscription on her forehead gives a reverse image of the holy inscription of the high priest."[19] Instead of holiness, the priests practiced abominations in the name of God because they rejected Jesus as God's Lamb.

Those first-century Israelite religious leaders who crucified Jesus and persecuted the saints had all the outward appearances of being God's true representatives, but they were hypocrites, "like whitewashed tombs which on the outside appear beautiful, but inside they are full of dead men's bones and all uncleanness" (Matt. 23:27). The high priest was a representative of God to the people. He had the responsibility to point people to true worship. Instead, he conspired with Rome to crucify "the Lord of glory" (1 Cor. 2:8; cf. Acts 2:22–23). This helps us identify "mystery Babylon" and understand the message of Revelation as God's covenant lawsuit against Jerusalem in the first century.

From this evidence we can conclude that the prophecies concerning the destruction of Old Testament Babylon have been fulfilled. The

Babylon of Revelation is used "mystically" (Rev. 11:8) to refer to an apostate *first-century* Jerusalem. The traits of pagan Babylon, the enemy of God's old covenant people, are used to describe first-century Jerusalem, the enemy of God's new covenant people.

First-century Rome is also a popular candidate for the Babylon designation in Revelation, and there is some evidence that can be read this way (Rev. 18:11–13).[20] But as Kenneth Gentry writes,

> Rome could not fornicate against God, for only Jerusalem was God's wife (Rev. 17:25, cp. Isa. 1:20; Jer. 31:31) . . . [In addition], there is an obvious contrast between the Harlot and the chaste bride (cp. Rev. 17:25 with Rev. 21:1ff.) that suggests a contrast with the Jerusalem below and the Jerusalem above (Rev. 21:2; cp. Gal. 4:24ff.; Heb. 12:18ff.). The fact that the Harlot is seated on the seven-headed Beast (obviously representative of Rome) indicates not identity with Rome, but alliance with Rome against Christianity.[21]

Whether Israel or Rome, the mystery of Babylon is found in the first century. There is no need for a rebuilt Babylon, just as there is no need for a rebuilt temple.

CONCLUSION

Tim LaHaye's *Prophecy Study Bible* concludes that the reference to Babylon in Revelation "does not refer to 'Babylon' literally, but rather figuratively." Rather, "the spirit of Babylon" is "characterized by rebellion and confusion." In this way, "Babylon is a symbol of rebellion against God." The question remains, Whose rebellion did God have in mind? The Bible tells us, "For it is time for judgment to begin with the household of God; and if it begins with us first, what will be the outcome for *those who do not obey the gospel of God*?" (1 Peter 4:17, emphasis added). Peter had his own countrymen in mind. Paul wrote something similar: "For after all it is only just for God to repay with affliction those who afflict you, and to give relief to you who are afflicted and to us as well when the Lord Jesus shall be revealed from heaven with His mighty angels in flaming fire, dealing out retribution to those who do not know God and to *those who do not obey the gospel of our Lord Jesus*" (2 Thess. 1:6–8, emphasis added). Earlier Paul had identified "those who do not obey the gospel of our Lord Jesus Christ." Those living in Thessalonica had endured suffering "at the hands of [their] own countrymen, even as they did from the Jews, who both killed the Lord Jesus and the prophets, and drove us out. They are not pleasing to God, but hostile to all men, hindering us from speaking to the Gentiles that they might be saved; with the result that they always fill up the measure of their sins. But wrath has come upon them to the utmost" (1 Thess. 2:14–16). The first-century Jews living in Jerusalem experienced God's wrath (Rev. 16:19; 17:4; 18:6).

8

THE ANTICHRIST

Let me warn you personally to beware of . . . a leader of humanity who may emerge from Europe. He will turn out to be a great deceiver who will step forward with signs and wonders that will be so impressive that many will believe he is of God. He will gain a great following among those who are left, and many will believe he is a miracle worker.

The deceiver will promise strength and peace and security, but the Bible says he will speak out against the Most High and will wear down the saints of the Most High. That's why I warn you to beware now of a new leader with great charisma trying to take over the world during this terrible time of chaos and confusion. This person is known in the Bible as Antichrist. He will make many promises, but he will not keep them.[1]

"I'm so discouraged. The world's a mess. Every time I pick up the newspaper or turn on the nightly news, there's always some reporter describing the latest global disaster."

"I know what you mean. It seems that evil is winning out over good."

"I agree. The time is ripe for the appearance of Antichrist. I've read a number of prophecy experts who believe that he's alive right now, ready to assume power after the Rapture. We must be living in the end times."

"I said it *seems* that evil is winning out over good."

"How can you say *seems?* Evil is winning!"

"The three Josephs would not agree."

"The three Josephs?"

"Let me tell you a true story that might help put things in perspective for you. Josef Ton, a Christian leader from Romania, was challenged in 1977 by a Christian friend to help set up an organization that would expose communism. Pastor Ton's answer was interesting. He maintained, 'Communism is an experiment that has failed. It wasn't able to fulfill any of its promises and nobody believes in it any more. Because of this, it will one day collapse on its own. Now, why should I fight something that is finished? I believe that our task is a different one. When communism collapses, somebody has to be there to rebuild society! I believe our job as Christian teachers is to train leaders so that they will be ready and capable to rebuild our society on a Christian basis.'"

"Who are the other two Josephs?"

"I'll get to them . . . As you might expect, his friend disagreed. He told Pastor Ton, 'Communism will triumph all over the world, because that is the movement of the Antichrist. And when the communists take over in the United States, they will then kill all the Christians. We have only one job to do: to alert the world and make ready to die.' Eventually, both men were forced to leave Romania. Pastor Ton started a training program in 1981 for Christian leaders who remained in Romania. His friend, as Pastor Ton tells it, 'has not done anything for Romania. He simply waited for the final triumph of communism and the annihilation of Christianity.'"

"What happened?"

"As you know, the Communist regime in Romania fell, and its president, Nicolae Ceausescu, and his wife were captured and found guilty of genocide. They were executed on December 25, 1989. Quite a Christmas present. The former Communists were swept from power in later elections. Pastor Ton trained more than a thousand people all over Romania. Today, these people are the leaders in churches, in evangelical denominations, and in key Christian ministries."[2]

"That's a fascinating story, and it offers me some encouragement. But what about the other Josephs?"

"Joseph was sold into slavery by his own brothers. He was put in prison on a false charge, but he ended up ruling Egypt. His admonition is instructive: 'As for you, you meant evil against me, but God meant it for good in order to bring about this present result, to preserve many people alive' (Gen. 50:20). Present-world conditions are not always indicators that we are living on the edge of history. Who would have thought that the Jews would grow into a mighty nation after spending hundreds of years as slaves in Egypt?"

"What about the third Joseph?"

"Jesus was buried in the tomb of Joseph of Arimathea. Neither the Romans nor the devil himself could keep Jesus a captive of death or the grave. In 1 John 3:8 we learn that 'the Son of God appeared for this purpose, that He might destroy the works of the devil.'"

"Won't Antichrist *eventually* take over?"

"The idea that the Antichrist will rule the world has been a popular belief for centuries. And there have been many Antichrist candidates. But can the modern Antichrist doctrine be found in the Bible? I don't believe it can. When each proposed biblical Antichrist figure is analyzed in context, Bible students will find that the modern Antichrist doctrine is a myth that has affected the way Christians live in the world and plan for the future."

If the central prophetic cities in LaHaye's *Left Behind* series are Babylon and Jerusalem, then the central prophetic character is the Antichrist. He makes his appearance in the first volume and is prominent in every volume thereafter. Nicolae Carpathia was "born in Romania." He is described as "blonde and blue eyed, like the original Romanians, who came from Rome, before the Mongols affected their race."[3] LaHaye's Antichrist must be Roman since he believes that the Antichrist arises out of a reconstituted Roman Empire. LaHaye tells us that many Romanians are of Italian descent. Though Nicolae was "born in Romania, his heritage is actually Italian." LaHaye stresses that "many native Romanians" are Italian.[4]

This smooth-talking, very clever Antichrist will use the unseen power of Satan to disarm the world powers, "empower the United Nations," and move the world to one currency with the ultimate goal of becoming a "global village" under his control.[5] Of course, at first, Nicolae is benevolent. He does not act the way that most people would envision an antichrist to behave. Chloe says, "He looks like a breath of fresh air to me. If he starts trying to weasel his way into power, I might be suspicious, but a pacifist, content to be president of a small country? His only influence is his wisdom, and his only power is his sincerity and humility."[6]

Separating fiction from fact when it comes to the Antichrist is difficult since no single place in the Bible provides a lengthy exposition of the subject as there is for the timing and events of the Tribulation (Matt. 24; Mark 13; Luke 21). The doctrine has to be pieced together from various biblical texts. So much fiction is wrapped up in LaHaye's Antichrist character that it's essential for us to turn to his nonfiction works on the subject to understand what he claims the Bible actually says about the Antichrist.

BUILDING AN ANTICHRIST

For Tim LaHaye, the Antichrist is "the king of Babylon" (Isa. 14:4), "Lucifer" (Isa. 14:12 KJV), "the son of destruction" (2 Thess. 2:3), "the prince who is to come" (Dan. 9:26), "the little horn" (Dan. 7:8; 8:9), "the man of lawlessness" (2 Thess. 2:3), "the beast" (Rev. 13), and several other biblical characters all rolled into one. LaHaye asserts, "Many titles are given to Antichrist in the Scriptures—at least twenty in number."[7] This futurized composite Antichrist supposedly will make himself known during the seven-year Tribulation period, after the rapture of the church. LaHaye maintains that he is European, specifically Roman, since he arises out of the midst of the "ten horns" on the head of the "fourth beast" (Dan. 7:7–8, 19–26). The fourth beast, like the fourth kingdom in Nebuchadnezzar's dream (Dan. 2), is said to be a distant future, revived Roman Empire. This is the same beast that rises out of the sea in Revelation (13:1–10).

As a man of peace, the Antichrist will make a covenant with the Jews guaranteeing them peace and security in their own land. In the middle of the covenant period, he will break his agreement and turn on the Jews. He will then make war with the Jewish saints and will overcome them (Rev. 13:17; Dan. 7:21). According to LaHaye, during this three-and-one-half-year period of time, two-thirds of the Jews living in Palestine will be killed (Zech. 13:8–9).

As a counterfeit Christ, the Antichrist will be given great power by the devil in an attempt to duplicate Jesus' miraculous works. He will even seek to match the Resurrection. He will seem to have suffered a mortal wound to the head but will then be miraculously resurrected (Rev. 13:3, 14). Of course, the world will be awestruck by this manifestation of supernatural power and follow him with undying loyalty and reverence.

According to this elaborate scenario, the world will be living under a tyranny directed by Satan through his Beast-Antichrist and False Prophet. Each and every person will be stamped with the dreaded identifying number 666 (Rev. 13:18)! This recipe for disaster will eventually lead to Armageddon where all the nations of the world will be brought against Israel (Rev. 16:13–16). Only the return of Christ will save Israel and the world.

When it is tested against sound biblical interpretation, will such a theory hold up? The issue of timing invalidates the entire modern Antichrist theory (Rev. 1:1, 3; 3:10; 22:10). Is it possible that what was prophecy when the New Testament was written is now history? Could the Beast of Revelation 13 and his attendant number 666 be referring to a well-known historical figure who played a prominent religious and political role during the time in which Revelation was written?

As we will see, LaHaye's modern doctrine of Antichrist is an amalgamation of biblical concepts, personalities, and events that are unrelated to one another or find their fulfillment in history. Trying to merge these divergent entities has led to consistent confusion for centuries in attempts to identify Antichrist. There have been literally hundreds of Antichrist candidates, everyone from Caligula and Domitian to Henry Kissinger[8] and Ronald (6) Wilson (6) Reagan (6).[9] All have one thing in common; all have been wrong.

THE BIBLICAL ANTICHRIST

It's curious to read LaHaye's material on the Antichrist and learn that he briefly mentions the only verses that actually use the term. The word *antichrist* appears in only two of John's epistles (1 John 2:18,

22; 4:3; 2 John 7), and the term's definition is clear and precise. LaHaye admits this, but then adds to the definition by claiming, "The Bible repeatedly predicts, however, that one person will arise as the embodiment of all anti-Christian attitudes, purposes, and motives that Satan has implanted in his emissaries throughout past centuries."[10] Yet one cannot reach this conclusion by studying John's *biblical* description of Antichrist. John's Antichrist is

- anyone "who denies that Jesus is the Christ" (1 John 2:22).

- anyone who "denies" the Father and Son (1 John 2:23).

- "every spirit that does not confess Jesus" (1 John 4:3).

- "those who do not acknowledge Jesus Christ as coming in the flesh. This is the deceiver and the antichrist" (2 John 7).

None of John's statements relate to the modern doctrine of the Antichrist as outlined by LaHaye and many other prophecy writers. LaHaye even has to admit "that the term *the Antichrist*, which has been universally accepted by fundamental Bible teachers and prophetic students, is nowhere in the Bible used in connection with a specific person."[11] Having written this, LaHaye spends thousands of pages in his *Left Behind* series applying the term to a specific person. John's Antichrist doctrine is a dispute over the nature of Jesus Christ. John did not have a particular individual in mind; he was referring to *individuals* who taught that Jesus Christ is not who the Bible says He is:

In one word, "Antichrist" meant for John just denial of what we should call the doctrine, or let us rather say the fact, of the Incarnation. By whatever process it had been brought about,

137

"Christ" had come to denote for John the Divine Nature of our Lord, and so far to be synonymous with "Son of God." To deny that Jesus is the Christ was not to him therefore merely to deny that he is the Messiah, but to deny that he is the Son of God; and was equivalent therefore to "denying the Father and the Son"—that is to say, in our modern mode of speech, the doctrine—in fact—of the Trinity, which is the implicate of the Incarnation. To deny that Jesus is Christ come—or is the Christ coming—in flesh, was again just to refuse to recognize in Jesus Incarnate God. Whosoever, says John, takes up this attitude toward Jesus is Antichrist.[12]

Is this interpretation possible? Aren't we supposed to look for a future apostasy out of which *the* Antichrist will arise? As the New Testament makes clear, apostasy was present in John's day. Paul had to counter a "different gospel" that was "contrary" to what he had preached (Gal. 1:6–9). He had to battle "false brethren" (Gal. 2:4, 11–21; 3:1–3; 5:1–12). He warned the Ephesian church leadership that "men will arise, speaking perverse things, to draw away the disciples after them" (Acts 20:28–30). Theological insurrection came from within the Christian community in the first century.

Many people prior to Jerusalem's destruction in A.D. 70 questioned and disputed basic Christian doctrines such as the Resurrection (2 Tim. 2:18). Some even claimed that the Resurrection was an impossibility (1 Cor. 15:12). Others within the church prohibited marriage (1 Tim. 4:1–3) and the goodness of God's creation (Col. 2:8, 18–23). The apostles found themselves defending the faith against numerous false teachers and "false apostles" (Rom. 16:17–18; 2 Cor. 11:13–14; Phil. 3:18–19; 1 Tim. 1:3–7; 2 Tim. 4:2–5). Apostasy increased to such an extent that Paul had to write letters to a young pastor who was experiencing the doctrinal disputes firsthand (1 Tim. 1:19–20; 6:20–21; 2 Tim. 2:16–18; 3:1–9, 13; 4:10, 14–16). Peter wrote, "False prophets also arose among the people, just as there will also be false teachers among you, who will secretly introduce destructive heresies, even denying the Master who bought them, bringing swift destruction upon themselves" (2 Peter 2:1).

John listed several movements that were affecting the church with false doctrines: "evil men" (Rev. 2:2), "those who call themselves apostles" but who are found to be "false" (2:2), a revival of "the teaching of Balaam" (2:14), those who "hold the teaching of the Nicolaitans" (2:15), and the toleration of the "woman Jezebel, who . . . leads [God's] bond-servants astray so that they commit acts of immorality and eat things sacrificed to idols" (2:20). An apostasy was alive and well on planet Earth in the *first* century (2 Thess. 2:3). John told us that those antichrists "went out from *us*, but they were not really of *us;* for if they had been of us, they would have remained with us; but they went out, in order that it might be shown that they all are not of us" (1 John 2:19, emphasis added). The Bible leaves us with no doubt: the Antichrist was a first-century movement.

CONSPICUOUS BY ITS ABSENCE

One of the arguments that LaHaye uses for his belief that the church is raptured before a future Tribulation period is that the word *church* does not appear after Revelation 4:1 when a voice told John, "Come up here." Following this logic, then, how does LaHaye support his claim that Revelation describes a future seven-year Tribulation period in which Antichrist is in control of the world, when the word *Antichrist* does not appear anywhere in Revelation? The absence of the word *Antichrist* is significant since the John who defined Antichrist for us in two of his short epistles is the same John who penned Revelation. Edward Hindson, one of four associate editors of LaHaye's *Prophecy Study Bible*, writes, "Ironically, the term 'antichrist' appears only in

1 John 2:18–22; 4:3; and 2 John 1:7."[13] Having acknowledged this, Hindson, like LaHaye, does not explain why John never uses the term in Revelation, even though Antichrist is the book's main evil character.

MORE THAN ONE

According to the Bible, Antichrist is not a single individual. John wrote, "Children, it is the last hour; and just as you heard that antichrist is coming, even now many antichrists have arisen; from this we know that it is the last hour" (1 John 2:18). It is possible that the early church "heard" that one man was to come on the scene who was to be *the* Antichrist. John seemed to be correcting this mistaken notion:

> John is adducing not an item of Christian teaching, but only a cur-
> rent legend—Christian or other—in which he recognizes an ele-
> ment of truth and isolates it for the benefit of his readers. In that
> case we may understand him less as expounding than as openly
> correcting it—somewhat as, in the closing page of his Gospel, he
> corrects another saying of similar bearing which was in circulation
> among the brethren, to the effect that he himself should not die
> but should tarry till the Lord comes [JOHN 21:18–23].[14]

In a similar manner, the people in Jesus' day had "heard" certain things that were only partially true. Jesus corrected them in their misreading of the Bible (Matt. 5:21, 27, 33, 38, 43).[15] Christians are bound by what is written in the Bible, not what people claim the Bible teaches.

THE LAST HOUR

Whether there was to be only one or many antichrists, John made it clear that "it is the last hour" or "the last time" for those who *first* read his letters (1 John 2:18). How do we know this? John said, "Even *now* many antichrists have arisen." And in case a reader missed his point, he repeated it: "From *this* we know that it *is* the last hour." John did not describe a period of time thousands of years in the future. The presence of antichrists in John's time was an indication that the end of the age was upon them. Previous predictions about those who would oppose Jesus as the Messiah were being fulfilled. The antichrists were manifesting themselves within the church community in John's day. Paul told his fellow Christians, "Beware of the dogs, beware of the evil workers, beware of the false circumcision" (Phil. 3:2). "The party of the circumcision" (Gal. 2:12) insisted that the shed blood of Jesus was not enough to save sinners. The Judaizers demanded that Old Testament blood rituals and ordinances had to be followed. For them, "Christ will be of no benefit" (Gal. 5:2). Because of the corruption of the gospel, John described the Judaizers as a "synagogue of Satan" (Rev. 2:9; 3:9).

John wrote that it was the "last hour" for *his contemporaries*. The fact that there were antichrists alive and well in his day was evidence that it was the last hour. Compare the straightforward statement of Scripture with LaHaye's interpretation of "the last hour": "In 1 John [2:18] the apostle speaks of 'the last hour.' He is referring here to the new economy of God's grace, warning that in this church age there would be 'many antichrists . . . by which we know that it is the last hour.' He was right: For two thousand years the church age has not been without false christs and antichrists sent by Satan to deceive the saints."[16]

LaHaye, who insists on interpreting the Bible literally, has turned "the last hour" or "the last time" into two thousand years of church history. Keep in mind that Jesus had told His disciples years before, John among them, that their generation would see the destruction of the temple and the city of Jerusalem (Matt. 24:1–34). John, writing close to the time when this prophecy was to be fulfilled, could point to the rise of "many antichrists" as evidence that it was the last hour for *his* generation. The fact that people were denying that Jesus had come in the flesh was proof enough that Jesus' prediction was true and on time (2 John 7).

Christians had heard that "the spirit of the antichrist" was coming. For them, *"now* it is *already* in the world" (1 John 4:3, emphasis added). Antichrists had arrived. It is inappropriate to look for a future political leader and describe him as *the* Antichrist when the Bible makes no such application.

An antichrist, therefore, is *anyone* who "denies that Jesus is the Christ," that is, *anyone* "who denies the Father and the Son" (1 John 2:22). *"Every* spirit that does not confess Jesus is not from God . . . *this* is the spirit of the antichrist" (1 John 4:3, emphasis added). "For *many* deceivers have gone out into the world, *those* who do not acknowledge Jesus Christ as coming in the flesh. *This* is the deceiver and the antichrist" (2 John 7, emphasis added). John's very exact definition does not apply to "the king of Babylon" (Isa. 14:4), "Lucifer" (Isa. 14:12 KJV), "the little horn" (Dan. 7:8; 8:9), "a king of fierce countenance" (Dan. 8:23 KJV), "the prince who is to come" (Dan. 9:26) or "the mighty king" (Dan. 11:36), since denying "that Jesus is the Christ," denying "the Father and Son," not confessing Jesus, and not acknowledging "Jesus Christ as coming in the flesh" were foreign concepts to them and their time.

THE BEAST

If the *antichrist* is a term that was used to describe anyone who did not believe that Jesus was God incarnate, and the term is not found in Revelation, then who or what is the Beast of Revelation 13? Actually two beasts conspire together to oppose the things of God: a sea beast (13:1–10) and a land beast (13:11–18). The time parameters of Revelation limit who the beasts can be. Because the events of

Revelation were to happen "shortly" (Rev. 1:1), the time was "near" (1:3) for those who first read the prophecy, and the temple was still standing (11:1–2), the list of Beast candidates must also be near in time to those who first picked up and read or heard the original scroll. Nero Caesar fits three essential criteria in determining the identity of the sea beast who will "make war with the saints" (13:7): the time of his reign (A.D. 54 to 68), the numerical value of his official name and title, and his character as a persecutor of "the saints."

THE BEAST'S NAME AND NUMBER

When trying to match "six hundred and sixty-six" with a historical figure, we need more than a plausible candidate; we need a relevant candidate. The first readers of Revelation were told to "calculate the number of the beast, for the number is that of a man; and his number is six hundred and sixty-six" (13:18). Since Revelation was written to a first-century audience, we should expect the first-century readers to be able to calculate the number with relative ease and understand the result. They would have had few candidates from which to choose. Notice that the number is "six hundred and sixty-six," not three sixes. LaHaye misidentifies the number when he writes, "The plain sense of Scripture tells us that it comprises the numbers: six, six, six."[17] The three Greek letters that make up the number represent 600, 60, and 6.

Ancient numbering systems used an alphanumeric method. This is true of the Latin (Roman) system that is still common today: I = 1, V = 5, X = 10, L = 50, C = 100, D = 500, M = 1,000. Greek and Hebrew follow a similar method: each letter of each alphabet represents a number. The first nine letters represent 1–9. The tenth letter represents 10, with the nineteenth letter representing 100 and so on. Since the book of Revelation is written in a Hebrew context by a Jew with numerous allusions to the Old Testament, we should expect the solution to deciphering the meaning of six hundred and sixty-six to be Hebraic. "The reason clearly is that, *while [John] writes in Greek, he thinks in Hebrew,* and the thought has naturally affected the vehicle of expression."[18]

Is there anything in John's writings, especially in Revelation, that hints at this use of both Greek and Hebrew? The "angel of the abyss" was described in two ways: "His name in Hebrew is Abaddon, and in the Greek he has the name Apollyon" (Rev. 9:11). Something similar was done with "Har-Magedon" (hill of Megiddo) or "Ar-Magedon" (city of Megiddo) (Rev. 16:16). Megiddo was an Old Testament city (1 Chron. 7:29), the place where King Josiah was killed (2 Chron. 35:20–27). In John's gospel, the place where Pilate sat down to judge Jesus was called "The Pavement," but John called attention to its Hebrew name "Gabbatha" (John 19:13). In the same chapter, John wrote how Pilate had an inscription placed on the cross above Jesus' head written in "Hebrew, Latin, and in Greek" (John 19:20). Going from Greek to Hebrew was typical and expected since Jews spoke Hebrew.

When Nero Caesar's name is transliterated into Hebrew, which a first-century Jew would probably have done immediately, he would have gotten *Neron Kesar* or simply *nrwn qsr,* since Hebrew has no letters to represent vowels. (The *w* represents the "o" sound and the *q* represents the "k" sound in Hebrew.) "It has been documented by archaeological finds that a first century Hebrew spelling of Nero's name provides us with precisely the value of 666. Jastrow's lexicon of the Talmud contains this very spelling."[19] When we take the letters of Nero's name and spell them in Hebrew, we get the following numeric values: n = 50, r = 200, w = 6, n = 50, q = 100, s = 60, r = 200 = 666.

Every Jewish reader, of course, saw that the Beast was a symbol of Nero. And both Jews and Christians regarded Nero as also having close affinities with the serpent or dragon . . . The Apostle writing as a Hebrew, was evidently thinking as a Hebrew . . . Accordingly, the Jewish Christian would have tried the name as he *thought* of the name—that is *in Hebrew letters*. And the moment that he did this the secret stood revealed. No Jew ever thought of Nero except as "*Neron Kesar*."[20]

How does the beast coming out of the earth or land fit into this equation? The land beast was most likely Jewish, probably the religious leaders who were continually fighting against their countrymen in Judea who embraced Jesus as the Messiah. He had "two horns like a lamb," but "he spoke as a dragon" (Rev. 13:11). Jesus warned His disciples about this character: "Beware of the false prophets, who come to you in sheep's clothing, but inwardly are ravenous wolves" (Matt. 7:15). They might present themselves as God's religious representatives, but underneath the "sheep's clothing," a dragon was present. The "beast coming up out of the earth" with the "two horns" most likely represents the Jewish high priest and the Herodian dynasty. It was "Herod the king" (Matt. 2:1), also called Herod the Great, who slaughtered "all the male children . . . from two years old and under" in an attempt to kill Jesus (2:16), "the King of the Jews" (2:2). "Herod the tetrarch" (Matt. 14:1), whom Jesus described as "that fox" (Luke 13:32), arrested John the Baptist and had him beheaded because John had been saying to him, "It is not lawful for you to have [your brother's wife as your own]" (Matt. 14:3–12). Herod Agrippa I killed James the brother of John (Acts 12:2) and was heralded as "a god" by the people and "did not give God the glory" (Acts 12:20–23).

The "Herodians" aligned themselves with the Pharisees against Jesus (Mark 3:6; 12:13). Philip Mauro's comments are especially helpful:

For history, both sacred and profane, sets before us a most notable character, one who appears upon the scene and occupies the center stage in Israel just at "the end" of the Asmonean era, and one who answers to *every item* of the prophetic description. We have reference to that strange, despotic, ungovernable and unspeakably cruel personage, whom the evangelists designate emphatically as— "Herod the King"—that remarkable character who was a usurper upon the throne of David when Christ, the true King, was born.[21]

The high priest oversaw the execution of Stephen (Acts 7:1, 54–60), and Herod "laid hands on some who belonged to the church in order to mistreat them. And he had James the brother of John put to death with a sword" (Acts 12:1–2). Notice that Herod was delighted "that it pleased the Jews" (Acts 12:3).

THE BEAST'S CHARACTER

Nero had his mother bludgeoned and slashed to death by marines ordered to do the job after his attempts to poison and drown her failed. A few years later, he had his wife, Octavia, killed so he could marry his mistress, Poppaea. He kicked Poppaea to death when she complained about him coming home late. The Roman historian Suetonius reported that Nero "castrated the boy Sporus and actually tried to make a woman of him; and he married him with all the usual ceremonies . . . and treated him as his wife."[22] His other sexual exploits are too degrading to put into print. But his persecution of Christians led the first-century church to regard Nero as Revelation's "beast" in confirmation of what they read in Revelation. Miriam Griffin, tutor in ancient history and Fellow of Somerville College, Oxford, writes, "In A.D. 64 came the most serious threat to Nero's popularity when the Great Fire broke out. It was widely believed that Nero first used the blaze as a backdrop for a virtuoso performance and then restarted it to clear the ground for his reconstruction of Rome. This time, force was used on a despised minority, the Christians, who were burned alive to illuminate circus games."[23]

Rumors circulated that Nero had set the fire. "Nero first attempted to quash the rumours by religious ceremonies designed to appease the supposedly angry gods."[24] He needed a scapegoat, "so he decided to fasten guilt on a human culprit, the Christians," using them as "human torches."[25] John said of the Beast, "It was also given to him to make war with the saints and to overcome them" (Rev. 13:7).

THE TESTIMONY OF THE CHURCH

Christian history supports the view that Nero was the Beast. "All the earliest Christian writers on the Apocalypse, from Irenaeus down to Victorinus of Pettau and Commodian in the fourth, and Andreas in the fifth, and St. Beatus in the eighth century, connect Nero, or some Roman Emperor, with the Apocalyptic Beast."[26] Although confusing the Antichrist with the Beast, Miriam Griffin writes that "Nero is the Anti-Christ whose persecution of the Christians heralds the destruction of Rome. This view of Nero as Anti-Christ continued to be celebrated by the Church Fathers and by later Christian writers. The picture of him as the incarnation of evil triumphed as Christianity triumphed."[27] Tertullian (ca. 155–220), in chronicling the sufferings of the apostles, wrote, "At Rome Nero was the first who stained with blood the rising faith."[28]

A curious variation on 666 adds validity to the argument that Nero was considered to be the sea beast of Revelation 13. Some Greek New Testament manuscripts read 616 instead of 666. Why would someone making a copy of the Revelation scroll make such a number change? "Perhaps the change was intentional, seeing that the Greek form Neron Caesar written in Hebrew characters (*nrwn qsr*) is equivalent to 666, whereas the Latin form Nero Caesar (*nrw qsr*) is equivalent to 616."[29] Keep in mind that there were no copy machines in the first century. If a person wanted a copy of a manuscript, someone had to copy it for him by hand. No matter how carefully a scribe worked, mistakes were inevitable. Some mistakes occurred when a scribe was making a copy of a known copy. He might have thought the copy he was copying was mistaken and it was up to him to correct it. A Latin copyist might have thought that 666 was an error because Nero Caesar did not add up to 666 when transliterated into Latin. He then changed 666 to 616 to conform to the Latin rendering since it was generally accepted that Nero was the Beast. In either case, a Hebrew transliteration nets 666, while a Latin spelling nets 616. Nero was the "man" and 666 was his number.

THE MAN OF LAWLESSNESS

LaHaye writes that of "all the titles given to him, the one used by the Apostle Paul in 2 Thessalonians 2:3, 'the man of lawlessness,' is the most descriptive. As 'the man of lawlessness' he will come on the scene in the last days as the embodiment of all the sinful people who have ever lived. Second Thessalonians 2:4 offers an appropriate description of his conduct: 'He will oppose and will exalt himself over everything that is called God or is worshipped, so that he sets himself up in God's temple, proclaiming himself to be God.'"[30]

Paul does not describe the "man of lawlessness" as someone who embodies "all the sinful people who have ever lived." The actions of the "man of lawlessness are not much different from those of Herod Agrippa I who had James the brother of John put to death (Acts 12:2) and thought of himself as a god. When Herod "put on his royal apparel," he "took his seat on the rostrum and began delivering an address" (Acts 12:21). He had assumed the role of a deity: "The people kept crying out, 'The voice of a god and not of a man!'" (Acts 12:22). Notice that the "man of lawlessness," like Herod before him, "takes his seat" (2 Thess. 2:4). God did to Herod what He would do to the man of lawlessness in the first-century temple: "And immediately an angel of the Lord struck him because he did not give God the glory, and he was eaten by worms and died" (Acts 12:23). In a similar way, the man of lawlessness was killed "with the breath of [God's] mouth" when he took his seat in the temple and proclaimed himself to be God prior to the temple's destruction in A.D. 70 (2 Thess. 2:8).

Although we are not told the identity of the man of lawlessness by name, we are told when he would appear. The "man of lawlessness" was said to take "his seat in the temple of God" (2 Thess. 2:4). When Paul wrote this letter to the Christians at Thessalonica, the temple was still standing. Paul did not write, "The man of lawlessness will take his seat in a rebuilt temple." Those who first read his letter would immediately have thought of the temple that was still standing in Jerusalem because Paul did not give them any reason to think any other way.

Paul's man of lawlessness was alive in his day since the restrainer was alive, and the Thessalonians knew the identity of the restrainer: "And *you know* what restrains him *now*" (2 Thess. 2:6, emphasis added). In the next verse, we read, "He who *now* restrains will do so until he is taken out of the way" (2:7, emphasis added). Paul wrote, "The mystery of lawlessness is *already at work*" (2 Thess. 2:7, emphasis added). Paul was not describing a distant antichrist figure; he had someone in mind who was alive in the first century.[31] This person was identified as "the son of destruction" (2 Thess. 2:3), like Judas (John 17:12). Therefore, it's reasonable to assume that the person Paul was describing was a Jew who occupied the temple during the siege before it was destroyed.

Since the man of lawlessness has not been revealed to us by

name, but by his time, we can only speculate about his identity. We should look for a first-century candidate. Southern Baptist evangelist and prophecy writer John Bray has identified a likely candidate. John Levi of Gischala "was the key man in the destruction of Jerusalem, the greatest instigator of the tribulation upon the Jews in the city, and an 'abomination' himself as he 'sat' in power in the Temple itself. And he was the cause of the ceasing of the daily sacrifices three and one half years after Vespasian came against the city. So far as the people were concerned, he had taken the place of God in the Temple!"[32] Following the first-century historian Josephus, Bray offers compelling historical evidence for his opinion, everything from murder to defilement of the temple. Mireille Hadas-Lebel recounts John's lawless deeds:

> Crimes against men were accompanied by what Josephus considered crimes against God. John of Gischala was especially guilty of these latter. Early in the siege he had used timber intended for the Temple to construct war machines. Next, he had all the sacred vessels melted down, including precious vases offered by the emperor Augustus and his wife. Then he had dipped into the Temple reserves of oil and wine.[33]

John Levi of Gischala was a prominent figure during the temple siege. His occupation of the temple followed the surrounding of Jerusalem by armies.

In the final analysis, the Bible does not identify the man of lawlessness, the beast, or the many antichrists by name. It's possible that even Paul did not know the identity of the man of lawlessness. He only knew that he was alive and being restrained as he wrote his letter. Tim LaHaye and other prophecy writers who share his views have the luxury of never having to identify the man of lawlessness, since in their prophetic scenario they and all other Christians will be raptured before he reveals himself.

CONCLUSION

While LaHaye paints a fascinating picture of an end-time world leader, whom he describes as Antichrist, we have to ask why the biblical definition of this figure does not match his amalgamated world leader. We also must ask why LaHaye insists on skipping over centuries of history in search of an "antichrist candidate" when there are a number of more likely candidates that fall within the time frame of first-century biblical history. Further, we have to ask why LaHaye's understanding of Antichrist is so certain when hundreds of speculative prophecy writers throughout the centuries were equally certain of their choice. Lastly, we must ask why LaHaye disagrees with Paul when he states that the "mystery of lawless was already at work," and John assured his first-century readers that the presence of antichrists in his day was evidence "that it is the last hour."

9

THE MARK

Suddenly, as if in a trance, Leon rose and began to speak. "Every man, woman, and child, regardless of their station in life, shall receive this mark on their right hands or on their foreheads. Those who neglect to get the mark when it is made available will not be allowed to buy or sell until such time as they receive it. Those who overtly refuse shall be put to death, and every marked loyal citizen shall be deputized with the right hand and the responsibility to report such a one. The mark shall consist of the name of His Excellency or the prescribed number."[1]

"Dad, listen to this."

"What is it?"

"This man says that the mark of the Beast is going to be a microchip implanted under the skin. He says that they're already using them on animals."

"That's true. It's a way for dairies to keep track of milking schedules. Pet owners are encouraged to use them in case their dog or cat is lost.[2] Machine-readable bar codes that can be read by laser are being used to track bees in the wild.[3] Clothes, books, tools, CDs, and other high-priced items carry 'source tags' as a way to counter theft."[4]

"What would happen if governments started requiring that microchips be embedded under our skin? What if social planners claimed that they could put all our financial and medical records on a chip? We wouldn't have to carry credit cards, cash, or checkbooks anymore. If we were in an accident, a hospital could retrieve our complete medical history from the chip in an instant. The chips would be presented as a good thing."

"It's one thing to be concerned about intrusive governments and the erosion of our freedoms. It's another thing to equate modern technology with the mark of the Beast. They are not the same thing. Adolf Hitler was thought to be the Antichrist. Tattooing numbers on the arms of Jews cinched it for lots of people. In fact, a book being sold today claims that Hitler is the Antichrist."[5]

"How can that be? Hitler's dead."

"According to the author who promoted this idea, Hitler will be raised from the dead. Of course, the ever-present Social Security number is thought to be the mark of the Beast. It's being used as a personal identification number. When you were born, a nurse wanted my Social Security number to put on your birth certificate."

"What did you say?"

"I told her no. I pointed out to her that my Social Security card reads: 'For Social Security and tax purposes—not for identification.' If you check your card, you will find that it does not include this line."

"So what does the Bible say about these things? What is the mark of the Beast?"

The number and mark of the Beast have been misidentified over the centuries as the sign of the cross, ordination of bishops, labels on products made by trade unions, and the red star of Communist nations.[6] In our day, Social Security numbers, universal product codes (bar codes),[7] worshiping on Sunday instead of Saturday,[8] and the World Wide Web have been singled out as the mark of the Beast.[9] According to LaHaye, the mark is a "miniature biochip" that "can be inserted as painlessly as a vaccination" under the skin.[10]

While computer chips and sophisticated tracking devices make for interesting fictional reading, biblical reality is far less mysterious but much more profound and theologically significant. Peter Lalonde, producer of the film version of *Left Behind* and a member of LaHaye's Pre-Trib Research Center, follows an interpretive methodology almost identical to LaHaye's. It seems that LaHaye and Jenkins created their fictional "biochip" scenario from the Lalondes' book *Racing Toward . . . The Mark of the Beast.* The authors claim that only today can the specific elements of Revelation 13 be fulfilled. This seems to be a standard argument. Peter and Paul Lalonde write, "As always, God is way ahead of the latest biometric engineers, smart card developers, and global communication systems planners . . . For the first time in history, the technology to easily fulfill this incredible prophecy exists."[11]

The technology existed in the first century to accomplish what LaHaye and the Lalondes maintain is required to fulfill the prophetic particulars of Revelation 13:16–18. A simple mark, for example, a visible tattoo or a brand, could easily have been made on the forehead and hand, if that is what the text is calling for. In fact, LaHaye's fictional Antichrist character, Nicolae Carpathia, in responding to Walter Moon's desire to be the first to bear the mark, asks, "You may just get your wish, and while I am touched by your sentiment, how do you know that I will not brand you with an iron like a head of cattle?" A literal interpretation, as LaHaye understands literalism, demands just such an external mark—nothing more and nothing less.

Thomas Ice and Timothy Demy, both contributors to LaHaye's

Prophecy Study Bible, insist, contrary to LaHaye and the Lalondes, that the mark is "like a tattoo . . . visible to the naked eye . . . on you, not in you."[12] Such an application would have been easy for a first-century audience to understand. Branding has been used for centuries to identify slaves, idolaters, and property. A late-seventeenth-century reference work, *Archaeologia Graeca,* published in two volumes by John Potter, includes significant background information on ancient marking systems:

> In this work Potter described the ancient custom of branding slaves, which according to him was usually done in the forehead. Soldiers, on the other hand, he informed his readers, were branded in the hand with the name or character of their general, a custom which he believed the Apostle Paul alluded to in Gal. 6.17.[13] Not only so, but he also wrote that it was likewise customary to stigmatize the worshippers and votaries of the ancient gods. This was done by means of symbolic tattoos: the thunderbolt for Jupiter, the trident for Neptune, and the ivy-leaf for Bacchus. But the particular mark of the sun was XH,[14] which had the numerical value of 608. Potter suggested that this was the background against which Rev. 13.16–18 was to be understood.[15]

The Bible has numerous examples of marking people on the right hand and forehead. A "certain man clothed in linen with a writing case" went through the city of Jerusalem to "put a mark on the foreheads of the men who sigh and groan over all the abominations which are being committed in its midst" (Ezek. 9:2, 4; cf. 2 Cor. 1:22; 2 Tim. 2:19; Rev. 7:2–3). Isaiah described any person who identified himself as "the LORD's" as one who wrote "on his hand 'B to the LORD'" (Isa. 44:5). Why don't these marks den application? As we we will see, such marks are often then we have to ask whether the seal on the foreheads of God's bond-servants are external tattoos or biochips (Rev. 7:3; 9:4).

While LaHaye and Jenkins pick a supertechnological mark as the fulfillment of Revelation 13:16-18, they choose a rather low-tech way to execute those who refuse the mark—the guillotine. The fact that beheading is the method of execution in Revelation (20:4), and not lethal injection or some other form of modern punishment, is a good indication that the persecution takes place during a pretechnological time. Beheading, most likely by the sword (Rom. 13:4; Heb. 11:34, 37; Rev. 19:21), was a common form of execution in the first century.

ADDING TO THE BIBLE

In an attempt to make Revelation 13:16–18 conform to the latest advances in technology because of his futuristic perspective, LaHaye must add to the biblical text. Once again, LaHaye follows an interpretation outlined by Peter and Paul Lalonde. In an advertisement for their *This Week in Bible Prophecy* television program, the prophecy authors write, "The Mark of the Beast—it's one of the clearest and most dramatic prophecies in the Bible. It states simply that in the last days[16] that no man will be able to buy or sell unless he has the mark IN his right hand or forehead." According to the Lalondes, the "IN" refers to an embedded microchip or something similar placed *under* the skin; they emphasize the word *IN*.

The Greek preposition *epi* (upon), not *en* (in), is used in Revelation 13:16 to describe where the mark was to be placed. *Epi* is best translated "on" or "upon." This is why the passage states that the mark was to be given *"on* their right hand or *on* their forehead," not *"in* their right hand or *in* their forehead."

The interpretation advocated by LaHaye and the Lalondes forces readers of *Left Behind* to believe that the message behind the mark of the Beast has been unintelligible for nearly two thousand years since computer chips and scanning technologies are late-twentieth-century innovations. Yet low-tech methods of screening a population have been quite effective throughout history, as the men from Ephraim found out when they could not pronounce "Shibboleth" (Judg. 12:4–7). During the reign of Caesar Augustus, Rome was able to identify and tax the entire empire without sophisticated scanning devices (Luke 2:1–4). And there was nothing high-tech about the numbering system Hitler used to identify and catalog Jews.

IS IT VISIBLE?

A more fundamental question needs to be asked, however: Is the "mark of the beast" a visible mark? Consider that none of today's prophetic techno-sensationalists compare the mark given to the 144,000 by the "Lamb" in Revelation 14:1 with the mark given by the "beast" in 13:16. The application of the marks has to be the same. Will Jesus implant a biochip in the foreheads of the 144,000? One writer claims that the Beast's mark needs to be visible because he does not have the ability to see what people believe. On the other hand, "Jesus Christ does not need some kind of a visible mark to help Him watch over the 144,000."[17] Of course, if this is true, then Jesus doesn't need an invisible mark either.

In a book filled with symbols, it should not surprise us that in a chapter filled with symbols we should encounter a symbolic mark. Should we look for a beast that literally comes "up out of the sea, having ten horns and seven heads" (13:1)? Is there a literal land beast that has "two horns like a lamb" and speaks "as a dragon" (13:11)? Furthermore, insisting that the mark of the Beast is actually a computer chip is not in any way a literal interpretation, becau͏ not a single place in the rest of the Bible where a mar͏ ized electronic device.

IS IT SYMBOLIC?

Most Bible commentators believe the mark of the Beast is symbolic because marking the forehead and hand is used symbolically in other parts of the Bible. John D. Hanna, chairman and professor of historical theology at Dallas Theological Seminary, shows the symbolic significance of marking the forehead and hand in his analysis of Exodus 13:9:

> Like the Passover ([Ex.] 12:26–27), the Feast of Unleavened Bread had great educational value in the home (13:8–9). The feast was like a sign on their hand or forehead, that is, it was a continual reminder of God's mighty deliverance from Egypt. Some orthodox Jews today interpret that passage (and Deut. 6:8; 11:18) literally and bind passages of the Law (viz., Ex. 13:2–10; Deut. 6:4–9; 11:13–21) on their arms and foreheads in small pouches, so-called phylacteries, though this was probably not God's intention.[18]

Hebrew scholar John J. Davis writes, "Many feel that the expressions found in [Ex. 13]:9, 16 are not to be interpreted literally but refer alone to symbolic action."[19] This is made even more clear when we read the instructions given to the Israelites as they were about to depart from Egypt: "It shall serve as a sign to you on your hand, and as a reminder on your forehead, that the law of the LORD may be in your mouth; for with a powerful hand the LORD brought you out of Egypt" (Ex. 13:9). The Shema of Israel states,

> Hear, O Israel! The LORD is our God, the LORD is one! And you shall love the LORD your God with all your heart and with all your soul and with all your might. And these words, which I am commanding you today, shall be on your heart; and you shall teach them diligently to your sons and shall talk of them when you sit

in your house and when you walk by the way and when you lie down and when you rise up. *And you shall bind them as a sign on your hand and they shall be as frontals on your forehead.* (Deut. 6:4–8, emphasis added)

Elmer Towns, a contributor to LaHaye's *Prophecy Study Bible*, states that "these verses are still carried out literally by many orthodox Jews . . . The intent of this passage is that the Word of God should be hidden in a person's heart and should constantly be a source of devotion and obedience to the Lord."[20] The comments of Old Testament scholars Keil and Delitzsch are especially helpful: "The line of thought referred to merely expresses the idea, that the Israelites were not only to retain the commands of God in their hearts, and to confess them with the mouth, but to fulfill them with the hand, or in act and deed, and thus to show themselves in their whole bearing as the guardians and observers of the law."[21] Commentators who generally share LaHaye's prophetic belief system, and other more standard Bible commentators believe, after a thorough study of the Old Testament, that marking the head and hand is a symbolic act.[22]

A study of the New Testament nets similar results. New Testament theologian George Eldon Ladd points out that "it is not at all clear that John is thinking of a literal brand visible on the person of the worshippers of the beast. The seal of God placed on the forehead of the 144,000 (7:3) is surely not meant to be a visible mark; it is a symbolic way of expressing divine protection (see Isa. 44:5). The mark of the beast may be intended to be a parody on the mark of God."[23] Commenting on the symbolic nature of marking the forehead and hand, J. E. Leonard makes the following point:

These signs were not literal marks on the skin—one cannot literally wear the observance of a festival on one's body—but were spiritual, visible only to God. (The phylacteries of the Jews in a later period were based on a materialistic interpretation of this passage.) As His Old Testament people were marked on hand and head as a sign of their covenant with the Lord who brought them out of slavery and made them a nation, so are those who give allegiance to the beast marked with his name.[24]

The symbolic nature of Revelation seems to demand such an interpretation. When God gives a mark to set apart His people, the mark is not visible to the eye. For example, in Revelation 3:12 we read, "He who overcomes, I will make him a pillar in the temple of My God, and he will not go out from it anymore; and I will write upon him the name of My God, and the name of the city of My God, the new Jerusalem, which comes down out of heaven from My God, and My new name."

Robert L. Thomas, also a contributor to LaHaye's *Prophecy Study Bible*, concludes correctly that the "pillar" language of Revelation 3:12 is "clearly metaphorical"[25] as is writing God's name on "he who overcomes." "To have 'the name of My God,'" Thomas writes, "was equivalent to belonging to God, being endowed with divine power (Moffatt). This sets the overcomer in utter contrast with the assumptions of the present Jewish persecutors (Beckwith)."[26] Having the "name of the city of My God" written upon the overcomer meant the a person had the right of citizenship in the New Jerusalem. "Christ's 'new name' symbolizes the full revelation of His character promised to the overcomer at Christ's second advent."[27]

Circumcision is a mark. In fact, circumcision is still required under the New Covenant: "He is a Jew who is one inwardly; and circumcision is that which is of the heart, by the Spirit, not by the letter; and his praise is not from men, but from God:" (Rom. 2:29). True circumcision takes place "with a circumcision made without hands" (Col. 2:11). Paul wrote, "Beware of the dogs, beware of the evil workers, beware of the false circumcision; for we are the true circumcision, who worship in the Spirit of God and glory in Christ Jesus and put no confidence in the flesh" (Phil. 3:2–3). Not all marks, therefore, are outward or physical. In fact the marks that truly matter are those found only on the heart.

With all these considerations, it is my belief and the belief of many fine scholars that the mark of the Beast, like the mark of the Lamb (14:1), is symbolic. Such a conclusion should not strike anyone as unusual since LaHaye himself acknowledges that there is a great deal of symbolism in Revelation. He notes that the woman of Revelation 12:1–2 is a symbol of Israel. The note on Revelation 13:2 in his *Prophecy Study Bible* points out that "the beast" is "used symbolically," and that it refers "to a king or a kingdom." LaHaye believes that "whenever the Bible uses a 'beast' symbolically (which is quite obvious by its description—seven heads, ten horns, and a mouth speaking blasphemy), it always means *government*."[28] He concludes that those "who have not been defiled with women, for they have kept themselves chaste" (14:4), should not be interpreted literally. "I do not, however, insist on a literal interpretation of this expression because nowhere does the Bible teach that sexual intercourse in marriage is defiling."[29]

In simple terms, the mark of the Beast is identification with Rome and apostate Israel against Christ. The mark of the Lamb is identification with Christ over and against the false religions of Rome and apostate Israel.

BUYING AND SELLING

The control of economic transactions drives modern claims of a one-world government dominated by the Antichrist during the Great Tribulation, which supposedly makes a visible mark of the forehead and hand necessary. This sensationalistic but popular view is outlined by Thomas Ice and Timothy Demy, both contributors to LaHaye's *Prophecy Study Bible*, in their book *The Coming Cashless Society:*

> Using every means at his disposal, including the technology of a cashless society, the Antichrist and his demands will bring the world into its greatest-ever moral and economic turmoil. Such chaos will make the stock market crash of 1929 look like a minor economic adjustment.
>
> Revelation 13:16, 17 is the biblical point of entry for discussion of the cashless society, a one-world government, global economics, and biblical prophecy.[30]

Revelation 13:16–17 says nothing about a cashless society. Having gone out on a limb with their prediction, the authors come back to biblical reality and write, "The Bible does not specifically predict computers, the Internet, credit cards, or any of the other trimmings that facilitate the modern electronic banking system."[31] In fact, Revelation 13:16–17 is describing not the control of financial transactions but access to the temple overseen by the Jewish anti-Christian religious establishment. The key to interpreting the passage is the prohibition "to buy or to sell" (13:17) if a person living in Israel did not profess allegiance to Caesar and the temple.

Jesus told the church of Laodicea, "I advise you to buy from Me gold refined by fire, that you may become rich" (Rev. 3:18). This shows that buying gold refined by fire is symbolic and is related to worship. It is reasonable, therefore, to assume that the reference to buying and selling in Revelation 13:17 is also symbolic. Once again, the Old Testament is helpful. Buying and selling, when related to worship, are symbolic like so many other things in Revelation:

Ho! Every one who thirsts, come to the waters;
And you who have no money come, buy and eat.

Come, buy wine and milk
Without money and without cost.
Why do you spend money for what is not bread,
And your wages for what does not satisfy?
Listen carefully to Me, and eat what is good,
And delight yourself in abundance. (ISA. 55:1–2; cf. JOHN 4:13–15;
   REV. 21:6)

Temple leaders controlled buying and selling to regulate access to the temple (Matt. 21:12). "This is established in [Revelation] 3:18 (and compare 21:6). When those who refuse the mark of the Beast are not allowed to buy and sell, it means that they are expelled from the synagogue and Temple. The merchants of the land in Revelation 18 are those who worshipped at the Temple and synagogue."[32] Jesus foretold that this would happen: "They will make you outcasts from the synagogue, but an hour is coming for everyone who kills you to think that he is offering service to God" (John 16:2). Keep in mind that the "beast coming up out of the earth" is involved in these events. The land beast is most certainly associated with first-century Israel, especially the priests who controlled access to the temple, which was finished during Nero's reign in A.D. 64.

Early in the church's history the disciples went to the temple to preach the gospel (Acts 5:20–21, 24, 42; 24:12). At first, they were welcomed (Acts 2:46). Peter and John frequented the temple during "the hour of prayer" (Acts 3:1). Jewish Christians continued to use the temple, even participating in some of its rituals (Acts 21:26). After the temple officials learned that those Jews were preaching that Jesus was the Messiah—the Lamb of God who takes away the sin of the world—Paul was "dragged . . . out of the temple; and immediately the doors were shut" (21:26–30).

During Jesus' ministry, the temple officials were "selling" and worshipers were "buying" access to the temple (Matt. 21:12), turning God's house into a "robbers' den" (Matt. 21:12–13). Only the Jews who aligned themselves with the priests (i.e., had the "mark of the beast"), the sacrificial system, and the temple buildings were allowed to enter the temple for worship.

To take the "mark of the beast" meant a person denied that Jesus was the Messiah, the true temple of God, the only sufficient sacrifice. Of course, Christian Jews avoided the "mark of the beast" and showed their true allegiance to Jesus, "having His name and the name of His Father written on their foreheads" (Rev. 14:1). With these names on their foreheads, they demonstrated public professions of faith and allegiance to Jesus. Those who carried the mark of the beast professed that they had chosen Caesar over Christ (John 19:15). When commanded not to speak to "any man in this *name*," Peter and John responded, "Whether it is right in the sight of God to give heed to you rather than to God, you be the judge; for we cannot stop speaking what we have seen and heard" (Acts 4:17–20). The proclamation that "Jesus is Lord" (1 Cor. 12:3) and "that there is another king, Jesus" (Acts 17:7) was a religious and political affront to those in power throughout the Roman Empire. Such proclamations were acts "contrary to Caesar" (17:7) and "against this holy place [i.e., the temple] and the Law" (6:13).

All of these passages fit together nicely since true redemption comes, not from Rome or earthly Jerusalem, but from where "the Lamb was standing," that is, Mount Zion. The writer of Hebrews describes Mt. Zion's location: "You have come to Mount Zion and to the city of the living God, the heavenly Jerusalem, and to myriads of angels" (Heb. 12:22). Revelation 13 and 14 contrast two ways of salvation: access to the temple through the mark of the Beast or through Jesus and the mark of the Lamb. Those who were circumcised in only their flesh followed the Beast, while those circumcised in the heart followed the Lamb.

While those opposed to Christ governed access to the earthly temple over which the two beasts conspired to resist the things of Christ and His church, John pointed believers to "the heavenly Jerusalem." In order to have access to the "Jerusalem above" (Gal. 4:26), a person must have the mark of the Lamb, which can be read only by God, who "sealed us and gave us the Spirit in our hearts as a pledge" (2 Cor. 1:22). Contrast this with earthly Jerusalem in the first century, which Paul describes as "present Jerusalem," which "is in slavery with her children" (Gal. 4:25). Those who continued to look to "present Jerusalem" for salvation were given the mark of a slave, "the mark of the beast."

THE BEAST LIVES AGAIN!

Revelation 13:3 states that one of the heads of the seven-headed "beast coming up out of the sea" suffered a fatal wound that was healed. LaHaye's *Prophecy Study Bible* offers the following commentary on this passage: "In the middle of the Tribulation, the Antichrist will be killed, lie in state briefly, and then actually be indwelt personally by Satan, who was cast out of heaven in the previous chapter." Not a single word of this is found in Revelation 13:3. John saw one of the beast's seven heads "as if it had been slain, and his fatal wound was healed." Nothing is said about an assassination or lying in state.

Without doubt, the sea beast is first-century Rome. The book of Daniel, on which Revelation 13 is based and derives its symbolic imagery, describes the fourth beast as "dreadful and terrifying and extremely strong; and it had large iron teeth. It devoured and crushed, and trampled down the remainder with its feet; and it was different from all the beasts that were before it, and it had ten horns" (Dan. 7:7). The four great beasts from Daniel came up from the sea (7:3): they were Babylon, Medo-Persia, Greece, and Rome.

The "ten horns" could represent the ten successive Roman emperors (kings) that made up the beastly empire[33] with the seven heads representing the Herodian dynasty that dominated the political life of Judea under the protection and favor of Rome.[34] We learn that one of the heads of the Beast appeared as if it had been slain, and the fatal wound was healed (Rev. 13:3). A wound to the head is a recurring theme in the Bible, reserved for God's enemies (Gen. 3:15; Judg. 4:21; 9:53; 1 Sam. 17:46–51; Ps. 74:13; Hab. 3:8–14; Matt. 27:33; Rom. 16:20). If the seven heads represent the seven Herods, then it's possible that the fatal wound refers to the death of Herod Agrippa I (Acts 12:20–23) and the apparent end of the Herodian domination of Israel. "For twenty years, ever since the execution of James son of Zebedee by Agrippa, and the attempted killing of Peter, the Church lived unmolested."[35] Soon after, however, Agrippa's son, Agrippa II, assumed the reins of power and did "his utmost to keep in with the Romans."[36] In addition to getting another Herod, Judea had to contend with Bernice, the sister of Herod Agrippa II (Acts 25:13, 23; 26:30). It was reported that she was involved in an incestuous relationship with her brother. Drusilla, who was Agrippa's sister, was married to Felix, the governor (Acts 24:24).

This interpretation is plausible, but others have suggested a different first-century fulfillment that still includes all the major New Testament characters who opposed the church. Since horns are typically metaphors for power (Dan. 7:7–8) and represent nations (8:20), "the number of seven heads and ten horns emphasizes the completeness of oppressive power"[37] of first-century Rome. Later in Revelation, we are told that "the seven heads are seven mountains on which the woman sits, and they are seven kings; five have fallen, one is, the other has not yet come; and when he comes, he must remain a little while" (Rev. 17:9–10).

The burning of Rome by Nero in A.D. 64 and his suicide at the age of thirty-one in A.D. 68 left Rome vulnerable and seemingly on the verge of collapse and open to attack from foreign forces. Mighty Rome looked "as if it had been slain" (13:3). The sixth king of Revelation 17:10 was alive when Revelation was written. John wrote that the sixth king "is." Nero was the sixth king in the line of Caesars. Galba followed Nero, but he reigned only a short time, approximately seven months, from June A.D. 68 to January A.D. 69. If Revelation is describing a period of prophetic history that is still in our future, then Revelation 17:10 makes no sense; the sixth king had to be alive when the book was written, because we are told that he was reigning at the time John received the prophecy.

Tacitus described the condition of the empire following Nero's death as anything but stable: "The period upon which I embark is one full of incident, marked by bitter fighting, rent by treason, and even in peace sinister. Four emperors perished violently. There were three civil wars, still more campaigns fought against the foreigner, and often conflicts which combined elements of both."[38]

Flavius Josephus noted that the Roman government at the time was "in a great internal disorder, by the continual changes of its rulers . . . [E]very part of the habitable earth under them was in an unsettled and tottering condition." The Germans and Gauls observed this weakness as an opportunity "to make a sedition, when the state of the Romans was so ill."[39] As if by a miracle, Rome came back to life. Rome's "fatal wound was healed. And the whole land was amazed and followed after the beast" (Rev. 13:3).

GIVING BREATH TO THE IMAGE

The second beast, the one that comes up out of the land, forces those who dwell in Israel "to worship the first beast" (Rev. 13:12). There is little doubt that the land beast is the religious leadership in first-century Israel. As has been pointed out earlier, the religious leadership in Israel worked with Rome on at least one project—the death of Jesus and the persecution of Jewish believers in Christ. Fearing Rome, "the chief priests and the Pharisees convened a council" (John 11:47–48) to determine how to appease their oppressors. The priests' hatred of Jesus was so great that they declared, in worshipful fashion, "We have no king but Caesar" (John 19:15). They brought false testimony to the courts and charged Jesus with political crimes: "And they began to accuse Him, saying, 'We found this man misleading our nation and forbidding to pay taxes to Caesar, and saying that He Himself is Christ, a King'" (Luke 23:2). Even when Pilate wanted to release Jesus, finding no fault in Him, "the Jews cried out, saying, 'If you release this Man, you are no friend of Caesar; everyone who makes himself out to be a king opposes Caesar'" (John 19:12).

What about the description of the land beast giving "breath to the image of the beast" (Rev. 13:15)? Milton Terry, author of *Biblical Hermeneutics*, the most widely used textbook on biblical interpretation, offers the following comments on this passage in his book *Biblical Apocalyptics*: "*To give breath to the image of the beast*—Or, *to give a spirit to the image*; that is, make it appear to be alive. It was the work of the local governors to make the Roman authority a very living thing to all its subjects, and the vigorous exercise of such power might in symbolic description be spoken of as a giving of life to the image of imperial sovereignty."[40]

The Bible clearly teaches that man-made images cannot come to life, even by the power of Satan: "Idols of gold and of silver and of brass and of stone and of wood . . . can neither see nor hear nor walk" (Rev. 9:20). The psalmist writes that idols "have mouths, but they cannot speak . . . They cannot make a sound with their throat" (Ps. 115:5, 7; cf. Isa. 46:7; Jer. 10:5). If John is describing a statue, he probably has an image of the emperor in mind. Images of the Roman emperor were common in Israel. The coin that the Pharisees and Herodians brought to Jesus carried Caesar's "image" (Matt. 22:20 KJV). False signs were common in the first century. Philip encountered Simon, "who formerly was practicing magic in the city, and astonishing the people of Samaria, claiming to be someone great" (Acts 8:9). Those who saw him perform believed that he was "the Great Power of God" (8:10) because "he had for a long time astonished them with his magic arts" (8:11). Paul faced "a certain magician, a Jewish false prophet whose name was Bar-Jesus" (13:6). Then there was the demon-possessed slave girl who was being used by her masters to make money for them by "fortune-telling" (16:16). Her skill was a form of ventriloquism, giving the impression to the superstitious that the gods spoke through her. George Eldon Ladd comments that the "power to make statues speak was well known in the ancient world. There grew up a cycle of legend around the person Simon Magus (Acts 8:9ff.), and early Christian literature relates stories of how he [seemingly] brought statues to life."[41] In fact, the literature of that era is abundant with stories of "speaking statues" and other "miracles":

> The ancient pagan priests had for centuries practiced deceiving superstitious worshipers into believing images made of stone, metal and wood could talk. Many of them used drugs or self-hypnosis to induce a trance in which they claimed to be speaking oracles from the gods or images. One such was the "oracle at Delphi," a Greek temple inhabited by priestesses and from which Alexander the Great demanded a revelation. Ventriloquism was a highly skilled and widely practiced art in heathen idolatry. Eurycles of Athens was the most celebrated of Greek ventriloquists. They were called *engastrimanteis*, or "belly prophets" because the ancients believed the voices came from the bellies of the oracles. Priests of ancient pagan religions were masters of this

art and to ventriloquism may be ascribed the alleged miracles of the "speaking statues" of the Egyptians, Greeks and Romans . . . Modern archaeologists have found devices used for secretly piping the human voice beneath altars bearing the statues of pagan gods.[42]

A study of the history of the first century abounds with accounts of events similar to those described in Revelation 13. "The command to perform idolatry alludes partly to the pressure placed on the populace and the churches in Asia Minor to give homage to the image of Caesar as a divine being. By the end of the first century A.D. all the cities addressed in the Apocalypse's letters had temples dedicated to the deity of Caesar, the first established in 29 B.C."[43]

LaHaye writes that "the False prophet will cause an image of the Antichrist to be built and will have power to 'give breath to the image of the first beast' (Rev. 13:14-15)."[44] It's puzzling to understand how in today's high-tech world there would be many people who would be impressed by a statue that speaks. Certainly some people would be fooled, but not enough to fulfill the worldwide impact that LaHaye imagines is to take place. Images of such things are daily occurrences in movies and entertainment attractions. Almost anyone who would see a statue speak, most likely via television, would assume that it was a trick, a sophisticated example of servomotorized animatronics or computer graphics. Caesar's Palace in Las Vegas, Nevada, has a likeness of Caesar that moves and speaks. As far as I know, no one believes it's real.

CONCLUSION

By taking the time texts seriously, assessing the historical context of the period, and relying on how the Bible applies its well-known

symbols to make theological points, we can come to no other conclusion than that Jesus was revealing to John prophetic events that
were "about to come upon the whole world" (Rev. 3:10) in his day.
There is no need for either sophisticated technology or reading into
the Bible to see things that just aren't there. This creates a future fulfillment of events that the Bible clearly says are to happen "shortly"
(1:1, 3).

The fiction of *Left Behind* allows LaHaye and Jenkins to speculate
well beyond the text of Scripture without being held accountable for
their speculation. Supposedly, nothing of what they maintain will
happen takes place until after every Bible-believing Christian is taken
off the earth. How can anyone ever claim that LaHaye is wrong when
all he has to say in defense is, "All these things are in the future that
none of us will ever see?" The approach that I have taken is open to
scrutiny since someone can always claim that there is no record of
these events having taken place. Of course, as I have pointed out,
there is much in the historical record that supports a first-century fulfillment. All the elements are present. Even so, where is the record of
Jesus being born of a virgin? Where is an extra-biblical account of
Jesus being raised from the dead? Where outside the Bible do we read
of Judas hanging himself, Paul's conversion, Herod being eaten by
worms, or Paul's shipwreck? We don't question these historical facts.
Therefore, why should we question the Bible when it tells us that the
events described in Revelation were to take place while those who
received the book were still alive?[45]

10

THE GREAT APOSTASY

The one-world religion was headed by the new Pope Peter, formerly Peter Mathews of the United States. He had ushered in what he called "a new era of tolerance and unity" among the major religions. The biggest enemy of Enigma Babylon, which had taken over the Vatican as its headquarters, were the millions of people who believed that Jesus was the only way to God.

To say arbitrarily, Pontifex Maximus Peter wrote in an official Enigma Babylon declaration, *that the Jewish and Protestant Bible, containing only the Old and New Testaments, is the final authority for faith and practice, represents the height of intolerance and disunity. It flies in the face of all we have accomplished, and adherents to that false doctrine are hereby considered heretics.*[1]

"You're on the air with Gary DeMar. Do you have a question for Gary?"

"It's not so much a question but an observation. It seems to me that we are moving toward a one-world religion, something that the Bible predicts."

"Can you tell me where the Bible predicts this one-world apostate religion?"

"Paul writes to the Christians at Thessalonica that the 'day of the Lord' will not come 'unless the apostasy comes first, and the man of lawlessness is revealed.' The apostasy hasn't come yet."

"Yes, it has. The New Testament is filled with examples of apostasy—everything from Paul's warning about 'savage wolves' who will arise from within the church 'speaking perverse things to draw away the disciples after them' to John's antichrists who 'have arisen.' In fact, John offers the presence of these antichrists as evidence 'that it is the last hour.' All the examples of heresy, apostasy, and just plain false doctrine that we read of in the New Testament were going on in the first century."

"But what about the apostasy that's going on around us today?"

"I could point to specific periods in every century and outline trends toward apostasy. Consider that before Martin Luther's bold challenge to the Roman Catholic Church in 1517, the church was deep in apostasy. Salvation by grace through faith and *sola scriptura* were considered doctrinal heresies by the church prior to Luther."

"I've always been taught to look for an end-time apostasy. I just assumed that when the New Testament discussed apostasy, it was predicting something in the distant future. Do you have time to present your case for a first-century apostasy?"

"Let's take a commercial break. After we come back, we'll give Gary some time to develop his position . . . Stay tuned."

The *Left Behind* series takes full advantage of a supposed end-time apostasy to create a scenario that allows the Antichrist to take political and religious control of the world. Nicolae Carpathia, through the agency of *Pontifex Maximus* Peter Mathews, creates an all-inclusive new world religion. At first, religious tolerance is the name of the game. Because of centuries of religious battles, this new world religion will be considered a good thing. Divisions among the various denominations and competing world religions will be eliminated as people embrace "an apostate one-world religion."[2] Factions and religious infighting will be over as Nicolae Carpathia unites the world under his benevolent dictatorship. Although this makes for interesting fiction, we must once again ask if the Bible teaches an end-time apostasy as outlined by LaHaye and Jenkins in *Left Behind*.

LaHaye dismisses an apostasy that the Bible says was going on as the New Testament writers penned their letters. No one doubts that the Bible describes an active falling away from the faith, an apostasy from the truth. As evidence that he and his readers were living near the end of the old covenant, a covenant that was "becoming obsolete and growing old" and "ready to disappear" (Heb. 8:13), John wrote, "Children, it is the last hour; and just as you heard that antichrist is coming, even now many antichrists have arisen; from this we know that it is the last hour" (1 John 2:18). This verse describes the *time* of the apostasy, an apostasy that had arisen in John's day.

THE BIBLE AND THE GREAT APOSTASY

The Greek word *apostasia* appears in only two places in the New Testament (Acts 21:21; 2 Thess. 2:3) and generally has two meanings in biblical literature: political revolt and religious defection. The Septuagint, the Greek translation of the Hebrew Scriptures, uses *apostasia* to describe both a political revolt (Ezra 4:12, 15, 19; Neh. 2:19; 6:6) and a religious defection (Josh. 22:22; 2 Chron. 29:19; 33:19; Jer. 2:19). H. Wayne House attempts to prove that *apostasia* means a "departure from earth," that is, a pretribulational Rapture.[3] House has to admit, however, that "the case is not conclusive."[4]

The Jewish historian Josephus uses the word *apostasia* to charac-terize the Jewish revolt against the Roman government.[5] If Paul, in 2 Thessalonians 2:3, was using *apostasia* to describe a political revolt, then this fits the historical context of the Jewish rebellion against Roman authority, known in history as the Jewish War. With this usage in mind, we could interpret the passage this way: "Let no one in any way deceive you, for the judgment on Jerusalem will not come until the Jews first rebel against the Romans and the man of lawless-ness is revealed."

The New Testament also uses *apostasia* to describe a religious rebellion. For example, Jews who questioned the sufficiency of Jesus' death to pay the penalty for sin believed that forsaking the customs of Moses—especially circumcision—was "apostasy" (Acts 21:21), a falling away, a departure from the ordinances of the old covenant. Unfortunately most Bible translations do not render the Greek word *apostasia* in Acts 21:21 as "apostasy." Here is a literal rendering of Acts 21:21: "Now the [believing Jews] have heard reports about you, how you teach all the Jews who live among the Gentiles *to commit apostasy against Moses*, telling them to stop circumcising their chil-dren and not to follow the customs [of Moses]."

For the Judaizers, apostasy was a rejection of the customs of Moses, which they believed were a condition for salvation even if one embraced Jesus as the Messiah. That controversy was settled at the first church council in Jerusalem (Acts 15:1–35). For Paul, apostasy was following the customs of Moses as a condition for salvation. Of course, Paul's def-inition of apostasy is the correct one. Paul told Timothy that "in later times some will fall away [*apostasontai*] from the faith" (1 Tim. 4:1). The apostates would reject the counsel of the apostles and claim that Gentiles who embraced Jesus as the Messiah must be circumcised and "observe the Law of Moses" (Acts 15:5). These "doctrines of demons"—apostasies—had already shown themselves in the first-century church

(Col. 2:16, 23; cf. 1 Tim. 4:3). F. F. Bruce writes that the first-century Christians "must withstand the temptation to return to Judaism; that was the sin of apostasy which by its very nature was irremediable, for (as they had already acknowledged) there was no other name in the world but the name of Jesus in which salvation could be found. Not only was such apostasy sin; it was folly."[6]

A FIRST-CENTURY APOSTASY

Jesus warned about an approaching apostasy that would escalate, and His disciples would have to confront it (Matt. 7:15, 22; 24:5, 10–12, 24). Paul cautioned the church at Ephesus that after his departure, "savage wolves will come in among you, not sparing the flock; and from among your own selves men will arise, speaking perverse things, to draw away the disciples after them" (Acts 20:29–30). This adds another dimension to the apostasy—Jews who were first attracted to the gospel but, after learning that it did not maintain old covenant ceremonies, rejected it (Heb. 6:4–8). Paul warned the Ephesians that this departure from the faith would affect them because the apostates would come "from among your own selves."

Paul spoke to the Corinthian church about "false apostles, deceitful workers" who disguise themselves "as apostles of Christ" (2 Cor. 11:13). He described them as "servants" of "Satan" (11:14–15). Those in Galatia were disturbed by those who "want to distort the gospel of Christ" and preach a gospel "contrary" to what they had received (Gal. 1:7–8). Instead of looking to the distant future for this apostasy to show itself, Paul wrote, "I am amazed that *you are so quickly* deserting Him who called you by the grace of Christ, for a different gospel" (1:6, emphasis added). The entire church was disturbed by "false brethren" who were desirous to bring Christians "into bondage" to the law (2:4). A "different gospel" (1:6) is an apostate gospel.

To the church at Rome, Paul urged the members to keep an eye "on those who cause dissensions and hindrances contrary to the teaching" that they had learned. Paul's admonition was to "turn away from them." Through their "smooth and flattering speech they deceive the hearts of the unsuspecting" (Rom. 16:17–18). Paul became more specific when he told the Philippians to "beware of the dogs, beware of the evil workers, beware of the false circumcision" (Phil. 3:2). They were "enemies of the cross of Christ, whose end is destruction" (Phil. 3:18–19).

Paul's personal counsel to Timothy was to "instruct certain men not to teach strange doctrines, nor to pay attention to myths and endless genealogies, which give rise to mere speculation rather than furthering the administration of God which is by faith" (1 Tim. 1:3–4). Again, Paul had unbelieving Jews in mind since they were those who wanted "to be teachers of the Law" (1:7). Even by Timothy's day, some had "suffered shipwreck in regard to their faith" (1:19). Of course, apostasy had been predicted by the Holy Spirit, who explicitly said "that in later times some will fall away from the faith, paying attention to deceitful spirits and doctrines of demons" (4:1). Deceit and unsound doctrine were present in Timothy's day: "O Timothy, guard what has been entrusted to you, avoiding worldly and empty chatter and the opposing arguments of what is falsely called 'knowledge'—which some have professed and thus gone astray from the faith" (6:20–21).

Further instructions to Timothy were to "preach the word; be ready in season and out of season; reprove, rebuke, exhort, with great patience and instruction. For the time will come when they will not endure sound doctrine; but wanting to have their ears tickled, they will accumulate for themselves teachers in accordance to their own desires; and will turn away their ears from the truth, and will turn aside to myths" (2 Tim. 4:2–4). Who were those people who distorted the faith?

There are many rebellious men, empty talkers and deceivers, *especially those of the circumcision,* who must be silenced because they are upsetting whole families, teaching things they should not teach . . . This testimony is true. For this cause reprove them severely that they may be sound in the faith, *not paying attention to Jewish myths and commandments of men who turn away from the truth* . . . They profess to know God, but by their deeds they deny Him, being detestable and disobedient, and worthless for any good deed. (Titus 1:10–11, 13–14, 16, emphasis added)

Peter described a similar apostasy: "False prophets also arose among the people, just as there will also be false teachers among you, who will secretly introduce destructive heresies, even denying the Master who bought them, bringing swift destruction upon themselves" (2 Peter 2:1). Peter was not looking down the corridors of the distant future. He was warning those who had "received a faith of the same kind as ours, by the righteousness of our God and Savior, Jesus Christ" (2 Peter 1:1).

John's epistles describe a contemporary apostasy, those who denied that Jesus had come in the flesh (1 John 2:22). False prophets were prevalent in John's day (1 John 4:1). He wrote, "For many deceivers have gone out into the world, those who do not acknowledge Jesus Christ as coming in the flesh. This is the deceiver and the antichrist" (2 John 7). John made it clear that for the first-century church, it was the "last hour" (1 John 2:18). He offered the following evidence to support his claim: "They went out from us, but they were not really of us; for if they had been of us, they would have remained with us; but they went out, in order that it might be shown that they all are not of us" (1 John 2:19).

Jude warned the "beloved" to "contend earnestly for the faith . . . For certain persons have crept in unnoticed, those who were long beforehand marked out for this condemnation, ungodly persons who turn the grace of our God into licentiousness and deny our only

Master and Lord, Jesus Christ" (vv. 3–4). Jude then recounted several judgment periods in Israel's history (vv. 5–17). The "certain persons" were those who "were spoken beforehand by the apostles of our Lord Jesus Christ" (v. 17). Their appearance in Jude's day was evidence that it was "the last time" (v. 18). The "mockers" who "crept in unnoticed" were alive in Jude's day. They would meet the same fate as those mockers described in verses 5–17. When would that take place? The judgment had to be leveled against them personally since Jude compared their fate to that of old covenant "mockers" (vv. 5–17). The judgment had to be near.

> [I]n this interpretation, the apostasy is obviously the great apostasy of the Jews, gradually filling up all these years and hastening to its completion in their destruction. That the Apostle certainly had this rapidly completing apostasy in his mind in the severe arraignment that he makes of the Jews in I Thess. ii. 14–16, which reached its climax in the declaration that they were continually filling up more and more full the measure of their sins, until already the measure of God's wrath was prematurely . . . filled up against them and was hanging over them like some laden thunder-cloud ready to burst and overwhelm them,—adds an additional reason for supposing his reference to be to this apostasy—above all others, "the" apostasy—in this passage.[7]

The book of Revelation begins with several warnings to first-century churches to be faithful to the gospel and not to apostatize. To the church at Ephesus, Jesus said, "I know your deeds and your toil and perseverance, and that you cannot endure evil men, and you put to the test those who call themselves apostles, and they are not, and you found them to be false" (Rev. 2:2). From the message to the church of Smyrna we know about "the blasphemy by those who say they are

Jews and are not, but are a synagogue of Satan" (2:9). We know the time because Jesus told the church, "Behold, the devil *is about to cast some of you into prison*, . . . and you will have tribulation ten days" (2:10, emphasis added). The church at Pergamum had members "who hold to the teaching of Balaam, who kept teaching Balak to put a stumbling block before the sons of Israel, to eat things sacrificed to idols, and to commit acts of immorality" (2:14).

The church at Thyatira tolerated "the woman Jezebel, who calls herself a prophetess" (Rev. 2:20). She was said to have led Jesus' "bond-servants astray, so that they commit acts of immorality and eat things sacrificed to idols" (2:20). The church at Philadelphia also had a "synagogue of Satan, who say that they are Jews, and are not, but lie" (3:9).

If we take into account the way the Jews aligned themselves with Rome to crucify Jesus (John 19:12–15) and their relentless persecution of the early church (Acts 13:50; 14:1–7), there does not seem to be a more prominent example of apostasy anywhere else in the annals of history. "The 'falling away' then refers to that of Jews after the ascension of Christ, rather than that of the Church in the end of this age."[8]

THE DAY OF THE LORD

Many students of Bible prophecy immediately project the great apostasy into the distant future after observing that Paul used "the day of the Lord" in describing the timing of the "apostasy" (2 Thess. 2:2–3). The Bible describes numerous "days of the Lord"; the "day of the Lord" does not always refer to what many prophecy writers consider an apocalyptic end-time event. Isaiah wrote, "Wail, for the day of the LORD is near!" (Isa. 13:6). He continued,

> *Behold, the day of the LORD is coming,*
> *Cruel, with fury and burning anger,*

> *To make the land a desolation;*
> *And He will exterminate its sinners from it.* (13:9)

That was "the oracle concerning Babylon," the Babylon of the Old Testament, the Babylon that suffered divine retribution (13:1). For Babylon, the "day of the LORD" is past.

The "day of the LORD" was to draw "near on all the nations" (Obad. 15)—all the nations then in existence. Zephaniah stated that "the day of the LORD is near" (Zeph. 1:7) and restated it in verse 14: "Near is the great day of the LORD, near and coming very quickly." For those of us who read this, this particular "day of the LORD" is past. The "day of the LORD" came to Israel in Babylon's sacking of Jerusalem in 586 B.C.

John Walvoord, a favorite prophecy writer of LaHaye, makes a valuable comment about the multifaceted nature and application of the "day of the Lord": "The 'Day of the Lord' is an expression frequently used in both the Old and New Testaments to describe any period of time during which God exercises direct judgment on human sin. The Old Testament records a number of times when Israel endured a day of the Lord, lasting a few days or, in some cases, several years."[9]

The "day of the Lord" was a day of God's judgment and vengeance. As a result, there could be many such days. Luke described the destruction of Jerusalem in A.D. 70 as "days of vengeance" (Luke 21:22), the fulfillment of Isaiah 61:2: "the day of vengeance of our God" (also see Isa. 63:4).

The Thessalonians thought that the day of the Lord had come. Paul exhorted his readers: do not be "quickly shaken from your composure or be disturbed either by a spirit or a message or a letter as if from us, *to the effect that the day of the Lord has come*" (2 Thess. 2:2, emphasis added). Paul was not correcting a belief of the Thessalonians that the day of the Lord was "near" or "at hand," as some translations have it (e.g., KJV and ASV). The Bible states without reservation that the day of the Lord was near (e.g., Rom. 13:12; James 5:8; Rev. 1:1, 3). "All the Apostles believed that the day was near (1 Cor. xv. 51; James v. 8, 9; 1 Pet. iv. 7; 1 John ii. 18; Rev. xxii. 20), and their watchword was 'Maranatha,' 'the Lord is *near*.'"[10]

Since the Christians at Thessalonica thought that the day of the Lord was in the past, there is no way that they were thinking about either a Rapture or the Second Coming. LaHaye is incorrect when he identifies 2 Thessalonians 2 with the pretribulational Rapture ("our gathering together to Him") since *not one Christian at Thessalonica had been raptured!* Remember, the Thessalonians believed that the day of the Lord *had come.* They believed that it was a *past* event (2:2). If no one had been raptured, and Jesus had not returned to set up His earthly kingdom, then why would they have thought that the day of the Lord had come?

Furthermore, the passage cannot be describing the Second Coming since the Thessalonians believed they had received "a message or a letter" that had been sent to them by Paul, informing them, to repeat the point, that "the day of the Lord *has come*" (2:2). If they had thought that either the Rapture or the Second Coming had taken place—as per Paul's supposed message or letter—would they not have asked themselves why Paul had not been raptured? How could Paul have written a letter after the Rapture or after the Second Coming if he was no longer on the earth?[11] It's obvious, therefore, that Paul had some other series of events in mind.

A PAST DAY OF THE LORD

In the case of 2 Thessalonians 2:2, the "day of the Lord" that the Thessalonians thought had already come was God's judgment upon the old covenant order localized in Jerusalem that occurred in A.D. 70 (John 4:21; Gal. 4:25). John Lightfoot wrote that "the Scripture and the apostle had spoken of 'the day of the Lord's coming'; when he should come to take vengeance of the Jewish nation, for their wickedness and unbelief."[12] Paul described this coming judgment in his first letter to the Thessalonians. He reminded them that the apostate Jews "killed the Lord Jesus and the prophets . . . They are not pleasing to God, but hostile to all men, hindering us from speaking to the Gentiles that they might be saved; with the result that they always fill up the measure of their sins. But wrath has come upon them to the utmost" (1 Thess. 2:15–16; cf. Matt. 23:31–32, 35–36; John 3:36).

The Jewish converts and "God-fearing Greeks" of Thessalonica (Acts 17:1–4) would have immediately picked up the old covenant allusions and their application to the then present Jewish apostasy. "The apostasy here described is plainly not of a civil, but of a religious nature; not a revolt from the government, but a defection from the true religion and worship, 'a departing from the faith,' (1 Tim. iv. 1,) 'a departing from the living God,' (Heb. iii. 12) as the word is used by the apostle in other places."[13]

THE LAST DAYS

When the Bible is not interpreted in terms of its historical context, prophecies can be made to fit almost any period of history. This is especially true when the phrase the "last days" is used. LaHaye insists that Paul's "apostasy" is an end-time event that takes place in the "last days." But when are the "last days"? At least three views have been offered: (1) a concentrated period of time just prior to Jesus' second coming, making the time yet future; (2) the period of time between

Jesus' first coming and second coming, what is typically and erro-neously called the church age; and (3) the forty-year period from a point in time just prior to Jesus' death, resurrection, and ascension to the destruction of Jerusalem in A.D. 70, what the Bible describes as a generation (forty years).

Which is the biblical view? The first view finds little support in Scripture since the writer to the Hebrews said, "God, after He spoke long ago to the fathers in the prophets in many portions and in many ways, *in these last days* has spoken to us in His Son, whom He appointed heir of all things, through whom also He made the world" (Heb. 1:1–2, emphasis added). It's obvious from this passage and others like it that the last days were operating in the first century. He was writing in the last days. Peter declared that the fulfillment of Joel's prophecy was in his day (Acts 2:17). James warned the corrupt rich of his day that they were storing up their treasure "in the last days" (James 5:3), that is, in the present day. Timothy was given instructions on how to live "in the last days" (2 Tim. 3:1).

We are left with views 2 and 3. While position 2 has its adherents, it seems extreme and very nonliteral to extend the last *days* over two thousand *years*. The best explanation of the "last days" fits the time period between Jesus' earthly ministry and the end of the old covenant order leading up to the destruction of Jerusalem in A.D. 70. The apostle Paul told the Corinthians that the *ends* of the ages had come upon them: "Now these things happened to [Israel] as an example, and they were written for our instruction, upon whom the ends of the ages have come" (1 Cor. 10:11). The writer to the Hebrews took a similar approach: "Otherwise, [Jesus] would have needed to suffer often since the foundation of the world; but now once at the con-summation of the ages He has been manifested to put away sin by the sacrifice of Himself" (Heb. 9:26).

"THE END OF ALL THINGS"

Related to the "day of the Lord" language of 2 Thessalonians 2:2, the Bible uses the phrase "the end of all things." John Brown, in his exceptional three-volume commentary on Peter's first epistle, gives the following interpretation of "the end of all things is at hand" (1 Peter 4:7):

> After some deliberation, I have been led to adopt the opinion of those who hold that "the end of all things" here is the entire and final end of the Jewish economy in the destruction of the temple and city of Jerusalem, and the dispersion of the holy people. That was at hand; for this epistle seems to have been written a very short while before these events took place, not improbably after the commencement of "the wars and rumours of war" of which our Lord spake. This view will not appear strange to any one who has carefully weighed the terms in which our Lord had predicted these events, and the close connection which the fulfillment of these predictions had with the interests and duties of Christians, whether in Judea or in Gentile countries.
>
> It is quite plain, that in our Lord's predictions, the expressions "the end," and probably "the end of the world," are used in reference to the entire dissolution of the Jewish economy [Matt xxiv. 3, 6, 14, 34; Mark xiii. 30; Luke xxi. 32].[14]

The first-century church was expecting "the end." Where did they get the idea that the "end of all things was at hand" and that they were living in the "last days"? They got it from the letters they had received from Holy Spirit–inspired prophets who brought the Word of God to them. There is nothing unusual in the language. There are ends to all sorts of things. Every time we watch a movie, the words "The End" appear. No one understands this as being the end of everything, the end of all movies, or even the end of the day, but only the end of what was just viewed. A similar concept is used of "the end" in the Bible. It happened that the old covenant was coming to an end in the first century. No longer would God's people be bound by the requirements of the law that demanded daily sacrifice, the bloody rite of circumcision, earthly and sinful priests interceding for them. It was also the end of a temple that had sunk its foundation deep in the land of Israel. Now the temple of God—Jesus Himself—would be with His people wherever two or three were gathered (Matt. 18:20).

CONCLUSION

Placing the apostasy mentioned by Paul in 2 Thessalonians 2:3 in the first century does not mean that the church is free from those who depart from the faith today. LaHaye is correct in identifying John Shelby Spong, an Episcopal bishop, as an apostate.[15] But even LaHaye admits that Spong's views are not new. LaHaye cites a review of Spong's *Why Christianity Must Change or Die,* which justifies his claim: "In fact, his views seem very much in keeping with the religious humanist variety of Unitarianism."[16] The Unitarian movement can be traced back to the Arian heresy of the fourth century. The Arians, Unitarians like Servetus in the sixteenth century, organized Unitarians in the eighteenth century, prominent individuals who denied the deity of Christ (e.g., Thomas Jefferson), and cultists in our own day (e.g., Jehovah's Witnesses and Mormons) share the same apostate beliefs. There will always be apostasy in the world, just as there will always be tribulation in the world, but as Jesus said, "I have overcome the world" (John 16:33). The specific apostasy described in the Bible, however, was ongoing in the first century and led up to the destruction of Jerusalem in A.D. 70.

11

WHAT DIFFERENCE DOES IT MAKE?

If you've gotten this far in *End Times Fiction*, or you just wanted to find out where I'm coming from before you started reading, you know or will know that Tim LaHaye and I disagree on lots of things when it comes to Bible prophecy. As anyone who is familiar with the Bible and church history understands, this is not uncommon in Christian circles. It wasn't unusual for the apostles in the early church to disagree among themselves (Gal. 2:11). In Acts 15 we read about a council that was called to clear up some doctrinal issues. God spoke to Peter to show him that the Gospel was not just for the Jews (Acts 10:9–23). Paul declares that "there must also be factions among you, in order that those who are approved may have become evident among you" (1 Cor. 11:19). Disagreements over doctrinal issues, if handled in the proper Christian spirit, should make us better students of the Bible. If *End Times Fiction* does this, then the time I've spent on this project has been worthwhile. "Let each man be fully convinced in his own mind" (Rom. 14:5).

CAN'T WE JUST GET ALONG?

Does a debate over Bible prophecy really matter? Can't we just agree to disagree? On some points, yes. But there is more to this issue than a simple difference of opinion. LaHaye has made it clear that the literal interpretation of the Bible, as he understands it, is fundamental to a study of Bible prophecy. A Christian who does not interpret the Bible literally, as he defines it, cannot understand the Bible. With this exclusionary judgment, LaHaye has drawn a doctrinal line in the sand.

At one level, it was difficult writing this book because there are millions of sincere Christians who believe that the interpretive system of *Left Behind* is the only one that is consistent with the Bible's own interpretive principles. Readers of LaHaye's books have been told that a person who does not interpret the Bible literally "must disregard the plain teaching of the Word of God by spiritualizing and allegorizing prophetic portions well beyond their literal meaning."[1] But does LaHaye practice what he preaches? As I've shown throughout *End Times Fiction*, he does not.

REDEFINING LITERALISM

Having made the claim that his method is based on literalism, LaHaye spends considerable time redefining what he means by literalism. He does this so he can account for the many symbols in Revelation and other parts of the Bible that he doesn't interpret in terms of his literalism definition (see Chapter 1). Surprisingly, LaHaye claims that the following are symbols found in Revelation:

These include terms such as "the Word of God" (1:2, 9ff.), "Son of man" (1:13; 14:14), "marriage supper" (19:9), "the Bride" (21:9;

22:17), "first resurrection" (20:5–6), and "second death" (2:11; 20:6, 14; 21:8).[2]

Throughout LaHaye's books on prophecy, especially his commentary on Revelation, we continually read why one thing after another is not to be interpreted literally (e.g., Rev. 12:1–2; 14:4). For example, while LaHaye states that "the word 'beast' is used thirty-four times in Revelation and many other times in Scripture," the word "is symbolic of either a king or kingdom (see Dan. 7–8)."[3] So then, these are not real beasts (animals). Why can't they be real flesh-and-blood beasts? As LaHaye states, "Is anything too hard for God?"[4] He insists that God will make a chain strong enough to hold Satan (Rev. 20:1). If so many things in Revelation are symbolic, isn't it possible that the key and chain used to bind Satan are also symbolic? Are there physical keys to the kingdom of heaven (Matt. 16:19)? What about the "keys of death and of hades" (Rev. 1:18)?

In Revelation 19:15 a sharp sword comes out of Jesus' mouth to "smite the nations." But according to John Walvoord, whom LaHaye quotes approvingly, the sword is not literal. Rather, it represents "a sharp instrument of war, with which Jesus will smite the nations and establish His absolute rule."[5] Jesus is said to return on "a white horse" (Rev. 19:11). If the horse is literal, then it conflicts with Acts 1:11, which states, "This Jesus, who has been taken up from you into heaven, will come in just the same way as you have watched Him go into heaven." Jesus was *not* taken to heaven on a horse (see Mark 16:19).

I could go on with even more examples, but you get the point. LaHaye would claim that even "though some prophetic passages should be interpreted symbolically, it is important to remember that symbols in the Bible depict real people, things, and events."[6] Once again, I agree. It's my guess, however, that most Christians don't really understand what LaHaye and other prophecy writers who insist on literalism actually mean by the term when they see it redefined this way. A sword is "a sharp instrument of war" in Revelation 19, but a chain is a literal chain in Revelation 20. Why can't they both be symbols?

Psalm 98:8 declares, by way of a figure of speech called "personification," that the "rivers clap their hands." I believe it is literally true that God's creation is blessed by God's presence and sustaining hand.[7] This does not mean that the Bible is teaching that rivers have hands or that mountains have vocal cords so they can "sing together." Literalism needs a better definition than the one put forth by LaHaye, and it needs to be more consistently applied if he's going to make it the foundation stone for his prophetic system.

> "Literalness" does not indicate the truth or falsity, nor the precision, of the statement. A literal statement can be false, or even fantastic ("there is a ghost in my closet"); and a non-literal statement can be true ("there is a skeleton in my closet"). Further, "literal" does not mean "expressed with scientific or mathematical precision." If the almanac reports that "The sun rises tomorrow at 6:08 AM.," the statement is not scientifically precise (the sun does not "rise" from the astronomical point of view), but is nevertheless literal *within the understood context.*
>
> In Scripture, the distinction between literal and non-literal is perhaps the most important, though sometimes the most difficult to make. It is here that much controversy in the church has been centered. Arguments arise over whether something is literal or non-literal (e.g., the "thousand years" of Revelation 20).[8]

LaHaye's interpretive methodology seems so basic on the surface, but his numerous deviations from a literal approach on key passages create a problem with new believers who want to understand the Bible.

After extolling the virtues of interpreting symbols in his *Prophecy Study Bible* and his Revelation commentary, he writes in one of his other published works on prophecy something entirely different: "In recent years a number of teachers have concluded that prophecy should usually be interpreted symbolically." This, he says, has brought "confusion to the church."[9] If LaHaye would just say that not every passage in the Bible can or should be interpreted literally, a great deal of confusion could be avoided and those of us who disagree on what is and is not a symbol would not be stigmatized as "allegorists." Of course, even Paul interpreted Scripture "allegorically" (Gal. 4:24), so it can't be all bad.

COMMON SENSE?

LaHaye creates additional problems for interpreters who try to follow his methods when he adds "common sense" to the mix in trying to determine what is or is not to be interpreted literally. Consider this example:

> One of the reasons the book of Revelation is difficult for some people to understand is that they try to spiritualize the symbols used in the book. However, since many Old Testament prophecies have already been literally fulfilled, such as God turning water to blood (Ex. 4:9; 7:17–21), it should not be difficult to imagine that future prophetic events can and will be literally fulfilled at the appropriate time. Only when symbols or figures of speech make absolutely no literal sense, should anything but a literal interpretation be sought.[10]

Think how many times Jesus argued with the religious leaders of His day over the issue of literalism. When Jesus said "temple," the

Jews thought "temple." But Jesus meant "the temple of His body," not a temple made of stones (John 2:18–22; cf. Matt. 26:61).

Jesus told Nicodemus, "You must be born again" (John 3:7). Is this a proof text for reincarnation? Some people think it is.[11] Nicodemus heard "born again" and asked a question that related to a literal understanding of what Jesus seemed to be implying (3:4). Jesus said to him, "Are you the teacher in Israel, and do not understand these things" (3:10). Nicodemus should never have even considered a literal interpretation. Jesus never said, "Don't take Me literally," or "Look for the symbolic interpretation." As a student of the Bible, Nicodemus should have known how to interpret Jesus' words.

The woman of Samaria was looking for physical "living water" she could drink so she did not have to come out to a public well (John 4:15). Jesus had something else in mind. Jesus sure seems to be describing physical water. "Whoever drinks of the water that I shall give him shall never thirst; but the water that I shall give him shall become in him a well of water springing to eternal life" (John 4:14). She didn't know how Jesus would do it, but she believed that He could.

The Jews were upset with Jesus when He told them that He was "the living bread that came down out of heaven" and that they should eat His flesh (John 6:51). "Truly, truly, I say to you, unless you eat the flesh of the Son of Man and drink His blood, you have no life in yourselves" (6:53). The Jews interpreted Jesus' words literally: "The Jews therefore began to argue with one another, saying, 'How can this man give us His flesh to eat?'" (6:52). Jesus' disciples considered it a "difficult statement" (6:60). Jesus never said that His words should not be interpreted literally.

None of the above examples are to imply that the Bible is not to be interpreted literally or that everything is an allegory or a symbol. Rather, they are to show that no one, not even Tim LaHaye, consistently interprets the Bible literally because the Bible does not always demand a literal interpretation of every text. Consider what Dave Hunt, a contributor to LaHaye's *Prophecy Study Bible*, writes concerning Jesus' words about eating His flesh and drinking His blood:

> It is not a question of whether one *believes* Christ's words, but of how those words are *understood*. There is no more reason to take Him literally when He said "This is my body" than when He said "I am the door." To take Him literally violates common sense, consents to breaking God's law through cannibalism and partaking of blood, and leads to the foolish heresy that in spite of Christ being in heaven in a resurrected and glorified immortal body, His pre-crucifixion body of mortal flesh and blood is being ingested again and again by Catholics and Lutherans.[12]

Like LaHaye, who asserts that "only when symbols or figures of speech make absolutely no literal sense, should anything but a literal interpretation be sought," Hunt adds his own qualifier: To take Jesus "literally violates common sense." There are lots of things in the Bible that at one level violate common sense. How could God always exist? How did God create the world out of nothing? How do dead people rise from the dead? How could Jesus ascend into heaven? How could Jesus appear at will? Such things "violate common sense." It is this commonsense approach that leads many people to reject the Bible. Common sense tells them, based on what they know about the Bible, that these things don't happen.

Of course, we can always claim that with God all things are possible. Why isn't it possible that God transforms bread and wine into the literal body and blood of Jesus? By comparing John 6 with other portions of Scripture, we learn that this is not what Jesus had in mind.[13] But it takes being familiar with *all* of Scripture to know this. What's true for John 6 is also true for many of the symbols in

Revelation and other prophetic portions of Scripture. I agree with LaHaye when he writes, "For symbolic passages, compare Scripture with Scripture."[14] But a question remains: What passages are symbolic and how should they be interpreted? The Bible says that the sun will turn into darkness and the moon into blood (Acts 2:20). If we follow LaHaye's logic on blood (see above), the entire moon will turn into blood. Is it possible? Sure it is. With God, all things are possible. "It is not a question of whether one *believes* Christ's words, but of how those words are *understood*."

CAN GOD TELL TIME?

You might be asking at this point, "How is it possible that someone like Tim LaHaye, who has studied the Bible for nearly fifty years, could be so inconsistent, contradictory, and, in my opinion, mistaken?" If you are struggling with this question, don't fret. As I pointed out earlier in *End Times Fiction*, the prophetic belief system championed by LaHaye in *Left Behind* is relatively new. No one before 1830 ever taught it. You won't find it in a commentary or sermon throughout the span of the past nineteen centuries. While it's true that LaHaye has been a longtime student of Bible prophecy, so have many others who disagree with him. Beginning with a faulty premise will lead to faulty conclusions, no matter how long you study a topic.

So you are in good company if you decide to question the premise of *Left Behind*. You might also be relieved to know that many Bible-believing Christians who once believed in a left behind theology came to realize, after a thorough study of the subject, that the Bible didn't teach it. Some might think that this change disrupted their faith in the Bible. On the contrary, they were strengthened in their faith because they didn't have to gerrymander certain texts to make them fit a preconceived system of interpretation. For example, when the Bible described the judgment coming of Jesus as "near," "soon," and "at hand," they didn't have to say something like, "Time for God is different from the way we tell time. While God may have said the 'time is near' and these things 'must shortly take place,' He really didn't mean to imply that the time is *really* near." Consider LaHaye's comments on Revelation 1:1 and the use of the word *soon:* "[W]e find that this is the revelation of Jesus Christ 'to show his servants what must soon take place.' Again we see that the emphasis of the book is on the future."[15] It's not just the future; it's the *near* future. How do we know this? Because of the way that "soon" is used elsewhere in the Bible. We also know this based on the way *LaHaye* uses "soon." He believes that there are a number of signs in Scripture that indicate that Jesus is "going to come pretty soon. . . . [W]ithin our lifetime."[16]

Ed Hindson, professor and dean of the Institute of Biblical Studies at Liberty University in Lynchburg, Virginia, and one of the editors of LaHaye's *Prophecy Study Bible*, writes that "there are no specific time indicators of when" the prophecies outlined in the book of Revelation "will be fulfilled."[17] After making this claim, Hindson makes a startling admission:

> The only indication of time is the phrase "the time is at hand" (Greek, *kairos engus*). This may be translated "near" or "soon." Taken with the phrase "come to pass shortly" (Greek, *en tachei*, "soon") in verse 1, the reader is left expecting the imminent return of Christ.[18]

Hindson admits that these time words, when interpreted the way they would be interpreted in ordinary conversation, lead to a belief in "the imminent return of Christ." *Imminent* means "approaching," "impending," "looming," "near," "pending," "threatening." It is obvious, therefore, that the prophetic events of Revelation refer to the judgment coming of Christ that took place in the first century if the time words are interpreted literally.

Remember what LaHaye wrote about interpreting symbols? "For symbolic passages, compare Scripture with Scripture." The same applies to interpreting time passages. For example, the Greek word *engus* is translated either "at hand" or "near" throughout the Bible. The standard Greek lexicon on the New Testament offers one word, "near," as the meaning.[19] The following are just a few of nearly a hundred examples:

- Jesus said, "Go into the city to a certain man, and say to him, 'The Teacher says, "My time is at hand; I am to keep the Passover at your house with My disciples."'" (Matt. 26:18)

- Then He came to the disciples, and said to them, "Are you still sleeping and taking your rest? Behold, the hour is at hand and the Son of Man is being betrayed into the hands of sinners. Arise, let us be going; behold, the one who betrays Me is at hand!" (Matt. 26:45–46)

- But when you see Jerusalem surrounded by armies, then recognize that her desolation is at hand. (Luke 21:20)

- And the Passover of the Jews was at hand, and Jesus went up to Jerusalem. (John 2:13)

- Now the Passover, the feast of the Jews, was at hand. (John 6:4)

- Now the feast of the Jews, the Feast of Booths, was at hand. (John 7:2)

- Jesus therefore said to them, "My time is not yet at hand, but your time is always opportune." (John 7:6)
- Now the Passover of the Jews was at hand, and many went up to Jerusalem out of the country before the Passover, to purify themselves. (John 11:55)

Philip Mauro once held to the prophetic system advocated by LaHaye and other modern prophecy writers. He abandoned the system after a thorough study of the Bible. In the following quotation, he sets forth his reasons why he believes words that deal with time, when Scripture is compared to Scripture, can only be interpreted one way, because that's the way they are used in every instance in the New Testament:

> [T]he very first verse [in Revelation] states that God's purpose in giving the revelation to Jesus Christ was that he might "show unto His servants things which must *shortly come to pass.*" These words are not at all ambiguous, and the simple-minded would never suspect that they could have been intended to convey any other than their ordinary and apparent meaning, namely, that the things foretold in "this prophecy" were to happen in the era that was just then beginning. The word here rendered "shortly" means *just that.* It is variously translated in other Scriptures by the words *quickly, speedily, soon.* Thus, in Acts 25:4, Festus, after commanding that Paul be kept at Caesarea, said that "he himself would depart *shortly* thither." In Philippians 2:19 Paul writes, "I trust to send Timotheus unto you *shortly.*" And so also in 1 Timothy 3:14; Hebrews 13:23; and 2 Peter 1:14. In Galatians 1:6 we have, "so *soon* removed"; in Philippians 2:33, "so *soon* as I shall see how it will go with"; and in 2 Thessalonians 2:2, "That ye be not *soon* shaken in mind."[20]

197

Based on the way "quickly," "near," "at hand," and "shortly" are used in the New Testament, including Revelation, *Left Behind* is fiction in more ways than one.

PROPHETIC IDEAS HAVE CONSEQUENCES

Prophecy, like all biblical doctrines, has consequences for the way we live in the present and plan for the future. "The way you look to the future determines your planning and your actions. It is the way you understand the times that determines what you are going to do."[21] Consider these statements by well-known prophecy writers:

- This world is not going to get any easier to live in. Almost unbelievably hard times lie ahead. Indeed, Jesus said that these coming days will be uniquely terrible. Nothing in all the previous history of the world can compare with what lies in store for mankind.[22]

- What a way to live! With optimism, with anticipation, with excitement. We should be living like persons who don't expect to be around much longer.[23]

- I don't like cliches but I've heard it said, "God didn't send me to clean the fish bowl, he sent me to fish." In a way there's a truth in that.[24]

Ted Peters writes that for some Christians this kind of thinking "functions to justify social irresponsibility."[25] While not everyone who believes in the end-time scenario outlined by LaHaye in *Left Behind* thinks this way, there are many who do. A form of "prophetic inevitability" has set in that "portrays the present evil world as beyond improvement or redemption, and predicts instead that it will deteriorate steadily until the coming of Jesus, who will then set up his millennial reign on earth. If the world is getting worse, and if only Jesus at his coming will put it right, the argument runs, there seems no point in trying to reform it meanwhile. Adopting political programs is 'like cleaning the staterooms on the Titanic after it has hit the iceberg . . . It is far more important simply to preach the Gospel and to rescue souls for the next life.'"[26] If this approach is taken, and a hundred or two hundred years pass without the return of Christ, what will our world look like and how will Christians respond in the face of an even more degenerate world? Some might argue that no one really connects an end-time theology to present-day affairs. It's more prevalent than one might think:

> "Do you realize," a student asked Tom Sine during one of his futurology seminars in the United States, "if we start feeding hungry people, things won't get worse, and if things don't get worse, Jesus won't come?" She was utterly sincere, writes Tom Sine. He continues: "The response of the (student) . . . reflects what I call the Great Escape View of the future . . . The irony of (this) approach to the future is that, while it claims to take God seriously, it unwittingly moves God outside history, insisting that even he is powerless 'in these last days.' . . . It unintentionally fashions him into an impotent absentee landlord, who has lost control of his world and of human history . . . The Great Escape becomes an incredible copout from all Christ called us to be and to do."[27]

Then there are the extremists. The FBI was unprepared for the end-time logic of Vicki and Randy Weaver in the Ruby Ridge disaster. The Weavers were treated like fringe political extremists who were tied to white supremacist, anti-Semitic, and Aryan Nation groups rather than believers in an imminent apocalypse that they (the Weavers) concluded would be led by governmental powers ("the Beast").

The Weaver family's flight to Ruby Ridge was greatly influenced by *The Late Great Planet Earth*. Though Vicki Weaver, the family's spiritual leader, was also influenced by H. G. Wells and Ayn Rand, it was Lindsey's prophetic work, coupled with her home-spun visions, that convinced her to pack up her family and move to Ruby Ridge. She believed that the enemies of God predicted by Lindsey were prepared to strike at any moment.[28]

The Weavers mixed conspiracy theories, apocalypticism, and paranoia to conclude that the end was near.[29] You can imagine what the Weavers thought as they saw armed soldiers attacking their homestead. Was this happening everywhere? Was this the prelude to the end that they had read so much about in popular prophecy books and expected in their lifetime? The events described in Revelation were being acted out right before their eyes, so they thought.

While LaHaye writes that Christians should "avoid speculations that go beyond the intent of Scripture, and not make them mean more than is indicated,"[30] and that "any time a person sets a specific date we know he is wrong,"[31] he still leaves a compelling impression with his readers that it is our generation that will see the return of the Lord.

LaHaye does not name the "day or the hour" of Christ's return, but he is convinced that "it is near, even at the doors,"[32] that we are living "within the 'season,' or generation" of Christ's return.[33] He states "that, while we cannot say dogmatically that Jesus will return in our generation, we can say that our generation has more legitimate reasons for believing it than any previous generation . . . [T]he coming of Christ could be at hand . . . This is the first generation to see the possible fulfillment of that end-time prophecy."[34]

The history of date-setting is long and tortuous. Francis Gumerlock catalogs more than a thousand false predictions over the past two millennia, everything from the identity of the Antichrist to the date of Christ's coming. Two common streams run through all of them: they were sure of their prediction and they were wrong.[35] The track record for pointing out even the "season" or "generation" of Jesus' return is dismal as well: a 100 percent failure rate by everyone who claimed that they were living in the "terminal generation."

> During the late Middle Ages, before the dawning of the Renaissance, the plague swept across Europe, killing an estimated ⅓ to ½ of the continent's total population. The Hundred Years War between Britain and France dragged on, and even during periods of peace, armed bands roamed the countryside, looting and pillaging. Unsurprisingly, people seemed obsessed with death, as their art and literature attests. Many believed the events foretold in the book of Revelation were unfolding before their eyes.[36]

The majority of people who read *Left Behind* are being led to believe that Jesus is coming in their lifetime. The series would not have such mass appeal if LaHaye did not leave this distinct impression, even though he is careful to use words like "could," "more reason," "possible," and "cannot be dogmatic." Consider this interview with Larry King on CNN on June 19, 2000:

LaHaye: But I think another reason people are interested in [*Left Behind*] . . . is because it talks about the future. We're living at a time when people look at the future and think of it as rather precarious. In fact, there's a popular book out a couple of years ago on the death of history,[37] and it's not from a Christian perspective. And so people recognize that something is about to happen. And the Bible has a fantastically optimistic view of the future.

KING:	But weren't people saying this in 1890 and 1790? "It's coming. Boy, the apocalypse is coming. The end is near." They've always been saying it.
LaHAYE :	Well, we have more reason to believe that. Until Israel went back into the promised land, we couldn't really claim that the end times were coming. But ever since 1948, in subsequent years, we've realized that things are getting set up. It's stage setting for these momentous events.
KING :	Do you believe that some sort of end is coming?
LaHAYE:	Yes.
KING :	You believe that that will happen?
LaHAYE :	In fact, I believe there are a number of signs in Scripture that indicate it's going to come pretty soon. We say maybe within our lifetime.

While LaHaye does not put forth a specific day or year, he states unequivocally that Scripture "indicates it's going to come pretty soon." LaHaye believes that there are "Twelve Reasons Why This Could be the Terminal Generation." In the "Overview" that introduces LaHaye's article on the twelve reasons, we read: "Are we only a few years away from the second advent of Jesus Christ? Many believe that we are. Without saying that we are, the author [LaHaye] provides 12 reasons why he thinks this generation could be living on the verge of Christ's return."[38] What makes LaHaye so sure since the signs he lists have been with us for two thousand years?

THE "SUPER SIGN" OF CHRIST'S RETURN

LaHaye claims that the interpretive key to understanding when the coming of Jesus is near is the "super sign." According to LaHaye, the "super sign" is related to the national status of Israel in the twentieth century. Depending on which edition of LaHaye's books one reads, the key dates are either the November 2, 1917, signing of the Balfour Declaration[39] and the advent of World War I, or the world recognition by the United Nations of Israel's statehood in 1948.

Where is this "super sign" found in the Bible? Not in the New Testament. There is not a single verse in the entire New Testament that says anything about Israel becoming a nation again. Nothing prophetic in the New Testament depends on Israel becoming a nation again. If Israel becoming a nation again is such "a significant sign," then why doesn't the New Testament specifically mention it?

A super sign requires a super text to support it. Many prophecy writers find their needed support in Matthew 24:32–33 where Jesus tells His disciples: "Now learn the parable from the fig tree: when its branch has already become tender, and puts forth its leaves, you know that summer is near; even so you too, when you see all these things, recognize that He is near, right at the door." The fig tree putting forth leaves supposedly is Israel becoming a nation again in 1948. This interpretation was made popular by prophecy writer Hal Lindsey, and LaHaye agrees with it:

> The most important sign in Matthew has to be the restoration of the Jews to the land in the rebirth of Israel. Even the figure of speech "fig tree" has been a historic symbol of national Israel. When the Jewish people, after nearly 2,000 years of exile, under relentless persecution, became a nation again on 14 May 1948 the "fig tree" put forth its first leaves.
>
> Jesus said that this would indicate that He was "at the door," ready to return. Then He said, "Truly I say to you, *this generation* will not pass away until all these things take place" (Matthew 24:34, NASB).[40]

Not everyone agrees with Lindsey on this point. For example, John Walvoord concludes that the fig tree representing Israel "is not so used in the Bible . . . Accordingly, while this interpretation is held by many, there is no clear scriptural warrant. A better interpretation is that Christ was using a natural illustration."[41]

Even the editors of LaHaye's own *Prophecy Study Bible* agree with Walvoord that "the fig tree is not symbolic of the nation of Israel." LaHaye, however, contradicts Walvoord and his own editors when he writes, "When a fig tree is used symbolically in Scripture, it usually refers to the nation Israel. If that is a valid assumption (and we believe it is), then when Israel officially became a nation in 1948, that was the 'sign' of Matthew 24:1–8, the beginning 'birth pangs'— it meant that the 'end of the age' is 'near.'"[42] So who's right?

LaHaye has not always held the position that 1948 is the key date for the fulfillment of the "this generation" of Matthew 24:34. In the first edition of his *The Beginning of the End* (1972), LaHaye wrote, "Carefully putting all this together, we now recognize this strategic generation. *It is the generation that 'sees' the four-part sign of verse 7 [in Matt. 24], or the people who saw the First World War.* We must be careful here not to become dogmatic, but it would seem that these people are witnesses to the events, not necessarily participants in them. That would suggest they were at least old enough to understand the events of 1914–1918, not necessarily old enough to go to war."[43]

A number of things changed in the 1991 revised edition. The "strategic generation" has been modified significantly. It's no longer "the people who saw the First World War" but a later generation. "Carefully putting all this together, we now recognize this strategic generation. *It is the generation that 'sees' the events of 1948.* We must be careful here not to become dogmatic, but it would seem that these people are witnesses to the events, not necessarily participants in them." This change gives LaHaye another fifty years before this new generation passes away.[44]

If there is no New Testament text that points to Israel becoming a nation again, then where does LaHaye discover his biblical support? He attempts to find it in Ezekiel 37. When Ezekiel was given his revelation from God, the Jews had been overrun by the Babylonians. He would follow his countrymen into captivity in the second deportation to Babylon in 597 B.C. This means that Ezekiel 37 is describing the Jews' return to their homeland after seventy years of captivity (Jer. 25:11–12; Dan. 9:2). God promised to bring His people back "into the land of Israel" (37:12, 14), and He did. Of course, the ultimate fulfillment of this promise and other pledges in Ezekiel 37 take place in the New Testament era where Jesus, the descendant of David (37:24; cf. Matt. 21:9; 22:42; Luke 1:32, 69; Acts 2:32–36; Rev. 5:5; 22:16) is proclaimed the Shepherd of Israel (Ezek. 37:24; cf. Matt. 2:6; 26:31; John 10:11, 14, 16; Heb. 13:20). With all of this biblical evidence in view, it is not surprising, therefore, that the New Testament is silent about the prophetic significance of Israel becoming a nation again.

ALL CAME TO PASS

An additional point needs to be made on the subject of Israel. The claim is often made that all of the land promises regarding Israel have not been fulfilled. The Bible says otherwise:

- *"So the LORD gave Israel all the land which He had sworn to give to their fathers, . . . and no one of all their enemies stood before them; the LORD gave all their enemies into their hand"* (Josh. 21:43–44).

- *"Not one of the good promises which the LORD had made to the house of Israel failed; all came to pass"* (Josh. 21:45).

- *"And Thou didst find his heart faithful before Thee, and didst make a covenant with him to give him the land of the Canaanite, of the Hittite and the Amorite, of the Perizzite, the Jebusite, and the Girgashite—to give it to his descendants. And Thou hast fulfilled Thy promise, for Thou art righteous"* (Neh. 9:8).

God's Word could not be any more clear. Even after these unconfused statements, there are still those who insist that the land promises have not been fulfilled. Their assertion is based on passages from the prophets that indicate the Jews will be brought back to the land "a second time" (Jer. 29:14; Isa. 11:11–12). In order to discover the "second time," we have to determine the "first time." The "first time" was when God brought Israel into the land after their time of bondage in Egypt: "And there will be a highway from Assyria for the remnant of His people who will be left, just as there was for Israel in the day that they came up out of the land of Egypt" (Isa. 11:16). The second time was when the Jews returned "after seventy years" of captivity (Jer. 25:11, 12; 29:10; Dan. 9:2; Zech. 7:5).[45] There is no mention of a third time any place in the New Testament. This is a significant omission since a "super text" is needed to support a "super sign."

Any skeptic would be confused by all of this. He would find date setting and contradictions within LaHaye's own writings and from the editors of his own study Bible. A skeptic would wonder why the Bible says all the land promises have been fulfilled, while LaHaye and his supporters claim otherwise. A skeptic would point to history and wonder why the fulfillment of Matthew 24:32–33 was first said to be fulfilled during World War I, then it was Israel becoming a nation in 1948. Further skepticism arises as others point to Jerusalem's occupation of Jerusalem in 1967 or the 1993 peace accord.[46] If the Bible is so clear when it is interpreted literally, then why do the events and the dates that supposedly fulfill these prophecies keep changing?

CONCLUSION

Left Behind is a work of fiction. As long as it's read with this point in mind, there is no harm. But if the interpretive methodology set forth in the series is embraced as the Bible's method, then I believe many people will be disappointed and disillusioned when the scenario outlined by LaHaye does not come to pass.

CONCLUSION

"OK. I've read your book. I must admit, you've made a pretty strong case for your position."

"I appreciate your willingness to keep an open mind on the subject. Not everyone is so agreeable, even though we are to 'examine everything carefully' and to 'hold fast to that which is good.'"[1]

"Well, I want to know the truth. If it means abandoning a position that can't be supported by an appeal to the Bible, even if someone with the Christian character of Tim LaHaye believes it, I'm compelled to reevaluate what I believe. But I have to be convinced in terms of what the Bible says."

"You're in good company. The Bible says, 'Let each man be fully convinced in his own mind' (Rom. 14:5). Only a thorough study of Scripture will bring to light God's truth on this and every other subject."

"But I sill have one question . . . If so much has already been fulfilled, what's left on the prophetic horizon?"

A study of history has taught us that trying to predict prophetic events is a dubious and oftentimes dangerous practice. Even specifying an end-time "generation" has not been successful. C. Marvin Pate, professor of Bible at Moody Bible Institute, argues convincingly that "correlating current events" with Bible prophecies is "an obsession" that has "undoubtedly caused more harm than good."[2] Pate is not alone in his judgment. Dozens of examples of historians who have studied the subject could be cited. Francis X. Gumerlock, author of the most comprehensive study of two-thousand years of failed predictions, says it best in his book *The Day and the Hour*:

I originally intended the chronicle to be an article, which I estimated would be about ten pages in length. Twenty-one chapters later, *The Day and the Hour* illustrates century after century, year after year, the perennial fascination of those in Christendom who predicted a date for the Rapture, the Resurrection, or the Return of Christ; those who calculated the nearness of Armageddon, the Last Judgment, or the Millennium; those who announced a contemporaneous identity for the Two Witnesses, a last-days Elijah, the Antichrist, or some Beast from the Book of Revelation; and those who believed that their sect was the 144,000 or their generation the last.

In the course of this study, I have found that it was not only radicals and cultists who had engaged in this type of End-time date setting; almost no Christian denomination has been immune from it. Even some whom we consider heroes of the faith have mistakenly engaged in these sorts of vain speculations.[3]

With this knowledge before us, we can conclude that the prophetic system upon which the Left Behind series is based has a long and dubious history. Certainly it makes for fascinating reading. The same was probably true in 1643 when popular prophecy writer Joseph Mede declared in his *The Key to Revelation* that Spain was the Antichrist and the Native Americans comprised the end-time Gog and Magog of Ezekiel 38 and 39. No doubt people were equally fascinated when they picked up Edward Irving's *Babylon and Infidelity Foredoomed* and read that the Second Coming of Christ was very near.[4]

End Times Fiction is an attempt to put prophecy into biblical perspective, to serve as an antidote to the heartache of prophetic speculation. I have tried to show that the majority of prophetic material found in the Bible has already been fulfilled. Such a conclusion might be surprising to many students of the Bible, but a study of Bible commentators over the centuries will show that this has been a common and judicious way to interpret many prophetic texts. Of course, just because others have come to a conclusion similar to the one outlined in *End Times Fiction* does not make its position the right one. Even so, an appeal to the historical record does demonstrate that my position was not developed just to refute a popular prophecy writer.

If so much has already been fulfilled, Christians naturally ask, "Then what's left to happen and when will these events take place?" There is a companion question: "If so many prophecies are now history, then what application do the fulfilled parts of Scripture have for Christians today?" These are good and necessary questions. Let's take them one at a time.

WHAT'S ON THE PROPHETIC HORIZON FOR THE INDIVIDUAL?

For nearly two-thousand years Christians have asked this question. From the purely earth-bound perspective, their eschatological hopes did not materialize when the next prophetic event in their life was not as spectacular or comforting as a "pre-tribulational rapture." Without exception, death and immediate judgment awaited them: "It is appointed for men to die once, and after this comes judgment" (Heb. 9:27). For the Christian, death is the entry into a positive future, although death itself is not pleasant to think about or experience. "Jesus wept" over its effect on those left behind (John 11:35). The Bible describes death as a "sting" inflicted on us because of sin (1 Cor. 15:55). Even so, Paul could write, "but thanks be to God, who gives us the victory through our Lord Jesus Christ" (15:57). This is why Paul also wrote, "For to me, to live is Christ, and to die is gain" (Phil. 1:21). Odds are, knowing what we know about the span of centuries, the next prophetic event in our life is probably going to be death. This means that you and I must be prepared at this very moment to be ready to appear before the judgment seat of Christ, because we do not know when death will come (2 Cor. 5:10).

- But God said to him, "You fool! This very night your soul is required of you; and now who will own what you have prepared?" (Luke 12:20).

- Behold, now is "the acceptable time," behold, now is "the day of salvation" (2 Cor. 6:2).

- Believe in the Lord Jesus, and you shall be saved (Acts 16:31).

Being reconciled to God through Jesus Christ is every person's prophetic priority. Our eternal future depends on it.

WHAT'S ON THE PROPHETIC HORIZON FOR THE WORLD?

After Jesus rose from the dead and before His ascension into heaven, He gave a command to go and "make disciples of all the nations"

(Matt. 28:19). Even with the passage of two millennia, evangelism and discipleship efforts have only just begun. The discipleship process has taken a back seat to evangelism-only efforts. Many believe that once the gospel has gone around the globe, Jesus will return. This is a mistaken notion (see chapter 5). The command is *discipleship*, not simply evangelism. Leading people to Christ is only a required first step. No one is to remain a babe in Christ forever. The time comes when the maturing convert puts aside milk (1 Peter 2:2) and partakes of "solid food" (Heb. 5:13). The goal is to have the "senses trained to discern good and evil" (5:14). The ultimate goal for the Christian is take "every thought captive to the obedience of Christ" (2 Cor. 10:5). It was this kind of biblical thinking that changed the world throughout the centuries.[5] Until whole nations come under the sway of the gospel and are truly discipled, we should not expect the coming of the Lord.

WHAT'S ON THE PROPHETIC HORIZON FOR THE DEVIL?

We're often told that the devil controls the world, that he orchestrates the movements of history. This, too, is an unbiblical idea. The Bible says that Satan is defeated, disarmed, and spoiled (Col. 2:15; Rev. 12:7–17; Mark 3:27), "fallen" (Luke 10:18), and "thrown down" (Rev. 12:9). He was "crushed" under the feet of the early Christians (Rom. 16:20). He has lost "authority" over Christians (Col. 1:13) and has been "judged" (John 16:11). He cannot "touch" a Christian (1 John 5:18). His works have been "destroyed" (1 John 3:8). He has "nothing" (John 14:30). He "flees" when "resisted" (James 4:7) and is "bound" (Mark 3:27; Luke 11:20; Rev. 20:2).

The early Christians understood the place of the devil in God's sovereignly controlled universe. Our forefathers worked in terms of God as the Ruler of the kings of the earth, not in terms of Satan as the "ruler of this world," because "the ruler of this world" *has been* "cast out" (John 12:31). They took the Bible seriously when it said of God's people, "And Thou hast made them to be a kingdom and priests to our God; and they will reign upon the earth" (Rev. 5:10; compare 1 Peter 2:9–10). Paul tells us "that the saints will judge the world" (1 Cor. 6:2). And what of the evil in the world? Can it all be attributed to the devil? "But each one is tempted when he is carried away and enticed by his own lust. Then when lust has conceived, it gives birth to sin; and when sin is accomplished, it brings forth death" (James 1:14–15). Changed hearts and changed minds are in order, and these come only by way of regeneration.

WHAT'S ON THE PROPHETIC HORIZON FOR THE UNIVERSE?

The Nicene Creed of the fourth century states: "And He shall come again, with glory, to judge both the quick and the dead; Whose kingdom shall have no end . . . And I look for the Resurrection of the dead: And the Life of the world to come. Amen." This "coming" refers to Jesus' return to *judge*, not to *reign* on the earth. Jesus presently reigns over the universe from heaven (Acts 2:22–36). Heaven is His throne while earth is His footstool (2:35; 7:49). We also learn the end that relates to Jesus' "summing up of all things . . . things in the heavens and things upon the earth" take place "at His coming" when "He delivers up the kingdom to the God and Father, when He has abolished all rule and all authority and power. For He must reign until He has put all His enemies under His feet. The last enemy that will be abolished is death" (1 Cor. 15:23–26).

Does this mean that God's kingdom is some distant mirage? Scripture clearly teaches the *nearness* of the kingdom in Jesus' day (Matt 3:2; 4:17; 4:23; Mark 1:14–15; Luke 4:16–30; 4:43; 8:1 10:9; Col. 1:13), a definitive or present manifestation of the kingdom through Jesus' work (Matt. 11:2–6; Luke 4:21; Luke 11:20; 17:21), the continuing coming of the kingdom (Matt. 6:10), the progressive advance of the kingdom (Isa. 9:6–7; Dan. 2:31–34, 44–45; 1 Cor. 15:24; Matt. 13:31–33), and the consummation of the kingdom (Matt. 25; 1 Cor. 15:23–24; Rev. 21).

WHEN WILL THESE THINGS BE?

The Bible does not tell us when "the summing up of all things" will take place. The only signs that are yet to be fulfilled are the discipleship of the nations and Jesus putting all His enemies under His feet. When will these take place? The Bible does not say. The secret things belong to God (Deut. 29:29). In the meantime, Christians are to work out their salvation with fear and trembling; for it is God who is at work in you, both to will and to work for His good pleasure" (Phil. 2:12–13).

WHAT'S IN IT FOR ME?

"If so much of God's prophetic word is fulfilled, then how is it relevant for me today?" This often-asked question is surprising to me. There is so much of fulfilled prophecy we take for granted that has untold significance for every Christian throughout time. The Old Testament is filled with fulfilled prophecy, and yet we do not relegate it to the dust bin of history. The life, death, and resurrection of Jesus is a perfect example of the relevance of fulfilled prophecy. Jesus died nearly 2,000 years ago, but what He did for us so long ago applies to us today. Just because a prophecy has been fulfilled does not mean that it doesn't have any present-day application. Paul rehearses a bit of Israel's history and concludes, "Now these things happened to them as an example, and they were written for our instruction, upon whom the ends of the ages have come" (1 Cor. 10:11).

We can learn from fulfilled prophecy that God is faithful to His word. Like Paul's instruction to the Corinthians, we can learn from the mistakes of the past so that we do not repeat them. Furthermore, there are universal principles in fulfilled prophecy that are always applicable. Just because John was describing the attributes of first-century antichrists does not mean that there are not people today "who do not acknowledge Jesus Christ as coming in the flesh" (2 John 7). The beast of Revelation 13 raised his head in the first century, but this does not mean that there are not beast-like characters today. This is why Paul could write, "All Scripture is inspired by God and profitable for teaching, for reproof, for correction, for training in righteousness; that the man of God may be adequate, equipped for every good work" (2 Tim. 3:16–17).

The Bible calls on Christians to be discerning, to "test the spirits" (1 John 4:1). This is done by "examining the Scriptures daily to see whether" what is being taught, even by the most respected Christian, fits with biblical reality (Acts 17:11). Keep in mind that Christians in Thessalonica examined the Scriptures to see whether the views of Paul, an apostle called by God, lined up with the Bible. In another place, Paul calls on Christians to "examine everything thoroughly" (1 Thess. 5:21).

Too many Christians have only *heard* what some people *claim* the Bible teaches (Matt. 5:21). Because of what we know about prophetic claims and failed predictions over nearly two millennia, the task of biblical discernment is especially important when we consider the topic of Bible prophecy. The responsibility remains for each of us to be certain that what is being taught today is prophetic fact as actually found in the Bible.

NOTES

INTRODUCTION

1. From <www.leftbehind.com>—"Frequently Asked Questions for the Authors."
2. 6 April 1980.
3. William J. Petersen and Randy Petersen, *100 Christian Books That Changed the Century* (Grand Rapids, MI: Revell, 2000), 166.
4. Louise Cowan and Os Guinness, *Invitation to the Classics: A Guide to Books You've Always Wanted to Read* (Grand Rapids, MI: Baker, 1998), 173.
5. Lawrence E. Nelson, *Our Roving Bible: Tracking Its Influence Through English and American Life* (New York: Abingdon-Cokesbury Press, 1945), 99.
6. Ibid., 105.
7. There was a twenty-minute film produced in 1907.
8. John Tebbel, *Between Covers: The Rise and Transformation of American Publishing* (New York: Oxford University Press, 1987), 142.
9. Forrest Loman Oilar, *Be Thou Prepared for Jesus Is Coming* (Boston: Meador Publishing; New York: Oxford University Press, 1987), 142.1937, 7.
10. Pat Frank, *Alas, Babylon* (New York: Bantam Books, [1959] 1974).
11. Walter M. Miller Jr., *A Canticle for Leibowitz* (Philadelphia, PA: J. B. Lippincott, 1959).
12. Paul Brians, *Nuclear Holocausts: Atomic War in Fiction, 1895–1984* (Kent, OH: Kent State University Press, 1987), 261.
13. Edward E. Plowman, "Courtroom Tribulation," *World*, 10 March 2001, 51–52.
14. Tim LaHaye and David Noebel, *Mind Siege: The Battle for Truth in the New Millennium* (Nashville, TN: Word, 2000), 94.
15. Rick David, Letters to the Editor, *Charisma*, February 2001.
16. The movie came out late in 2000.
17. Quoted in Dave MacPherson, *The Three R's: Rapture, Revisionism, Robbery—Pretribulation Rapturism from 1830 to Hal Lindsey* (Simpsonville, SC: P.O.S.T. Inc., 1998), 140.
18. Michael Shermer, *How We Believe: The Search for God in an Age of Science* (New York: W. H. Freeman and Co., 2000), 1–7.

19. Tim Callahan, *Bible Prophecy: Failure or Fulfillment?* (Altadena, CA: Millennium Press, 1997), 204–29.

20. MacPherson, *The Three R's*, 109–14.

21. Merrill F. Unger, *Beyond the Crystal Ball* (Chicago, IL: Moody Press, 1973), 81–95.

22. Richard Abanes, *End-Time Visions: The Road to Armageddon?* (New York: Four Walls Eight Windows, 1998), 88.

23. Tim LaHaye and Jerry B. Jenkins, *Are We Living in the End Times?: Current Events Foretold in Scripture . . . And What They Mean* (Wheaton, IL: Tyndale, 1999), xi.

24. Tim LaHaye, gen. ed., *Prophecy Study Bible* (Chattanooga, TN: AMG Publishers, 2000), 7.

25. Floyd E. Hamilton, *The Basis of Christian Faith: A Modern Defense of the Christian Religion*, rev. ed. (New York: Harper & Row, 1964), 160.

CHAPTER 1

1. Tim LaHaye and Jerry Jenkins, *Left Behind: A Novel of the Earth's Last Days* (Wheaton, IL: Tyndale, 1995), 14.

2. This is not a description of a future technological battle or an ancient UFO sighting. It is "the appearance of the likeness of the glory of the LORD" (Ezek. 1:28) in symbolic terms.

3. Tim LaHaye, *No Fear of the Storm: Why Christians Will Escape All the Tribulation* (Sisters, OR: Multnomah, 1992), 240. *No Fear of the Storm* has been republished as *Rapture Under Attack.*

4. LaHaye and Jenkins, *Are We Living in the End Times?*, 84.

5. Tim LaHaye, "The Coming Wave," in *Future Wave: End Times, Prophecy, and the Technological Explosion,* by Ed Hindson and Lee Fredrickson (Eugene, OR: Harvest House , 2001), 7–8.

6. Margaret Coker, "Military luster fades in Russia, *The Atlanta Constitution* (May 9, 2001), B3.

7. LaHaye and Jenkins, *Are We Living in the End Times?*, v.

8. LaHaye and Jenkins, *Left Behind*, 10.

9. Ibid., 14.

10. Charles C. Ryrie, ed., *The Ryrie Study Bible* (Chicago, IL: Moody Press, 1978), 1285.

11. Some editions of the New American Standard Bible include "Rosh" in Isaiah 66:19: "Tarshish, Put, Lud, Meshech, Rosh, Tubal, and Javan." No other translation includes "Rosh" in this listing. The Hebrew text does not include "Rosh." The Lockman Foundation's on-line version of its updated translation of the NASB does not include "Rosh" in Isaiah 66:19. In response to my question regarding this discrepancy, the Lockman Foundation sent a lengthy and technical explanation, but in the final analysis admitted that the word *rosh* is not found in Isaiah 66:19 in either the Hebrew text or the Greek translation called the Septuagint (LXX).

12. E. W. Hengstenberg, *The Prophecies of the Prophet Ezekiel Elucidated* (Minneapolis, MN: James Publications, [1869] 1976), 333.

13. Hal Lindsey, *Late Great Planet Earth* (Grand Rapids, MI: Zondervan, 1970), 59–71.

14. Tim LaHaye, *The Beginning of the End*, rev. ed. (Wheaton, IL: Tyndale, 1991), 65.

15. *The Scofield Reference Bible*, ed. C. I. Scofield (New York: Oxford University Press, 1917), 883 n.

NOTES

16. Edwin M. Yamauchi, *Foes from the Northern Frontier: Invading Hordes from the Russian Steppes* (Grand Rapids, MI: Baker, 1982), 20.

17. Ralph H. Alexander, "Ezekiel," in *The Expositor's Bible Commentary*, ed. Frank E. Gaebelein, 12 vols. (Grand Rapids, MI: Zondervan, 1986), 6:930. For a discussion of five contemporary views of this battle, see Ralph H. Alexander, "A Fresh Look at Ezekiel 38 and 39," *Journal of the Evangelical Theological Society*, 17 (summer 1974), 162–65.

18. One of Benjamin's sons is named "Rosh" (Gen. 46:21), but no one identifies him with Russia. Russia was not settled by Jews from the tribe of Benjamin. The Benjamites settled in the most southern part of Israel. Paul was from the tribe of Benjamin (Rom. 11:1; Phil. 3:5).

19. Timothy J. Daily, *The Gathering Storm* (Tarrytown, NY: Revell, 1992), 166.

20. *The Moody Atlas of Bible Lands* (Chicago, IL: Moody Press, 1985), 5.

21. J. A. Thompson, *Deuteronomy*, Tyndale Old Testament Commentary Series (Downers Grove, IL: InterVarsity Press, 1974), 108.

22. Peter C. Craigie, *The Book of Deuteronomy*, NICOT (Grand Rapids, MI: Eerdmans, 1976), 141.

23. Rob Linsted, *The Next Move: Current Events in Bible Prophecy* (Wichita, KS: Bible Truth, n.d.), 41.

24. Harry Rimmer, *The Coming War and the Rise of Russia* (Grand Rapids, MI: Eerdmans, 1940), 48–51.

25. Ralph Woodrow, *His Truth Is Marching On: Advanced Studies on Prophecy in the Light of History* (Riverside, CA: Ralph Woodrow Evangelistic Association, 1977), 43.

26. James B. Jordan, *Esther in the Midst of Covenant History* (Niceville, FL: Biblical Horizons, 1995), 5.

27. Ibid., 5–7.

28. Note the figurative language: "like a storm . . . like a cloud."

29. Jordan, *Esther in the Midst of Covenant History*, 7.

30. An Agagite was a descendant of Amalek, one of the persistent enemies of the people of God. Numbers 24:20 records that "Amalek was the first of the nations, but his end shall be destruction." The phrase "first of the nations" takes us back to the early chapters of Genesis to Gomer, Magog, Tubal, Meshech, and their father, Japheth (Gen. 10:2), the main antagonist nations that figure prominently in Ezekiel 38–39. Amalek was probably a descendant of Japheth (Gen. 10:2).

31. Jordan, *Esther in the Midst of Covenant History*, 7. The word *haman* in Ezekiel "is spelled in Hebrew almost exactly like the name Haman . . . In Hebrew, both words have the same 'triliteral root' (*hmn*). Only the vowels are different. (Though in *hamon*, the vowel 'o' is indicated by the letter 'vav'" (7).

32. Lindsey quoted in LaHaye, *The Beginning of the End*, 80.

33. Of course, as any student of the Bible knows, these seemingly futurist depictions symbolize "the appearance of the likeness of the glory of the LORD" (1:28).

CHAPTER 2

1. LaHaye and Jenkins, *Left Behind*, 47–48.

2. LaHaye, *No Fear of the Storm*, 69.

3. Ibid., 188.

4. Advocates of a pretrib Rapture tell us that their version of the Rapture is like the doctrines

218

of the Trinity and the incarnate nature of Christ, "the product of biblical harmonization" (Thomas Ice and Timothy Demy, *The Truth About the Rapture* [Eugene, OR: Harvest House, 1996], 27). The incarnate nature of Christ can be proved by citing just two verses: "In the beginning was the Word, and the Word was with God, and the *Word was God* . . . And *the Word became flesh*, and dwelt among us, and we beheld His glory, glory as of the only begotten from the Father, full of grace and truth" (John 1:1, 14, emphasis added). The Trinity is equally easy to prove: the Father is God (1 Cor. 8:6); Jesus is God (John 1:1); the Holy Spirit is God (Acts 5:3–4); and there is only one God (1 Tim. 2:5). Unlike the pretrib Rapture, these two doctrines have been part of church history for centuries.

5. LaHaye and Jenkins, *Are We Living in the End Times?*, 113.

6. LaHaye refers to a book by Morgan Edwards, *Millennium: Last Days Novelties*, written in 1788, as evidence that the pretrib Rapture was taught before 1828. He says, "Although he saw only a three-and-a-half year Tribulation, he definitely saw the rapture occur before that Tribulation." At best, this makes Morgan a midtribulationalist. Then LaHaye tells us that Morgan "may have been influenced by John Gill before him or by others whose writings or teachings were available at that time *but have not been preserved*" (LaHaye and Jenkins, *Are We Living in the End Times?*, 113, emphasis added). How does he know this if their writings "have not been preserved"? LaHaye also refers to the work done by Grant Jeffrey in his book *Apocalypse*, which supposedly shows that the pretrib Rapture was taught prior to the nineteenth century. Jeffrey's work offers no such evidence, even though he selectively references numerous sources. Not one of these sources mentions a pretrib Rapture.

LaHaye also mentions Pseudo-Ephraem (probably a seventh-century composition) for historical support. While the sermon *On the Last Times, the Antichrist, and the End of the World* claims to be authored by Ephraem of Nisibis (306–73), no one really knows who wrote it or when it was written. Even so, pretribulationists believe that it contains two early pretrib Rapture statements (Timothy J. Demy, "Pseudo-Ephraem," in *Dictionary of Premillennial Theology*, ed. Mal Couch [Grand Rapids, MI: Kregel, 1996], 329; also see Demy and Thomas D. Ice, "The Rapture and an Early Medieval Citation," *Bibliotheca Sacra* [July/September 1995], 306–17, and Grant R. Jeffrey, "A Pretrib Rapture Statement in the Early Medieval Church," in *When the Trumpet Sounds*, ed. Thomas Ice and Timothy Demy [Eugene, OR: Harvest House, 1995], 105–25). For a refutation, see Bob Gundry, "'Pseudo-Ephraem' on Pretrib Preparation for a Posttrib Meeting with the Lord," in *First the Antichrist: Why Christ Won't Come Before the Antichrist Does* (Grand Rapids, MI: Baker, 1997), 16–18.

7. LaHaye, *No Fear of the Storm*, 154.

8. H. A. Ironside, *The Mysteries of God* (New York: Loizeaux Brothers, 1946), 50–51.

9. Not only are there five rapture positions, but there are at least four millennial positions: premillennialism, dispensational premillennialism, amillennialism, and postmillennialism. For a study of the various millennium views see: C. Marvin Pate, gen. ed., *Four Views on the Book of Revelation* (Grand Rapids, MI: Zondervan, 1998); Darrell L. Bock, gen. ed., *Three Views on the Millennium and Beyond* (Grand Rapids, MI: Zondervan, 1999); and Steve Gregg, ed., *Revelation: Four Views—A Parallel Commentary* (Nashville, TN: Thomas Nelson Publishers, 1997).

10. Thomas D. Ice, "The Origin of the Pretrib Rapture: Part II," *Biblical Perspectives*, March/April 1989, 5, emphasis added.

NOTES

11. Ironside, *The Mysteries of God*, 52.

12. LaHaye and Jenkins, *Are We Living in the End Times?*, 47.

13. Marvin Rosenthal, *The Pre-Wrath Rapture of the Church: A New Understanding of the Rapture, the Tribulation, and the Second Coming* (Nashville, TN: Thomas Nelson, 1990), 280.

14. William Sanford LaSor, *The Truth About Armageddon: What the Bible Says About the End Times* (Grand Rapids, MI: Baker, 1982), 134.

15. John F. Walvoord, *The Prophecy Knowledge Handbook* (Wheaton, IL: Victor Books, 1990), 481.

16. LaHaye and Jenkins, *Are We Living in the End Times?*, 95–96.

17. Paul wrote that Christians had been "raised up" with Jesus in such a way that they were "seated . . . with Him in the heavenly places, in Christ" (Eph. 2:6; cf. 1:20). That was not something that was going to happen; it was an event that had taken place in the first century. This verse is rarely discussed by advocates of a pretrib or any other Rapture position who claim to interpret the Bible literally.

18. Anthony A. Hoekema, *The Bible and the Future* (Grand Rapids, MI: Eerdmans, 1979), 168.

19. LaHaye and Jenkins, *Are We Living in the End Times?*, 96.

20. Ibid., 98.

21. For an alternate view, see Gary DeMar, *Last Days Madness: Obsession of the Modern Church*, 4th ed. (Powder Springs, GA: American Vision, 1999), chap. 17.

22. John F. Walvoord, *The Prophecy Knowledge Handbook: All the Prophecies of Scripture Explained in One Volume* (Wheaton, IL: Victor Books, 1990), 496.

23. Ronald A. Ward, *Commentary on 1 and 2 Timothy and Titus* (Waco, TX: Word Books, 1974), 260.

24. R. C. H. Lenski, *The Interpretation of St. Paul's Epistles to the Colossians, to the Thessalonians, to Timothy, to Titus and to Philemon* (Minneapolis, MN: Augsburg, [1937] 1961), 922.

25. C. Summer Wemp, "The Epistle to Titus," in *Liberty Bible Commentary: New Testament*, ed. Edward E. Hindson and Woodrow Michael Kroll (Lynchburg, VA: Old-Time Gospel Hour, 1982), 657.

26. LaHaye and Jenkins, *Left Behind*, 209.

27. Ibid.

28. C. I. Scofield, *Scofield Reference Bible* (New York: Oxford University Press, [1909] 1945), 1016 n. 1.

29. LaHaye, *No Fear of the Storm*, 177.

30. Ibid., 65.

31. Ibid., 74. See Tim LaHaye, *Revelation Unveiled*, rev. ed. (Grand Rapids, MI: Zondervan, 1999), 51–91.

32. LaHaye, *Revelation Unveiled*, 84.

33. William Hendriksen, *More Than Conquerors: An Interpretation of the Book of Revelation*, 2d ed. (Grand Rapids, MI: Baker, [1940] 1982), 60.

34. LaHaye, *Revelation Unveiled*, 99.

35. Ibid., 100.

36. The words *church* and *churches* are used eighteen times.

37. LaHaye, *Revelation Unveiled*, 100.

38. Kenneth L. Gentry Jr., "A Preterist View of Revelation," in *Four Views on the Book of Revelation*, ed. C. Marvin Pate (Grand Rapids, MI: Zondervan, 1998), 57 n. 49.

39. Robert H. Gundry, *The Church and the Tribulation* (Grand Rapids, MI: Zondervan, 1973), 78. Also see Gundry, *First the Antichrist*, 84–87.

40. If Bible interpretation is based on word counts, then the book of Esther does not belong in the Bible: "There can be no doubt that the historicity and canonicity of Esther has been the most debated of all the Old Testament books. Even some Jewish scholars questioned its inclusion in the Old Testament because of the absence of God's name" (Edward G. Dobson, "Esther," in *Liberty Bible Commentary: Old Testament*, ed. Edward E. Hindson and Woodrow M. Kroll [Lynchburg, VA: Old-Time Gospel Hour, 1982], 909).

41. George Eldon Ladd, *A Commentary on the Revelation of John* (Grand Rapids, MI: Eerdmans, 1972), 72.

42. D. A. Carson, *The Gospel According to John* (Grand Rapids, MI: Eerdmans, 1991), 488.

43. LaHaye and Jenkins, *Are We Living in the End Times?*, 97.

44. Tim LaHaye, gen.ed., *Prophecy Study Bible* (Chatanooga, TN: AMG Publishers, 2000), 1479.

45. LaHaye, *Revelation Unveiled*, 306.

CHAPTER 3

1. LaHaye and Jenkins, *Left Behind*, 309.

2. Henry M. Morris, *The Revelation Record* (Wheaton, IL: Tyndale, 1983), 28–30. Morris lists "seven years of judgments" (11:3; 12:6, 14; 13:5). Not one of these references mentions "seven years."

3. LaHaye identifies the "forty-two months" of Revelation 11:2 and 12:6 as describing the same period of time. See LaHaye, *Prophecy Study Bible*, 1380, 1383.

4. Ibid., 1375.

5. Ibid., 1380.

6. Tim LaHaye, "Reasons for a Pretribulation Rapture," *Prophecy Study Bible* (Chatanooga, TN: AMG Publishers, 2000), 1479.

7. LaHaye, *Are We Living in the End Times?*, 364.

8. John Walvoord, *The Revelation of Jesus Christ: A Commentary* (Chicago: Moody Press, 1966), 178.

9. Kenneth L. Gentry Jr., *Before Jerusalem Fell: Dating the Book of Revelation*, 3d ed. (Atlanta, GA: American Vision, 1998), 253.

10. LaHaye and Jenkins, *Are We Living in the End Times?*, 149.

11. Ibid., 153.

12. J. Barton Payne, *Encyclopedia of Biblical Prophecy: The Complete Guide to Scriptural Predictions and Their Fulfillment* (New York: Harper & Row, 1973).

13. J. Barton Payne, *The Imminent Appearing of Christ* (Grand Rapids, MI: Eerdmans, 1962), 148–49.

14. Philip Mauro, *Seventy Weeks and the Great Tribulation* (Swengel, PA: Reiner, n.d.), 74.

15. Philip Mauro, *The Wonders of Bible Chronology* (Swengel, PA: Reiner, 1970), 97.

16. The "he" of Daniel 9:27 refers to "Messiah" in verse 26, not "the prince who is to come." "Messiah" is the subject throughout 9:24–27, while "prince who is to come" is a subordinate clause of "the people": "The people of the prince who is to come." Let's suppose, however, that the "prince" of verse 26 is not the Messiah. Why does he have to be the

NOTES

Antichrist? Why couldn't he be Titus, the Roman general whose armies destroyed the "holy city" in A.D. 70?

17. There are thirteen instances of forty-year time periods in the Bible with no gaps (Deut. 8:2; Judg. 3:11; 5:31; 8:28; 13:1; 1 Sam. 4:18; 2 Sam. 5:4; 1 Kings 11:42; 2 Chron. 24:1; Ezek. 29:11; Acts 7:23, 30; 13:21). In addition to the forty-year intervals of time, there are thirteen forty-day time periods found in Scripture. In each case, no gap is implied (Gen. 7:4, 12; 50:3; Ex. 24:18; 34:28; Num. 13:25; Deut. 9:18, 25; 1 Sam. 17:16; 1 Kings 19:8; Ezek. 4:6; Matt. 4:2; Acts 1:3).

18. Jacques Doukhan, "The Seventy Weeks of Dan. 9: An Exegetical Study," *Andrews University Seminary Studies* 17 (spring 1979), 8. Quoted in J. Randall Price, "Prophetic Postponement in Daniel 9 and Other Texts," in *Issues in Dispensationalism*, ed. Wesley R. Willis and John R. Masters (Chicago, IL: Moody Press, 1994), 148. Price does not follow this methodology.

19. E. J. Young, *The Prophecy of Daniel: A Prophecy* (Grand Rapids, MI: Eerdmans, 1949), 216.

20. E.W. Hengstenberg, *Christology of the Old Testament and a Commentary on the Messianic Predictions,* 4 vols. (Grand Rapids, MI: Kregel, [1872–76] 1956), 3:143.

21. Milton S. Terry, *Biblical Apocalyptics: A Study of the Most Notable Revelations of God and of Christ* (Grand Rapids, MI: Baker, [1898] 1988), 201.

22. Stuart Olyott, *Dare to Stand Alone* (Welwyn, Hertfordshire, England: Evangelical Press, 1982), 125.

CHAPTER 4

1. Tim LaHaye and Jerry Jenkins, *Tribulation Force: The Continuing Drama of Those Left Behind* (Wheaton, IL: Tyndale, 1996), 373–74.

2. LaHaye, *No Fear of the Storm,* 240. Also see LaHaye and Jenkins, *Are We Living in the End Times?,* 5.

3. The Greek word translated "world" (*oikoumene*) in Revelation 3:10 is best translated "inhabited earth" or "Roman Empire." The usual word for "world" (*kosmos*) is not used. The Greek word *oikoumene* is also used in Luke 2:1 and is often translated "inhabited earth" or "Roman Empire" in modern translations because the tax decree included only the Roman Empire, what was generally known of the world at that time. The Greek word for "earth" (*ges*, from which we get the word *geography*) is best translated "land" when Israel is the subject. In this case, the context determines the best translation.

4. LaHaye, *Revelation Unveiled,* 25.

5. Thomas Ice and Randall Price, *Ready to Rebuild: The Imminent Plan to Rebuild the Last Days Temple* (Eugene, OR: Harvest House, 1992), 197–98.

6. LaHaye and Jenkins, *Are We Living in the End Times?,* 122.

7. LaHaye, *Prophecy Study Bible,* 879, note on Ezekiel 40:3.

8. LaHaye, *Revelation Unveiled,* 182.

9. Thomas Ice, "Preterism and the Date of Revelation," in LaHaye's *Prophecy Study Bible,* 1484.

10. G. K. Beale, *The Book of Revelation: A Commentary on the Greek Text* (Grand Rapids, MI: Eerdmans, 1999), 20–21.

11. LaHaye, *Revelation Unveiled,* 27.

12. The disputed sentence, in italics, can be read this way: "We will not, however, incur the risk of pronouncing positively as to the name of Antichrist; for if it were necessary that his name should be distinctly revealed in this present time, it would have been announced by him who beheld the apocalyptic vision. *For it [the apocalyptic vision] was seen no very long time since, but almost in our day, toward the end of Domitian's reign.*"

Or it can be read this way: "We will not, however, incur the risk of pronouncing positively as to the name of Antichrist; for if it were necessary that his name should be distinctly revealed in this present time, it would have been announced by him who beheld the apocalyptic vision. *For he [John] was seen no very long time since, but almost in our day, toward the end of Domitian's reign.*"

"Was seen" is a third-person singular that can be translated either as "it was seen" or "he was seen." In Greek, the subject is incorporated in the verb. Since "it would have been announced" refers to "the name of Antichrist" in the first sentence and not "this present time," we can assume that "he [John] was seen" refers to "by him who beheld" and not "the apocalyptic vision."

13. Gentry, *Before Jerusalem Fell*, 67.

14. LaHaye, *Revelation Unveiled*, 26.

15. Kenneth L. Gentry Jr., *The Beast of Revelation* (Powder Springs, GA: American Vision, 2001), chap. 14.

16. LaHaye, *Revelation Unveiled*, 27.

17. Ibid.

18. Quoted in Gentry, *Before Jerusalem Fell*, 321.

19. Gentry, *Before Jerusalem Fell*, 322.

20. LaHaye and Jenkins, *Are We Living in the End Times?*, 31, emphasis in original.

21. LaHaye, *Prophecy Study Bible*, 1038, note on 24:15.

22. D. A. Carson, "Matthew," in *The Expositor's Bible Commentary*, ed. Frank E. Gaebelein, 12 vols. (Grand Rapids, MI: Zondervan, 1985), 8:507.

23. LaSor, *The Truth About Armageddon*, 122.

24. LaHaye, *Prophecy Study Bible*, 1040, note on Matthew 24:34.

25. The Greek word *genea* is translated "generation," while *genos* is translated "race." *Genea* is used in Matthew 1:17: "Therefore all the generations from Abraham to David are fourteen generations; and from David to the deportation to Babylon fourteen generations; and from the deportation to Babylon to the time of Christ fourteen generations." Try substituting "race" for "generation." It does not make sense.

CHAPTER 5

1. LaHaye and Jenkins, *Left Behind*, 418.

2. Thomas Ice and Timothy Demy, *The Truth About the Signs of the Times* (Eugene, OR: Harvest House, 1997), 8. Quoted in LaHaye and Jenkins, *Are We Living in the End Times?*, 16.

3. Ralph Woodrow, *The Great Prophecies of the Bible* (Riverside, CA: Ralph Woodrow Evangelistic Association, 1971), 54. See Flavius Josephus, *The Antiquities of the Jews,* in *The Works of Josephus,* trans. William Whiston (Peabody, MA: Hendrickson Publishers, 1987), 20.5.1, 531.

4. Alexander Keith, *Evidence of the Truth of the Christian Religion, Derived from the Literal Fulfillment of Prophecy; Particularly as Illustrated by the History of the Jews and by the Discoveries of Recent Travelers* (Edinburgh: William Whyte & Co., 1844), 60.

NOTES

5. Thomas Newton, *Dissertations on the Prophecies, Which Have Remarkably Been Fulfilled, and at This Time Are Fulfilling in the World* (London: J. F. Dove, 1754), 333.

6. The Greek word often translated "affliction" or "persecution" in Acts 11:19 is the same word translated "tribulation" (*thlipsis*) in Matthew 24:9.

7. In Colossians 1:6, the Greek word *kosmos* is used. Even if Jesus had used *kosmos* in Matthew 24:14, Colossians 1:6 would be its fulfillment. The same is true for Romans 1:8.

8. Edward Hayes Plumptre, "The Gospel According to St. Matthew," in *A New Testament Commentary for English Readers*, ed. Charles John Ellicott, 3 vols. (London: Cassell and Co., 1897), 1:147.

9. Flavius Josephus, *The Wars of the Jews,* in *The Works of Josephus*, ed. William Whiston (Peabody, MA: Hendrickson Publishers, 1987), 4.3.6–10 and 4.5.4, 671–72, 680.

10. William L. Lane, *Commentary on the Gospel of Mark* (Grand Rapids, MI: Eerdmans, 1974), 469.

11. Josephus, *The Wars of the Jews,* 5.1.3, 697.

12. Martin Hengel, *The Zealots: Investigations into the Jewish Freedom Movement in the Period from Herod I until 70 A.D,* trans. David Smith (Edinburgh: T. & T. Clark, [1976] 1989), 305.

13. LaHaye, *Prophecy Study Bible,* 1118, note on Luke 21:24.

14. Ibid., 1119, note on Luke 21:35–36.

15. Robert L. Thomas and Stanley N. Gundry, *A Harmony of the Gospels* (Chicago, IL: Moody Press, 1978), 195–201.

16. Josephus, *The Wars of the Jews,* 6.5.2, 742–43.

Chapter 6

1. LaHaye and Jenkins, *Left Behind,* 221.

2. Daniel is called "son of man" once (Dan. 8:17).

3. LaHaye, *Revelation Unveiled,* 198.

4. Ibid., emphasis added. Also see LaHaye, *Prophecy Study Bible,* 47, note on Genesis 37:6–11, and 1383, note on Revelation 12:1–5.

5. Woodrow, *Great Prophecies of the Bible,* 81.

6. "'And the stars in the sky fell to the earth, as late figs drop from a fig tree when shaken by a strong wind' (Rev. 6:13). This verse indicates that meteors will fall to the ground and hit as hard, unripe things [*sic*]." (LaHaye, *Revelation Unveiled,* 147).

7. George Eldon Ladd, *Jesus and the Kingdom: The Eschatology of Biblical Realism* (New York: Harper & Row, 1964), chap. 2.

8. LaHaye, *Prophecy Study Bible,* 1040, note on Matthew 24:29–31.

9. "Hereafter" does not mean "at the Final Judgment" when everybody will see Jesus, when at the name of Jesus every knee will bow and every tongue will confess "that Jesus Christ is Lord, to the glory of God the Father" (Phil. 2:11).

10. LaHaye and Jenkins, *Are We Living in the End Times?,* 225.

11. James Glasgow, *The Apocalypse Translated and Expounded* (Edinburgh: T. & T. Clark, 1872), 126–27.

12. LaHaye and Jenkins, *Are We Living in the End Times?,* 57.

13. LaHaye, *Prophecy Study Bible,* 1040, note on Matthew 24:32–33.

14. John Calvin, *Commentary on a Harmony of the Evangelists, Matthew, Mark, and Luke,* 3 vols. (Grand Rapids, MI: Eerdmans, 1957), 1:152.

15. Henry Hammond, *A Paraphrase, and Annotations Upon all the Books of the New Testament, Briefly Explaining all the Difficult Places Thereof* (London: Printed for John Nicholson, at the King's-Arms in Little Britain, 1702), 102.

16. John Lightfoot, *A Commentary on the New Testament from the Talmud and Hebraica*, 4 vols. (Oxford: Oxford University Press, [1658–1674] 1859), 2:320.

17. Philip Doddridge, *The Family Expositor; or, A Paraphrase and Version of the New Testament; with Critical Notes, and a Practical Improvement of each Section*, 6 vols. (Charlestown, MA.: Ethridge and Company, 1807), 1:377.

18. Newton, *Dissertations on the Prophecies, Which Have Remarkably Been Fulfilled*, 377.

19. John Gill, *An Exposition of the New Testament*, 3 vols. (London: Mathews and Leigh, 1809), 1:296.

20. Thomas Scott, *The Holy Bible Containing the Old and New Testaments, According to the Authorised Version; with Explanatory Notes, Practical Observations, and Copious Marginal References*, 3 vols. (New York: Collins and Hannay, 1832), 3:111.

21. Robert G. Bratcher and Eugene A. Nida, *A Translator's Handbook of the Gospel of Mark* (New York: United Bible Societies, 1961), 419.

22. William L. Lane, *Commentary on the Gospel of Mark* (Grand Rapids, MI: Eerdmans, 1974), 480.

23. Carson, "Matthew," 8:507.

CHAPTER 7

1. LaHaye and Jenkins, *Left Behind*, 352.

2. LaHaye and Jenkins, *Are We Living in the End Times?*, 134.

3. Ibid., 135.

4. Ibid., *Are We Living in the End Times?*, 136.

5. Joseph Addison Alexander, *The Prophecies of Isaiah*, 2 vols. (Grand Rapids, MI: Zondervan [1846–47] 1977), 1:281.

6. Charles H. Dyer, *The Rise of Babylon: Sign of the End Times* (Wheaton, IL: Tyndale, 1991), 19.

7. Ronald Showers, "The Biblical Concept of the Day of the Lord," *Israel My Glory*, April/May 1992, 30.

8. Edwin Yamauchi, "Updating the Armageddon Calendar," *Christianity Today*, 29 April 1991, 51.

9. Tony Horwitz, "Paranoia Runs Deep in Iraqi Sands," *Washington Post*, 20 November 1988, E1. Quoted in Dyer, *The Rise of Babylon*, 129.

10. LaHaye and Jenkins, *Are We Living in the End Times?*, 137–38.

11. LaHaye, *Revelation Unveiled*, 188.

12. Ibid., 70.

13. "Now I have given all these lands into the hand of Nebuchadnezzar king of Babylon, My servant, and I have given him also the wild animals of the field to serve him" (Jer. 27:6).

14. Arno Froese, "The Figurative Babylon," in *Prophecy Study Bible*, 703, emphasis added.

15. LaHaye and Jenkins, *Are We Living in the End Times?*, 143.

16. Dave Hunt, *A Woman Rides the Beast: The Roman Catholic Church and the Last Days* (Eugene, OR: Harvest House, 1994). Dave Hunt is one of the contributors to LaHaye's *Prophecy Study Bible*, x, 1303. LaHaye takes a similar position in describing "Religious Babylon." See LaHaye, *Revelation Unveiled*, 26–77.

17. Mal Couch and Joseph Chambers, "Babylon," in *Dictionary of Premillennial Theology*, ed. Mal Couch (Grand Rapids, MI: Kregel, 1996), 61–62.

18. Gentry, *Before Jerusalem Fell*.

19. Gentry, "A Preterist View of Revelation," 77.

20. When looked at in purely economic terms, these items point to a world trading power. Looked at theologically, the "cargoes" relate to the temple, priesthood, and sacrificial system, as if to say that these items are used for trade rather than the sanctuary and worship. Although it's true that Rome trafficked in slaves, Israel had its own sform of slave trade (Matt. 23:13–15; Gal. 4:22–25).

21. Gentry, *Before Jerusalem Fell*, 241.

CHAPTER 8

1. LaHaye and Jenkins, *Left Behind*, 212–13.

2. Josef Ton, "The Cornerstone at the Crossroads," *Wheaton Alumni*, August/September 1991, 6–7.

3. LaHaye and Jenkins, *Left Behind*, 70.

4. Ibid., 270.

5. Ibid., 274.

6. Ibid., 275.

7. LaHaye, *Revelation Unveiled*, 207.

8. Salem Kirban, *Kissinger: Man of Peace?* (Huntington Valley, PA: Salem Kirban, 1974).

9. Francis X. Gumerlock, *The Day and the Hour: Christianity's Perennial Fascination with Predicting the End of the World* (Powder Springs, GA: American Vision, 2000), 10, 89, 115, 231, 286. Also see Christopher Hill, *Antichrist in Seventeenth-Century England* (London: Oxford University Press, 1971).

10. LaHaye, *Revelation Unveiled*, 207.

11. Ibid.

12. Benjamin B. Warfield, "Antichrist," in *Selected Shorter Writings of Benjamin B. Warfield*, vol. 1, ed. John E. Meeter (Nutley, NJ: Presbyterian and Reformed, 1970), 360–61.

13. Edward Hindson, "Antichrist," in *Prophecy Study Bible*, 1291.

14. Warfield, "Antichrist," 357.

15. Gary DeMar, *"You've Heard It Said": 15 Biblical Misconceptions That Render Christians Powerless* (Atlanta, GA: American Vision, 1991).

16. LaHaye and Jenkins, *Are We Living in the End Times?*, 17.

17. LaHaye, *Revelation Unveiled*, 22–27.

18. R. H. Charles, *A Critical and Exegetical Commentary on the Revelation of St. John*, 2 vols. (New York: Charles Scribner's Sons, 1920), 1:cxliii.

19. Gentry, *The Beast of Revelation*, chap. 3. Also see Charles, *A Critical and Exegetical Commentary on the Revelation of St. John*, 1:367.

20. Frederic W. Farrar, *The Early Days of Christianity* (New York: E. P. Dutton, 1882), 471.

21. Philip Mauro, *The Seventy Weeks and the Great Tribulation: A Study of the Last Two Visions of Daniel, and of the Olivet Discourse of the Lord Jesus Christ*, rev. ed. (Swengel, PA: Reiner, 1944), 13–40.

22. Suetonius, *The Lives of the Twelve Caesars: Nero*, 28. Quoted in Gentry, *The Beast of Revelation*, chap. 1.

23. Miriam T. Griffin, *Nero: The End of a Dynasty* (New Haven, CT: Yale University Press, 1984), 112.

24. Ibid., 132–33.

25. Ibid., 133.

26. Farrar, *Early Days of Christianity*, 472.

27. Griffin, *Nero*, 15.

28. Tertullian, "Scorpiace: Antidote for the Scorpion's Sting," in "The Writings of Tertullian," 2.8, *The Ante-Nicene Fathers* (Grand Rapids, MI: Eerdmans, 1956), 3:648.

29. Bruce M. Metzger, *A Textual Commentary on the Greek New Testament* (London: United Bible Societies, 1971), 751–52.

30. LaHaye, *Revelation Unveiled*, 208.

31. For a verse-by-verse exposition of 2 Thessalonians 2, see DeMar, *Last Days Madness*, 273–311.

32. John Bray, *The Man of Sin of II Thessalonians 2* (Lakeland, FL: John Bray Ministries, 1997), 26. See Paul L. Maier, *Josephus: The Essential Writings* (Grand Rapids, MI: Kregel, 1988), 347–54, for a description of John Levi's lawless exploits.

33. Mireille Hadas-Lebel, *Flavius Josephus: Eyewitness to Rome's First-Century Conquest of Judea*, trans. Richard Miller (New York: Macmillan, [1989] 1993), 165.

CHAPTER 9

1. Tim LaHaye and Jerry Jenkins, *The Mark: The Beast Rules the World* (Wheaton, IL: Tyndale, 2000), 85.

2. The Humane Society in Athens, Georgia, promotes a program where "a microchip containing an identification number that can be implanted into an animal's skin between its shoulder blades" so "any chip-equipped animal . . . can be traced back to its owner in minutes" ("Society Offers Microchip Implant for Dogs," *Marietta Daily Journal*, 4 July 1994, 3B). Also see Shelley Emling, "Super Bar Codes," *Atlanta Journal/Constitution*, 13 May 2001, Q1, 10.

3. "Bee Bar Code," *Popular Science*, December 1989, 54.

4. Katherine Hobson, "Hey, Security Tag Makers: You're It," *U.S. News & World Report*, 14 May 2001, 34.

5. Robert Van Kampen, *The Sign of Christ's Coming and the End of the Age*, rev. ed. (Wheaton, IL: Crossway Books, 1999), 22–25.

6. Gumerlock, *The Day and the Hour*, 225.

7. Gary H. Kah, *En Route to Global Occupation* (Lafayette, LA: Huntington House, 1991), 12.

8. A full-page advertisement paid for by the Eternal Gospel Church of Seventh-Day Adventists that appeared in *USA Today* (August 10, 1999), 13A. This is a relatively old view. See Albertus Pieters, *Studies in the Revelation of St. John* (Grand Rapids, MI: Eerdmans, 1950), 212.

9. Zola Levitt writes in his April 1999 ministry newsletter that after attending a prophecy conference, he "started looking into the Hebrew language and certain computer designations" and linked the World Wide Web and 666: "To begin with, the familiar symbol for the Internet, World Wide Web or 'www', would be rendered in Hebrew as *vav, vav, vav* (the Hebrew alphabet does not have a 'w' and Hebrew speaking people use the *vav*, or 'v', in place of our 'w'). The interesting part is that since Hebrew letters also have numerical values (Hebrew speakers do not prefer Arabic numerals), we have a number of the letter *vav*. Since it is the sixth letter of the alphabet, the expression 'www', in Hebrew, is 666." Of course, this has not stopped Zola Levitt from using the World (6) Wide (6) Web (6).

10. LaHaye and Jenkins, *The Mark*, 85.

11. Peter Lalonde and Paul Lalonde, *Racing Toward . . . The Mark of the Beast* (Eugene, OR: Harvest House, 1994), 87, 103.

12. Thomas Ice and Timothy Demy, *The Coming Cashless Society* (Eugene, OR: Harvest House, 1996), 131.

13. "From now on let no one cause trouble for me, for I bear on my body the brand-marks of Jesus" (Gal. 6:17; see Isa. 44:5).

14. These two Greek letters represent 600 (X) and 8 (H).

15. David Brady, *The Contribution of British Writers Between 1560 and 1830 to the Interpretation of Revelation 13.16–18 (The Number of the Beast): A Study in the History of Exegesis* (Tubingen, Germany: J. C. B. Mohr, 1983), 167. "We read in 3 Macc. ii. 29, of Ptolemy Philopater, that he ordered the Jews of Alexandria to be forcibly enrolled, and when enrolled, to be marked with a red-hot brand on their body, with the sign of Bacchus the Ivy-weaver. And Philo mentions idolaters who confessed their idolatry by branding themselves with indelible marks" (Henry Alford, *The New Testament for English Readers* [Chicago, IL: Moody Press, 1889]).

16. Actually nothing is said about "the last days" in Revelation 13. But even if Revelation 13 did use "the last days" to designate the time in which the prophetic events were to take place, other passages indicate that "the last days" were in the first century (see Heb. 1:1–2 and James 5:3).

17. Larry Spargimino, *The Anti-Prophets: End-time Prophecy and the Challenge of Preterism* (Oklahoma City, OK: Hearthstone Publishing, 2000), 25.

18. John Hanna, "Exodus," in *The Bible Knowledge Commentary: Old Testament*, ed. John F. Walvoord and Roy B. Zuck (Wheaton, IL: Victor Books, 1985), 130.

19. John J. Davis, *Moses and the Gods of Egypt: Studies in Exodus*, 2d ed. (Grand Rapids, MI: Baker, 1986), 163.

20. Elmer L. Towns, "Deuteronomy," in *Liberty Bible Commentary: Old Testament*, 338.

21. C.F. Keil and F. Delitzsch, *Biblical Commentary on the Old Testament: Pentateuch*, 3 vols. (Grand Rapids, MI: Eerdmans, 1951), 3:37.

22. John I. Durham, *Word Biblical Commentary: Exodus* (Waco, TX: Word, 1987), 178; W. H. Gispen, *Bible Student's Commentary: Exodus* (Grand Rapids, MI: Zondervan, 1982), 133, 135; R. Alan Cole, *Tyndale Old Testament Commentaries: Exodus* (Downers Grove, IL: InterVarsity Press, 1973), 114; James G. Murphy, *A Critical and Exegetical Commentary on the Book of Exodus with a New Translation* (Minneapolis, MN: Klock & Klock [1866] 1979), 141; C. F. Keil and F. Delitzsch, *Biblical Commentary on the Old Testament: Pentateuch*, trans. James Martin, 3 vols. (Grand Rapids, MI: Eerdmans 1951), 2:36–37; Philip C. Johnson, "Exodus," in *The Wycliffe Bible Commentary*, ed. Charles F. Pfeiffer and Everett F. Harrison (Chicago, IL: Moody Press, 1962), 63; Hywel R. Jones, "Exodus," in *The New Bible Commentary: Revised*, ed. Donald Guthrie and J. A. Motyer (Grand Rapids, MI: Eerdmans, 1970), 128.

23. George Eldon Ladd, *A Commentary on the Revelation of John* (Grand Rapids, MI: Eerdmans, 1972), 185.

24. J. E. Leonard, *Come Out of Her, My People: A Study of the Revelation to John* (Chicago, IL: Laudemont Press, 1991), 105.

25. Robert L. Thomas, *Revelation 1–7: An Exegetical Commentary* (Chicago, IL: Moody Press, 1992), 292.

26. Ibid., 293.

27. Ibid.

28. Tim LaHaye, *Understanding the Last Days: The Keys to Unlocking Bible Prophecy* (Eugene, OR: Harvest House, 1998), 57.

29. LaHaye, *Revelation Unveiled*, 233.

30. Ice and Demy, *The Coming Cashless Society*, 69–70.

31. Ibid., 85.

32. James B. Jordan, *A Brief Reader's Guide to Revelation* (Niceville, FL: Transfiguration Press, 1999), 19.

33. Julius Caesar, Augustus Caesar (Octavian), Tiberius Caesar, Gaius Caesar (Caligula) Claudius Caesar, Nero Caesar, Galba, Otho, Vitellius, and Vespasian.

34. Herod the Great, Archelaus, Herod Antipas, Herod Philip I, Herod Philip II, Herod Agrippa I, and Herod Agrippa II.

35. Stewart Perowne, *The Later Herods: The Political Background of the New Testament* (London: Hodder and Stoughton, 1958), 105.

36. Ibid., 106.

37. Beale, *The Book of Revelation: A Commentary on the Greek Text*, 684.

38 *Tacitus: The Histories,* trans Kenneth Wellesley, 1:11 (London, England: Penguin Books, 1990), 2–3.

39. Flavius Josephus, *The Wars of the Jews*, 7.4.2, 754.

40. Milton S. Terry, *Biblical Apocalyptics: A Study of the Most Notable Revelations of God and of Christ* (Grand Rapids, MI: Baker Book House, [1898] 1988), 400.

    Terry's further remarks are interesting: "There may also in this connection be an allusion to such well-known claims and feats of miraculous power as Simon Magus puts forth in the Recognitions of Clement (iii, 47), where he is represented as saying: 'I have flown through the air; I have been mixed with fire, and been made one body with it; I have made statues move; I have animated lifeless things'" (400).

41. George Eldon Ladd, *A Commentary on the Revelation of John* (Grand Rapids, MI: Eerdmans, 1972), 184. "Simon was deemed a god at Rome and honored as a god with a statue in the River Tiber between two bridges." For an account of Simon Magus, see Paul L. Maier, ed., *Eusebius: The Church History: A New Translation with Commentary* (Grand Rapids, MI: Kregel, 1999), 71–72. *The Church History* of Eusebius was written in the fourth century and relies on the works of earlier writers.

42. Paul T. Butler, *Thirteen Lessons on Revelation*, 2 vols. (Joplin, MO: College Press Publishing Co., 1982), 2:21.

43. Beale, *The Book of Revelation: A Commentary on the Greek Text,* 710.

44. LaHaye, *Revelation Unveiled*, 225.

45. Gary DeMar, *Thinking Straight in a Crooked World: A Christian Defense Manual,* (Powder Springs, GA.: American Vision, 2001).

CHAPTER 10

1. LaHaye and Jenkins, *Tribulation Force,* 401, emphasis in original.

2. LaHaye and Jenkins, *Are We Living in the End Times?*, 67.

3. H. Wayne House, "Apostasia in 2 Thessalonians 2:3: Apostasy or Rapture?" in *When the Trumpet Sounds*, 262–96.

4. Ibid., 286.

5. Flavius Josephus, *The Life of Flavius Josephus*, in *The Works of Josephus*, trans. William Whiston (Peabody, MA: Hendrickson Publishers, 1988), 4.

6. F. F. Bruce, *The Spreading Flame: The Rise and Progress of Christianity from Its First Beginnings to the Conversion of the English* (Grand Rapids, MI: Eerdmans, 1958), 152.

7. Benjamin B. Warfield, "The Prophecies of St. Paul," in *Biblical and Theological Studies*, ed. Samuel G. Craig (Philadelphia, PA: Presbyterian and Reformed, 1968), 474.

8. Bruce E. Hoyt, "What About the Antichrist?" *Presbyterian Journal*, 17 May 1978, 8.

9. John F. Walvoord, *Prophecy: 14 Essential Keys to Understanding the Final Drama* (Nashville, TN: Thomas Nelson, 1993), 114–15.

10. F. W. Farrar, *Texts Explained or Helps to Understand the New Testament* (Cleveland, OH: F. M. Barton, 1899), 178. The Greek word translated "is present" is found in six places in the New Testament in addition to 2 Thessalonians 2:1. In each case, "is present" and not "is near" is the best translation (Rom. 8:38; 1 Cor. 3:22; 7:26; Gal. 1:4; 2 Tim. 3:1; Heb. 9:9). E. J. Bicknell writes that "'is now present'. . . is the only possible translation of the Greek . . . Attempts are made to soften down the translation because of the difficulty of seeing how any one could suppose that the Day of the Lord had actually arrived" (E. J. Bicknell, *The First and Second Epistles to the Thessalonians* [London: Methuen and Co., 1932], 74).

11. For a similar discussion of this point, see N. T. Wright, "Jerusalem in the New Testament," in *Jerusalem Past and Present in the Purposes of God*, ed. P. W. L. Walker (Grand Rapids, MI: Baker, 1994), 64.

12. John Lightfoot, *The Whole Works of the Rev. John Lightfoot*, ed. John Rogers Pitman, 13 vols. (London: J. F. Dove, 1822), 3:231.

13. Newton, *Dissertations on the Prophecies*, 389.

14. John Brown, *Expository Discourses on the First Epistle of the Apostle Peter*, 3 vols. (Marshallton, DE: The National Foundation for Christian Education, n.d.), 3:84–85. See his equally fine comments on the passing of "heaven and earth" in *The Discourses and Sayings of our Lord*, 3 vols. (London: Banner of Truth Trust, [1852] 1967), 1:171–74.

15. LaHaye and Jenkins, *Are We Living in the End Times?*, 68.

16. Patricia Klein, reviewer, on-line review, <www.amazon.com> (1998). Quoted in LaHaye and Jenkins, *Are We Living in the End Times?*, 68.

CHAPTER 11

1. Tim LaHaye, *No Fear of the Storm: Why Christians Will Escape All the Tribulation* (Sisters, OR: Multnomah Press, 1992), 243.

2. Tim LaHaye, "How to Study Bible Prophecy," *Prophecy Study Bible* (Chattanooga, TN: AMG Publishers, 2000), xiii.

3. Ibid.

4. Tim LaHaye, *Revelation Unveiled*, rev. ed. (Grand Rapids, MI: Zondervan, 1999), 323.

5. John F. Walvoord, *The Revelation of Jesus Christ* (Chicago: Moody Press, 1966), 277. Quoted in LaHaye, *Revelation Unveiled*, 307.

6. LaHaye, "How to Study Bible Prophecy," xiii.

7. Joseph Addison Alexander, *The Psalms Translated and Explained* (Grand Rapids, MI: Baker Book House, [1873] 1975), 402.

8. Dan McCartney and Charles Clayton, *Let the Reader Understand: A Guide to Interpreting the Bible* (Wheaton, IL: Victor Books/A BridgePoint Book, 1994), 120. For many interpreters, the number "thousand" is thought to be figurative of a "very long period of

time," since "thousand" is often used in Scripture to mean more than a thousand (Ex. 20:6; Deut. 1:11; 7:9; 32:30; Joshua 23:10; Judges 15:15; Ps. 50:10; 90:4; 91:7; 105:8; Ecc. 6:6; Isa. 30:17; 60:22; 2 Pet. 3:8).

9. Tim LaHaye and Jerry Jenkins, *Are We Living in the End Times?: Current Events Foretold in Scripture . . . And What They Mean* (Wheaton, IL: Tyndale House Publishers, 1999), 6.

10. LaHaye, "How to Study Bible Prophecy," xiii.

11. Norman L. Geisler and J. Yutaka Amano, *The Reincarnation Sensation* (Wheaton, IL: Tyndale House Publishers, 1986), 142–43.

12. Dave Hunt, *A Woman Rides the Beast: The Roman Catholic Church and the Last Days* (Eugene, OR: Harvest House, 1994), 384.

13. James G. McCarthy, *The Gospel According to Rome: Comparing Catholic Tradition and the Word of God* (Eugene, OR: Harvest House Publishers, 1995), 138–44.

14. LaHaye, "How to Study Bible Prophecy," xiii.

15. LaHaye, *Revelation Unveiled*, 25.

16. An interview with Tim LaHaye and Jerry Jenkins on Larry King Live, "Is the Apocalypse Coming?" (June 19, 2000).

17. Ed Hindson, *Approaching Armageddon: The World Prepares for War with God* (Eugene, OR: Harvest House, 1997), 36.

18. Hindson, *Approaching Armageddon*, 36.

19. W. F. Arndt and F. W. Gingrich, eds., *A Greek-English Lexicon of the New Testament and Other Early Christian Literature*, 4th ed. (Chicago: University of Chicago, 1957), 213.

20. Philip Mauro, *Things Which Soon Must Come to Pass: A Commentary on the Book of Revelation* (Swengel, PA: Reiner Publications, [1925] 1984), 24–25. Emphasis in original.

21. Josif Ton, "The Cornerstone at the Crossroads," *Wheaton Alumni* (August/September 1991), 6–7.

22. Charles C. Ryrie, *The Living End* (Old Tappan, NJ: Revell, 1976), 21.

23. Hal Lindsey, *The Late Great Planet Earth* (Grand Rapids, MI: Zondervan, 1970), 145.

24. Hal Lindsey, "The Great Cosmic Countdown," *Eternity* (January 1977), 21.

25. Ted Peters, *Futures: Human and Divine* (Atlanta, GA: John Knox, 1978), 28.

26. John R. W. Stott, *Human Rights and Human Wrongs: Major Issues for a New Century* (Grand Rapids, MI: Baker Books, 1999), 23.

27. Stott, *Human Rights and Human Wrongs*, 30–31. See Tom Sine, *The Mustard Seed Conspiracy* (Waco, TX: Word, 1981), 69–71.

28. Paul T. Coughlin, *Secrets, Plots & Hidden Agendas: What You Don't Know About Conspiracy Theories* (Downers Grove, IL: InterVarsity, 1999), 145–46.

29. Jess Walter, *Every Knee Shall Bow: The Truth and Tragedy of Ruby Ridge and the Randy Weaver Family* (New York: Regan Books/Harper Collins, 1995).

30. Tim LaHaye, "Twelve Reasons Why This Could be the Terminal Generation," *When the Trumpet Sounds*, eds. Thomas Ice and Timothy Demy (Eugene, OR: Harvest House Publishers, 1995), 429.

31. Ibid.

32. Ibid.

33. Ibid., 443.

34. Ibid., 429, 436, 442.

35. Francis X. Gumerlock, *The Day and the Hour: Christianity's Perennial Fascination with Predicting the End of the World* (Atlanta, GA: American Vision, 1999).

36. "In the Spotlight," *World* (June 16, 2001), 22. For a detailed historical account of the era, see John Aberth, *From the Brink of the Apocalypse: Confronting Famine, Plague, War and Death in the Later Middle Ages* (New York: Routledge, 2001).

37. Francis Fukuyama, *The End of History and the Last Man* (New York: The Free Press, 1992).

38. LaHaye, "Twelve Reasons Why This Could be the Terminal Generation," 427.

39. LaHaye calls it the "Balfore Treaty." (LaHaye, "Twelve Reasons Why This Could Be the Terminal Generation," 432).

40. Lindsey, *The Late Great Planet Earth*, 53–54.

41. John F. Walvoord, *Matthew: Thy Kingdom Come* (Chicago, IL: Moody, [1974] 1980), 191–92.

42. LaHaye and Jenkins, *Are We Living in the End Times?*, 57.

43. Tim LaHaye, *The Beginning of the End* (Wheaton, IL: Tyndale House Publishers, 1972), 165, 168. Emphasis added.

44. Tim LaHaye, *The Beginning of the End*, rev. ed. (Wheaton, IL: Tyndale House Publishers, 1991), 1993. Emphasis added. For a side-by–side analysis of LaHaye's change, see Richard Abanes, *End–Time Visions: The Road to Armageddon?* (New York: Four Walls Eight Windows, 1998), 295.

45. William Hendriksen, *Israel in Prophecy* (Grand Rapids, MI: Baker Book House, 1968), 16–31.

46. Paul Boyer, *When Time Shall Be No More: Prophecy Belief in Modern American Culture* (Cambridge, MA: The Belknap Press of Harvard University, 1992); James Randi, "Forty-Nine End-of-the-World Prophecies—That Failed," *An Encyclopedia of Claims, Frauds, and Hoaxes of the Occult and Supernatural* (New York: St. Martin's Press, 1995), 257–67; Dwight Wilson, *Armageddon Now!: The Premillenarian Response to Russia and Israel Since 1917*, 2d ed. (Tyler, TX: 1991).

CONCLUSION

1. 1 Thessalonians 5:21.

2. Quoted in Jeffery L. Sherer, "Dark Prophecies," *U.S. News & World Report* (December 15, 1977), 69. Also see C. Marvin Pate and calvin B. Haines, Jr., *Doomsday Delusions: What's Wrong with Predictions About the End of the World* (Downers Grove, IL: InterVarsity Press, 1995).

3. Francis X. Gumerlock, *The Day and the Hour: Christianity's Perennial Fascination with Predicting the End of the World* (Powder Springs, GA: American Vision, 2000), 2.

4. Arnold Dallimore. *The Life of Edward Irving: The Fore-Runner of the Charismatic Movement* (Carlisle, PA: Banner of Truth Trust, 1983), 62.

5. D. James Kennedy and Jerry Newcombe, *What If Jesus Had Never Been Born* (Nashville, TN: Thomas Nelson, 1994); *What if the Bible Had Never Been Written?* (Nashville, TN: Thomas Nelson, 1998); Alvin J. Schmidt, *Under the Influence: How Christianity Transformed Civilization* (Grand Rapids, MI: Zondervan 2000).